NO MORE CHERRY BLOSSOMS

Sisters Matsumoto and Other Plays

NO MORE CHERRY BLOSSOMS

SISTERS MATSUMOTO AND OTHER PLAYS

PHILIP KAN GOTANDA

Foreword by Stephen H. Sumida

UNIVERSITY OF WASHINGTON PRESS
Seattle and London

No More Cherry Blossoms: Sisters Matsumoto and Other Plays is published with the assistance of a grant from the NAOMI B. PASCAL EDITOR'S ENDOWMENT, supported through the generosity of Janet and John Creighton, Patti Knowles, Mary McLellan Williams, and other donors.

Designed by a.k.a. design
Printed in the United States of America
10 09 08 07 06 05   5 4 3 2 1

University of Washington Press
P.O. Box 50096, Seattle, WA 98145
www.washington.edu/uwpress

Library of Congress Cataloging-in-Publication Data

Gotanda, Philip Kan.
   No more cherry blossoms : Sisters Matsumoto and other plays / Philip Kan Gotanda ; foreword by Stephen Sumida.
      p. cm.
   ISBN 0-295-98501-1 (pbk. : alk. paper)
      1. Asian American women—Drama.   I. Title.
PS.3557.07934N6   2005
812'.54—dc22   2004028990

The paper used in this publication is acid-free and recycled from 10 percent post-consumer and at least 50 percent pre-consumer waste. It meets the minimum requirements of American National Standard for Information Sciences—Permanence of Paper for Printed Library Materials, ANSI Z39.48-1984.

For Diane and Catherine

CONTENTS

Foreword by Stephen H. Sumida   ix

Preface   xv

Sisters Matsumoto   3

The Wind Cries Mary   77

Ballad of Yachiyo   157

Under the Rainbow, a Play of Two One Acts

    Natalie Wood Is Dead   223

    White Manifesto and Other Perfumed Tales of
    Self-Entitlement, or, Got Rice?   250

FOREWORD

Sisters Matsumoto, The Wind Cries Mary, Ballad of Yachiyo, and *Under the Rainbow* come from a compact period of playwriting for Philip Kan Gotanda, which overlapped and continued beyond his writing of *Fish Head Soup and Other Plays* (1995), his first published collection of plays. The span of the historical settings of these plays reveals Gotanda's vision for presenting a multigenerational Japanese America within a multicultural America. In expressing this vision he draws upon a sense of history and a method and aesthetic of evocation. Gotanda draws from us what we know and do not know we are carrying in our cultural memories and in our feelings shaped by experience and history. If we are not viewers and readers who have learned or experienced Japanese American history and culture, then Gotanda's artistic, intellectual method works by drawing us into the experience of his plays so that we, too, may come to know his subject.

The protagonists in almost all the plays are women, each responding to and acting upon her historical time of transition. *No More Cherry Blossoms* intimates multiple senses in which the "cherry blossoms," as idealizations of Japanese women especially and of Asian women generally, are "no more" in the American settings of the plays. The image is an American stereotype, unfit for any individual's identity. Yet Gotanda's evocation and critique of the stereotype is not a simple rebellion against it. The apprehension of the cherry blossom's beauty not at full bloom but at the moment it blows off the branch must rest somewhere in Gotanda's sense of the beautiful, while the peacefulness in the image is "no more" in the heroic and tragic lives of Gotanda's characters. The title Gotanda gives to this collection evokes too the winds and spring squalls that lift and scatter the petals from the branches and trees, which continue their cycles of growth and decline.

Although the four plays are set in times of transition, Gotanda's choices of writing from historical sources intimate that all times are transitional—certainly his own, as he writes. History is not the freezing of time for purposes of study, but is the flow of time in continual change. In historical order, *Ballad of Yachiyo* would come earliest, with its setting in 1919 on the island of Kaua'i, Hawai'i. Yachiyo's parents, immigrant workers on a sugar plantation, send her to learn "tea" and serve an artist, and improve her life by doing so. The artist, Takamura, is a potter and a powerfully unconventional fellow. *Yachiyo* is Gotanda's visually most bold and evocative play, its force evidently coming in part from the shock of imagining or discovering a tragedy his own family had kept quiet for seven decades. *Sisters Matsumoto* would be next in historical order. Set in late 1945 near Stockton, California, where three sisters try to resettle after their release from the Japanese American concentration camp at Rohwer, Arkansas, this drama is Gotanda's presentation of what in general is the most public narrative in Japanese American history—the internment and its aftermath. Gotanda pulls away from this general theme to draw characters with sharp features, relationships, and conflicts. *The Wind Cries Mary* follows, set in San Francisco, 1968. It was the time of student uprisings, especially at San Francisco State University, where the loud birth cries of ethnic studies and Asian American studies rose up to resound through the decades. The social and political turbulence, however, changes the conditions that the protagonist, Eiko Hanabi (Mary), has strengthened herself to oppose and control. Who then is she in the new times and personal conditions she did not predict? *Under the Rainbow* is the most contemporary of the plays. In *Natalie Wood Is Dead*, the first of the two one-act plays that make up *Under the Rainbow*, a mother and her daughter summon an entire history of Asians and mixed-race Asian Americans in the American entertainment industry during the second half of the twentieth century. The play performs tacitly as a partner with Gotanda's two-generation, male-centered earlier play, *Yankee Dawg You Die*.

The second one-act play of *Under the Rainbow—White Manifesto and Other Perfumed Tales of Self-Entitlement, or, Got Rice?*—is a monologue, virulent and pathetic, delivered by a self-proclaimed white master of seducing Asian women. The history evoked here is of Western attempts to dominate Asia for centuries as both symbolized and enacted in Western sexual domination of women.

The order in which Gotanda places these works in this collection, however, is different from the chronological order suggested by their settings. Their order of appearance in this volume resists a cliché that Japanese American history is a story of how life has gotten better. Certain rifts, fractures, discriminations, and conflicts in Japanese American culture and society persist regardless of chronological orderings. These include rifts between Japanese Americans and others in American society, between Japanese Americans of the continent and of Hawai'i, between the American- and the Japanese-educated of the Nisei generation, between those considered Japanese of the "main" islands of that nation and those of Okinawan origin, between interpretations of Japanese American history as a sunshine history and as a tragic history or a history of continuing struggle, and issues that persist between women and men.

In Gotanda's plays it is male characters who sometimes serve to dramatize some of these persistent issues or dynamics in Japanese American culture. There is Bola in *Sisters Matsumoto*, a character rooted in Hawai'i and a distinctive history that brought him together with the Matsumotos in the Arkansas concentration camp and now in Stockton. There is another brother-in-law in that play, Hideo, a Kibei Nisei, born in America and educated in Japan, whose critical stance toward America puts him at odds with Bola and the eldest of the sisters, Grace, Hideo's wife. There is Yachiyo's boyfriend, Willie Higa, who embodies and dramatizes a discrimination that has endured for a century among Japanese Americans in Hawai'i, the marking of differences between "Japanese" and "Okinawans" on the plantations, where sugar planters used ethnic divisiveness to disunite and rule the workers. Willie's zeal as a labor organizer and a uniter—a dangerous, illegal activity on the sugar plantations in 1919—may be thought of as fueled by his heightened awareness of social injustice because of how others regard him dismissively as "that Okinawan boy." Absent from these issues, meanwhile, are conflicts between generations as consequences of so-called cultural differences between Japanese and Americans. Japanese Americans are Americans. Insofar as certain issues have been germane to Japanese American culture through more than three generations of history, it may be inferred that all generations alike have been participating in living, suffering, and perpetuating them. They are American issues—that is, historical constructions of Japanese Americans, whose culture begins, Gotanda assumes and accordingly writes, with the immigrants themselves.

In his body of works, Gotanda is constructing a Japanese America that is held together despite this community's loss of actual residence and neighborhoods in what before World War II were the Nihonmachi, Japantowns, and Little Tokyos of American cities. Such as it is, Japanese America is a connection among people (and Gotanda's characters) scattered from Hawai'i to New York, with the West Coast and Chicago in between. Gotanda evokes these connections sometimes in aesthetic ways, as when characters in more than one of his plays appreciate pottery and the artistic processes and skills that go into its creation. There would seem to be no other "connection" but a valuing of this art between Masi, in Gotanda's earlier play and film *The Wash*, and Yachiyo and the potter Takamura in *Ballad of Yachiyo*.

Gotanda also evokes in bluntly concrete ways a Japanese America that is otherwise discontinuous in historical space and time. But for some readers or viewers of Gotanda's plays to feel the impact of his method even when it is blunt, it is necessary to experience several of Gotanda's plays and to remember them along the way. For example, the Matsumoto sisters in this collection have the same surname as Masi and Nobu Matsumoto in *The Wash*, the Matsumoto family in *Song for a Nisei Fisherman* (also in Gotanda's earlier collection), and the same as the tragic Yachiyo Matsumoto, whom Gotanda memorializes in *Ballad of Yachiyo*. The questions evoked as to whether these sets of characters are "related" in Gotanda's fictive, dramatic world are made more curious again when Gotanda dedicates *Ballad of Yachiyo* to "the Memory of Yachiyo Gotanda, 1902–1919." There are evidently not only aesthetic connections among the Matsumoto sisters, Yachiyo, Nobu, and Masi, and the playwright, but also familial ones in some actual or symbolic way. Aside from the history of Gotanda's families, Gotanda is building up recognition, familiarity, and evocation by a repetition of names of characters who are related by this repetition within Gotanda's broad fictive community.

Another example of this connectivity is found in Dr. Frank Nakada in *The Wind Cries Mary,* who has the same surname as Shigeo Nakada (the protagonist who goes by the pseudonym Vincent Chang) in Gotanda's *Yankee Dawg You Die.* How an interpretation of one Nakada may be affected by an intepretation of the other opens intriguing lines of inquiry. Both are of the "older generation." Both have respectable stature. But they cannot be entirely alike in their inner lives. The Dr. Nakada in *The Wind Cries Mary* parallels Judge Brack in Henrik Ibsen's *Hedda Gabler,* the source that Gotanda "loosely adapted" to write *Mary.* It is interesting to consider how the scoundrel Dr. Nakada may also be one of the faces worn by Shigeo Nakada in *Yankee Dawg,* and how Shigeo Nakada's complicated, forever compromising idea and performance of "dignity" may be an aspect of Dr. Nakada in *Mary.*

A further kind of evocation occurs where Gotanda connects Japanese America internally by drawing upon its shared connections—or possible connections—with the cultures, arts, and histories of the national American and international worlds of Japanese Americans. Ibsen's Hedda Gabler powerfully inspires Gotanda's characterization of Eiko Hanabi in *The Wind Cries Mary.* But Eiko's parallel with Hedda would be nothing without Gotanda's insight about Eiko as a Japanese American woman at once ahead of her time yet now caught in changing times. Eiko's surname, Hanabi, means "fireworks" (literally, "fire flowers") and also sounds close to the term *hanabiri* (flower petals), which may evoke the title Gotanda gives to this book. *Sisters Matsumoto* evokes Anton Chekhov's *Three Sisters* and *The Cherry Orchard.*

In the sisters' attachment to the land through their awareness of the family's fairly recent history there, *Sisters Matsumoto* evokes Jun'ichirō Tanizaki's *Makioka Sisters* (Sasameyuki). In Gotanda's play and Tanizaki's novel, the sisters are the heads of their families, into which their husbands have married and, in Tanizaki's novel, have taken on the Makioka name.

The literary allusions or evocations I name here are ones that Gotanda himself has identified. They augment a sense that when reading or viewing Gotanda's plays, we are in touch with a wider world and experience than the plays' local settings seem to represent. As collections of his plays, Gotanda's two volumes so far suggest that he is dramatizing a larger vision and fiction of time and space called Japanese America that is related to Faulkner's Yoknapatawpha County, Toni Morrison's Ohio, O. A. Bushnell's Hawai'i, or August Wilson's Pittsburgh. These fictive places have been created out of each writer's vision to tell, interpret, and express through literary art an epic and the localized story—requiring many books, chapters, or plays to be told—that inspires them.

PREFACE

No one is ever just one thing: the label that's been given them, the definition that one has accepted and lives within. Nonetheless, so much of what we work and live by seems based on these seemingly transparent assumptions. I am a playwright, I am an American playwright, I am an Asian American playwright, I am an Asian American playwright of Japanese descent. They serve their purpose. They served their purpose.

In the end we're all beings in flux, in continual invention and reformation. We must use social labels and self-defining names as they should be used, as convenient constructs to get a handle on the shifting world, to be replaced by more suitable ones as the world shifts again, as we shift again.

It's an always present, seen and unseen exchange going on between the external and the internal. The process involves keeping the two in sync so one has better knowledge of the described world. The artist can then by the simple act of attention make an action in the direction of keenness, relevancy, and liberation.

We all do many things. We are all many things. I never quite know what I'll be doing tomorrow. If I will travel or stay at home. Be with others or alone. If it will be a play, a film, a song, or a pot.

What I try to do is get up each day and give my body the chance to speak. In whatever format, language, medium it chooses. I try to be a harsh judge of the work and brutally honest in its appraisal. It should represent the truth of that moment for me. The exact articulation of my whole being—hair to bone, bowels to skin, historical to contemporaneous, emotional to intellectual, all that can be seen and all that can be dreamt—in as artful a gesture as possible.

Of course one can never do exactly that. One comes as close as one can. That's the challenge.

Here's some of that work. It covers a period of about five to six years and gives a sense of the types of work I've been doing in theater. It's a good companion to my book, *Fish Head Soup and Other Plays*. It's a good companion to my films and screenplays. It's a good companion to my Web site (www.philipkangotanda.com). It's a good companion to hearing a performance of my spoken-word retro jazz ensemble, *the new orientals*.

The world shifts. The label no longer fits. We go to sleep, wake up, and try it again. Hopefully with new eyes.

The Plays

The four plays selected for this collection have Asian American women as their themes. They take place in different decades of American history. I never consciously attempted to write plays with *women's* themes, they simply were the stories I wrote when I sat down to write. They were chosen from other plays, however, in that they lend themselves to an inherent narrative for the collection.

The image of cherry blossoms, while on the one hand an intoxicating picture of temporal beauty, has also unfortunately become associated with the fantasized world of *oriental* tradition where Asian women can only serve, defer, and follow. I felt *No More Cherry Blossoms* was a fitting title for this collection of plays.

1. *Sisters Matsumoto* (1998) follows the lives of three grown sisters returning to their rural home in the Stockton, California Delta region after being released from an internment camp in Arkansas. Prior to the war they had been wealthy and privileged, the well-regarded daughters of a successful and influential potato farmer, Togo Matsumoto, moving easily in both the Japanese American community and white society circles. Now with their father dead and the family fortune gone, they must return to a world where money and class can no longer shield them from the now overt prejudice the war has awakened. It is in this climate that the Matsumoto sisters struggle to rebuild their once

proud lives and, in the process, come to understand what it means to be American.

I'd always been interested in the period right after the camps and what families had to go through in reintegrating back into American society. Also, this period has not been explored extensively in literature. Another area of interest to me was the internal class structures of "ethnic" communities and their relationships to the larger culture. In *Sisters Matsumoto* I have explored these themes. This story mirrors the history of my mother's life.

2. *The Wind Cries Mary* (2002) is based loosely on Ibsen's *Hedda Gabler*. The play is set on a college campus in the late sixties amidst turbulent antiwar demonstrations and the beginnings of Asian American identity politics. I was intrigued by the idea of exploring a character who had invested into a life based on a series of assumptions about her society only to have that world abruptly shift, suddenly displacing the old order's beliefs with a new set of options she would never have allowed herself to entertain.

The play contains a reference to the film *El Topo*. I put it in knowing that it was released a year after the date of the play's setting. Rob Hurwitt, the *San Francisco Chronicle* critic, noted the discrepancy. I thought, what the hell, I love the reference and felt it gave more than it took. I also originally included a reference to *The Brady Bunch* as being the perfect American *whiteface*. After the first preview I received two notes, a letter, and a phone call that all noted, in a friendly manner, that *The Brady Bunch* debuted a year later than the play's date. That reference was taken out.

3. *Ballad of Yachiyo* (1994) takes place around 1919 on the island of Kauai and follows the coming of age of a seventeen-year-old girl who is sent to live with a potter and his wife on the other side of the island. With the backdrop of labor unrest and the traditional Japanese approach to pottery making, we follow the changing dynamic of Yachiyo's relationship with the man and

his wife to its tragic end. I'm quite drawn to visual imagery in my stage work. With *Ballad of Yachiyo* I had the idea to write a play that would incorporate the visual elements of film and yet be totally theatrical in its aesthetic. *Yachiyo* tells much of its story through visual images, utilizing stage techniques that allow for cross-fades, dissolves, super impositions, etc. However, more than just pretty pictures, these visual scenes are intended to further the narrative as any scene with spoken dialogue would. They were clearly formulated in my head as I put them to paper, and I depicted them in a very precise textual manner. I wrote this play and developed its production with my long-time collaborator, director Sharon Ott, to create cinematic theatricality in the story-telling. It's based on a true story. And yes, they're cherry blossoms, but the idea is to create that image and then undercut it with the subsequent supertitles, erasing the romanticism and substituting the brutal reality of her real life and death. The play was last updated in 1996.

4. *Under the Rainbow* (2001) consists of two one-act plays. This is my most recent play and has yet to have a production at the time of this writing. I don't find this to be a problem in relation to its publication, as the play on page and the play on stage are ultimately two very different things. Many times the final production script does not read as a complete experience of the work, as it has been edited and made subservient to production. The play is all about the live performance and moment-to-moment interaction of the text through the instrument of the actors with the audience, a kind of mini-improvisation within the definitions of text. Much is left out of the script, as it is no longer needed by the actors, director, and designers, who are aware of the writer's intent yet discard parts of the text by the end of rehearsals. Given this process, why not have a script that's better suited as a literary instrument of the play rather than the live performance's blueprint?

White Manifesto and Other Perfumed Tales of Self-Entitlement, or, Got Rice? is a provocative foray into the phenomenon of white male fascination with Asian women. It explores issues of racial and gender entitlement. *Natalie Wood Is Dead* examines a mother and daughter relationship within the context of Hollywood and what each does or chooses not to do to survive. I always meant to write a two-female companion piece to my earlier work, *Yankee Dawg You Die*. This is it.

Philip Kan Gotanda
San Francisco
February 2005

NO MORE CHERRY BLOSSOMS

Sisters Matsumoto and Other Plays

Sisters Matsumoto

Writing of this play was funded by the Civil Liberties Public Education Fund.

Author's thanks to Diane Takei, Sharon Ott, Diane Matsuda, Manabi Hirasaki, Judi Nihei, Chris and Richard E. T. White, Bessie Takei, and Lila Matsumoto. Special thanks to Carl Mulert and the Joyce Ketay Agency.

For Catherine

Sisters Matsumoto had its world premiere as a co-production between the Berkeley Repertory Theatre, the San Jose Repertory Theatre, and the Asian American Theater Company in 1998–99.

DIRECTOR: Sharon Ott

CAST –
Grace Matsumoto: Kim Miyori
Chiz Matsumoto: Lisa Li
Rose Matsumoto: Michi Barall
Bola: Stan Egi
Hideo: Nelson Mashita
Henry Sakai: Ryan Yu
Mr. Hersham: Will Marchetti

Set Design: Kate Edmunds
Lighting Design: Nancy Schertler
Costumes: Lydia Tanji
Original Music: Dan Kuramoto

Characters
GRACE, 35 years old
HIDEO, husband to Grace
CHIZ, 32 years old
BOLA, husband to Chiz
ROSE, 26 years old
HENRY, suitor to Rose
MR. HERSHAM, neighbor and family friend

Time
1945, late fall into winter

Place
Stockton, California Delta region

ACT ONE

Scene One

Lights up. For a moment we hold on a large Victorian farmhouse. It's a once proud lady, now fading and gray. Weeds grow, the fields surrounding her appear abandoned. On a corner of the house is crudely painted "Japs Go Home." The distinctive call of the red-winged blackbird, a common Delta region species. We hear voices, car doors opening, luggage being unloaded.

    GRACE *stands for a moment looking out over the fields.*

BOLA *(off)*: Geez, my legs—I can stretch them . . .

CHIZ *(off)*: Bola, the luggage in the trunk. Careful . . .

BOLA: *(off)*: I got it, I got it.

HIDEO *(off)*: I think the car is dead.

CHIZ *(off)*: You'd think after all Papa did for him, Mr. Bedrosian would loan us his Cadillac.

    (GRACE *turns and sees "Japs Go Home" painted on the wall.* ROSE *enters and comes up behind* GRACE. ROSE *stares at the vandals' message.*)

    (CHIZ *enters carrying the baby, followed by* HIDEO *carrying two suitcases. Trailing is a struggling* BOLA, *laden with luggage.*)

HIDEO: I can look at the engine later.

CHIZ: And did you see the way he looked at us? Like he was doing us a favor loaning us that old Pontiac—

    (*They all come up behind* GRACE *and stop when they see the painted words. Silence. They exchange looks.* GRACE *moves away.*)

BOLA: I'll get rid of it later.

GRACE: Check in the supply shed, there might be some whitewash left.

BOLA: Jesus, look at the fields. I'm gonna look around.

HIDEO: I'd better go with you Bola.

ACT ONE, SCENE ONE

(BOLA and HIDEO *exit.* GRACE, ROSE *and* CHIZ *are alone. They look out over the fields.)*

CHIZ *(grimacing)*: Peat dirt. Lovely . . . *(beat)* I forgot how big this place was.

GRACE: I haven't forgotten.

ROSE: It seems smaller somehow . . .

GRACE: I remember everything.

ROSE: Not as majestic . . .

CHIZ: And dustier. This peat dirt covers everything. *(Looking out at the fields)* Criminy, what's the going price for weeds these days?

GRACE: The boy just let it go. I'm glad Papa can't see this. It would break his heart.

CHIZ: Oh look, my badminton net.

ROSE: It's like a ghost, just fluttering in the wind.

CHIZ: We can just restring it or use a clothesline—I'll look in the garage for the rackets. Bola!

(CHIZ exits. GRACE *and* ROSE *look on in silence.)*

ROSE: Grace?

GRACE: Hmm? *(Pause)* Rose?

ROSE: I was thinking about Papa. All alone in the Camp cemetery. Can we move him? Back here to Stockton? Maybe bury him on the farm?

GRACE: Let's talk about that later. Rohwer, Arkansas, is a long, long ways off.

(They enter the house. GRACE *looks around.* ROSE *notices a chair, takes off the white sheet covering it.)*

ROSE: Papa's chair. *(Feeling the contours)* It still has his shape. *(ROSE sits in it.)*

GRACE: Papa told me he bought this house for Mama. It was his gift to her. They had just enough for the down payment. It was pretty run down.

ROSE: Mama said that it snowed once and there was enough to build a snowman in the living room. I can't imagine them living like that!

GRACE: Mama was pulling your leg. It doesn't snow in Stockton. By the time you were three or four we'd already moved in to the big house in town.

Michi Barall (as Rose), Kim Miyori (as Grace), and Lisa Li (as Chiz) say farewell to their family farm in *Sisters Matsumoto*, Seattle Repertory Theatre, 1998–99.

Photo by Chris Bennion, courtesy Seattle Repertory Theatre

Kim Miyori (as Grace) is struck with the truth about the sale of her father's farm in *Sisters Matsumoto*, Seattle Repertory Theatre, 1998–99.

(Handwritten margin note:) hard-working father. Now that life's gone, it seems the security is lost

ROSE: We came out here on weekends. I remember playing outside in the wet tule fog. My eyelashes would get so wet it was like looking through a prism.

GRACE: Papa would work sun up to sun down on his tractor and sometimes late into the night. He hung big lanterns on the cab. Mama'd have to make him come in. Gradually things got better for them. Papa figured out potatoes grew well in this type of soil. He bought more land. They grew more potatoes. *(Looks up at the ceiling.)* We should keep the umbrellas handy, we may need them again.

> *(BOLA and HIDEO enter with more suitcases. BOLA balances, holding the phonograph. CHIZ follows.)*

CHIZ: Be careful, Bola.

BOLA: I got it, I got it. See all those sticks with red flags? Someone's been out here.

HIDEO: Government's probably doing some surveying.

BOLA: Where do you want all this stuff?

GRACE: Right there is fine for now, Bola.

BOLA: That Daugherty kid ought to be taken out and shot.

HIDEO: He just abandoned the place.

> *(HIDEO exits back to the car.)*

GRACE: Mr. Daugherty wanted to keep his son safe from the draft. Running a farm was essential wartime work.

CHIZ: Knowing how patriotic Papa was, I'm surprised he went along with that.

GRACE: Papa was a businessman, too. Mr. Daugherty helped Papa make a lot of money in the stock market.

HIDEO *(returning with more packages)*: He didn't rotate the crops at all. Just corn for three years.

BOLA: One of the tractors he left in the middle of the field to rust. And I looked in the sheds—the equipment's in bad shape.

GRACE: We can take inventory later, see what we have.

CHIZ: Wait, wait, let's take a picture. Rose, Grace—come on, come on . . . *(Announcing)* The Matsumoto Sisters return home.

GRACE: Chiz, not now—we have too many things to do.

ROSE: Oh, come on.

CHIZ: Come on, Grace. You know you're the one who always pulls

out the family photo albums. *(Hands* HIDEO *the baby.)* Here.
(Hands BOLA *the camera.)* Here.

HIDEO: Do you still know how to use one of those things?

BOLA: It's been almost four years—let's see if I still have my touch.

(GRACE, ROSE *and* CHIZ *line up.* HIDEO *enjoys having the baby.*
BOLA *puts a flash bulb in the camera.)*

BOLA: Ready?

*(They immediately compose themselves. There is an ease to their
pose that suggests that they are used to this kind of attention. Flash.
They immediately return to the tasks at hand.)*

CHIZ *(taking the baby from* HIDEO*)*: Esther likes you, huh?

HIDEO: She's a good baby. I'm going to miss the boys—running
all around, though.

CHIZ *(laughing)*: Yeah . . . But I'm glad we dropped them off with
Bola's sister in L.A. More Japanese there. Safer. I want to make
sure it's okay here, first.

HIDEO: How was the bus ride up? Any trouble?

CHIZ: No, just got right on. Some GIs stared at us in the depot,
but that was about it. I had to pull Bola away. You know these
Hawai'i boys.

HIDEO: I heard they burned down the White Star Sodaworks.

CHIZ: Down in L.A.? In Little Tokyo?

HIDEO *(nodding)*: Un-huh.

CHIZ: Geez . . . Bola? When can we call your sister? Check in
on the boys?

BOLA: Tomorrow. Old Man Sato's place, the Europa Hotel, has
a telephone we can use.

CHIZ: I'm not going in that old place, the roof might cave in.

HIDEO: I noticed he had it up for sale.

CHIZ: Who'd buy that place?

BOLA *(to* HIDEO*)*: You think the car will be okay?

HIDEO: I'll go look at it.

CHIZ: I wouldn't set a foot in there.

HIDEO *(exiting)*: Your father told me he stayed there after he quit
working the railroads.

BOLA: He said it was too cold in Montana and they didn't serve
him rice.

CHIZ: Bola, we got to get the phone hooked up, too.

BOLA (*exiting*): I'm gonna go out back, look in the warehouse. Check the stuff we stored from the house in town.

CHIZ (*going up the stairs with the baby*): Hey, let's each stay in our old rooms, like when we were kids. Come on, Rose . . .

(CHIZ *and* ROSE *exit up the stairs.* HIDEO *enters.*)

GRACE: Maybe we can get some of Papa's old workers to help out.

HIDEO: You think they're even around? Some have their own places now.

GRACE: They lost everything, too.

HIDEO: I can go into town later and ask at the Buddhist church. They should know who's around.

(GRACE *begins to open all the windows.*)

HIDEO: I heard Jimmy Kaneko bought the Chongs' old laundry down on Lafayette Street. He's going to make tofu. He took some money out of the *tanomoshi* fund. I know your father didn't believe in those things but it's helping the folks who don't have much. Jimmy got all his supplies to start up the business that way.

GRACE: The Chongs. Remember the sign they put up in their window? "We Are Chinese."

HIDEO: We have to start thinking about the future. We need to decide on what businesses we want to start. Now's the time. Everybody's coming back and if we wait too long everything's going to be taken up.

GRACE: I just don't think a newspaper is such a good idea . . .

HIDEO: But we need our own newspaper. Look, I know your father and I didn't always see eye to eye on things.

GRACE: Papa helped you. What about the aqua farming? Papa gave you money for that, didn't he? He supported you.

HIDEO: Did he? Or did he do it to help you?

GRACE: I just can't think about selling this place right now. I can't. Let's all get settled first.

HIDEO: How can we, all six of us cramped together under one roof?

GRACE: We were all living together in town. Right after Bola and Chiz returned from his internship. We all lived there together, didn't we?

Sisters Matsumoto

[handwritten note: they were obviously a wealthy family (@ one point)]

[handwritten note: girls = very proud of their family & name]

[handwritten note: Hideo → taking on role of father figure — kind of domineering & impatient]

HIDEO: That was your house in town, it was huge.

GRACE: We all lived here growing up, all of us and Mama, too.

HIDEO: You were kids Grace, we're all adults now. Bola needs a place to start his medical practice, I want to start my newspaper, and all that takes money. And what about Rose? We have to find her a husband, and you think a family's going to be impressed driving all the way out here to this farmhouse?

GRACE: This is the Matsumoto family, Hideo. We don't need to impress anyone. My father built the Japanese community here. If somebody thinks they're too good for us, we don't want them in our family.

HIDEO: I'm sorry, I shouldn't have said that.

GRACE: Who's going to want to read a newspaper in Japanese, Hideo? Who? You and your Kibei friends have to face up to it. Japan lost the war.

HIDEO: I know, I know . . .

GRACE: America won, we live here and we're Americans not Japanese. We read American newspapers, we want to know American news.

HIDEO: That's not what I'm talking about . . .

GRACE: And even if you get some of the Issei and Kibei to read it, can we make a living off of it? I don't want to live like we just got off the boat. I want nice things, things that we had before the war.

HIDEO: Holding on to this farm isn't going to bring things back the way they used to be.

GRACE: Someone's got to try.

(CHIZ *and* ROSE *re-enter from upstairs.*)

CHIZ (*to* ROSE): I'll check on the baby later.

BOLA (*off*): Professor, I need some help . . .

CHIZ (*to* GRACE): The upstairs isn't bad. Everything was shut, so it's not too dusty.

(BOLA *enters, struggling to carry a large ornate* obutsudan *(Buddhist shrine) and a pile of kimono . . .* HIDEO *exits.*)

CHIZ: Oh—the obutsudan . . .

(ROSE *helps* BOLA *set it down.*)

GRACE: What happened to it?

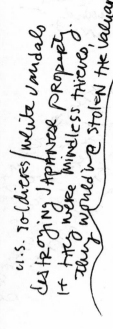

U.S. soldiers/white vandals destroying Japanese property. It they were mindless thieves they would've stolen the valuable china, etc.

BOLA: Part of the top got banged up a little.

GRACE: Mama loved this one. I'd go into the bedroom and we would offer incense.

BOLA: The warehouse is all broken into. Everything's thrown around, smashed.

CHIZ: The kimono?

BOLA: Water leaked into the crates from the bottom—they're all ruined.

ROSE: All of them?

BOLA: All rotted out.

(HIDEO *pushes his way in through the door, carrying a pile of kimono. He sets them down. Ciz moves forward and lifts one up. It's a beautiful kimono that is water stained and damaged.*)

CHIZ: Oh Grace, your favorite.

ROSE: How about Mama's *imari* ware?

BOLA: All broken. I can't tell, it's such a mess. Some more stuff was written on the walls, too.

HIDEO: More?

BOLA: I'll clean it up after I do the front of the house.

(BOLA *grabs the suitcases and moves towards the stairs.* HIDEO *doesn't feel comfortable and decides to exit.*)

HIDEO *(exiting)*: I'll go look at the car.

CHIZ *(to* BOLA*)*: Put them in the middle room.

BOLA: I don't like the middle room.

CHIZ: We're all staying in our old rooms—

BOLA: The back one gets more fresh air.

CHIZ: Yeah, but—

BOLA: I want air, I need air.

CHIZ: Okay, okay, okay, honey. Don't worry. I know how to handle him.

(BOLA *continues upstairs.*)

ROSE: Things aren't the same, are they?

GRACE: Rose?

ROSE: I kept hoping they would be. I prayed that they would be. (ROSE *is upset*) On the train coming back from Arkansas, I wouldn't get off at any of the stops.

GRACE: Hideo said you weren't feeling well.

ACT ONE, SCENE TWO

ROSE: I thought if I could make it to Stockton, just make it here, walk down Main Street, say hello to people, see them look back and smile . . . I don't know who I am anymore, where we fit in.

(GRACE *opens the* obutsudan. *As she speaks,* ROSE *rummages through a suitcase.*)

GRACE: That's why we have to stay who we are. Not lose ourselves. Always remember we are Matsumotos. That's the only thing we can hold on to. The only thing nobody can take from us. We are Matsumotos.

(ROSE *has found two photos. One of their father and one of their mother. She places them in the shrine.* CHIZ *reaches into her pocket and takes out a riceball wrapped in wax paper. She puts it in the shrine as an offering.*)

(GRACE *and the two sisters stare at their parents' faces and the shrine.* CHIZ *glances around the house.*)

(*Dim to darkness*)

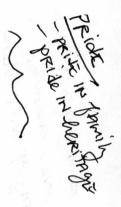

Scene Two

Night. The fireplace comes up. We see HIDEO *in front of it.* ROSE *enters and moves towards the fire.*

ROSE *(surprised)*: Oh, Hideo.

HIDEO: I started a fire. I was cold.

ROSE: I was wondering who was up.

HIDEO: Couldn't sleep, too?

ROSE *(shaking her head)*: Un-uh.

HIDEO: Grace is sleeping like a baby.

ROSE: She's always been like that.

(HIDEO *starts to get up.*)

HIDEO: Well. I have to get up early to work on the car. Everybody wants to go to town now.

ROSE: Can you stay for a bit? I was thinking about waking up Grace. I just can't be by myself in this house.

(HIDEO *settles back down. Awkward silence.*)

ROSE: If you want to go to bed, I'm sorry . . .

HIDEO: No, no, I just didn't want to make you uncomfortable.

ROSE: No, no . . .

(Pause.)

HIDEO: So do you have any plans?

ROSE: Mr. Kusaba opened his drugstore. Grace wants me to help over there.

HIDEO: Finally you get to use your pharmacy degree. Your father would be happy.

ROSE: I was helping Bola at the infirmary. In Camp?

HIDEO: Oh yeah, yeah . . .

ROSE: That was more nursing, though—we didn't have much medicine to dispense. You remember when Bola and Dr. Arao performed that emergency appendectomy on that little boy? No anesthesia or anything, just made him drink a half a bottle of homemade *saké.*

HIDEO: Like the cowboy movies. John Wayne.

ROSE: That's where Bola got the idea. It worked. I kept throwing up, though. I wasn't used to the blood. *(Beat)* What are your plans?

HIDEO: I don't know.

ROSE: You going to try the aqua-farming again?

HIDEO *(shakes head)*: I'm not cut out for any kind of farming. I think everybody knows it. Everybody except Grace. I thought farming sea urchins would be a new industry for Japanese in California. They were experimenting with it in Kobe, why not Morro Bay? *(Beat)* Your father knew I wasn't a farmer. I never understood why Grace chose to marry me, a college teacher.

ROSE: Because the other boys Papa brought home all looked like Saint Bernards. She thought you were sophisticated and handsome.

(They laugh. Calm down.)

HIDEO: She used to enjoy listening to me talk about the Japanese authors—Tanizaki, Natsume Soseki . . .

ROSE *(overlapping)*: Oh, I like him.

HIDEO: . . . Yes, I know . . .

ROSE: Your favorite author, his belief in the individual.

ACT ONE, SCENE TWO

HIDEO: Un-huh. *(Pause)* But after a while . . .
    (Pause.)
HIDEO: I'm not sure I want to be here. Back in Stockton.
    (Pause.)
ROSE: Does Grace know?
HIDEO: I wanted to move to Los Angeles. There are lots of Japanese down there. I could find partners, easily set up. But you know Grace.
ROSE: I can't imagine her anywhere else. There are lots of Japanese here, too. And with everyone coming back, there'll be plenty of opportunities.
    (Pause.)
HIDEO: Grace ran into Mrs. Okubo while we were in town. I should have told you.
ROSE: Oh no, already?
HIDEO *(getting up)*: She said she'd start coming up with some more suitable names by next week.
    (HIDEO takes an envelope from the table and hands it to ROSE.)
ROSE: I'm not ready for this yet. All these boys parading in . . .
HIDEO: It's been almost two years, Rose.
ROSE *(opening envelope and taking out the photos)*: I know . . .
HIDEO: It's time to move on with your life.
    (Silence. She stares at a photo.)
ROSE: I can still see his face. As if there's a picture of him inside of my head. I just close my eyes . . . *(closes eyes)* . . . and there he is . . . *(slowly opens her eyes)*. When his mother told me he'd been killed over in Italy—I just couldn't let him go, I thought I would die if I let him go. So I began to imagine his face. Night after night, his eyes, his mouth, every curve, angle—I would hold his image there. Hold it because I thought I would die if I didn't. *(Pause.)* But after a while . . . after some time had passed? I began to realize I wouldn't die.
    (Pause.)
ROSE: I still hold his image there. *(Closes her eyes for a beat, then opens them.)* Because I want to.
    (A sleepy GRACE walks in and sees them. They notice her. GRACE is momentarily thrown by seeing the two together.)

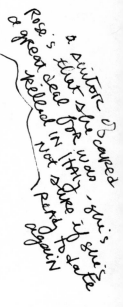

Rose's suitor a great deal that she was killed for in Italy, not like this. Read it state again

(handwritten margin note: This is more awkward than it should be... Hideo gets out of there As Fast As possible)

HIDEO: Grace. We couldn't sleep.

ROSE: Hideo wanted to go to bed but I made him keep me company.

GRACE: Cold weather makes me thirsty. Funny, huh?

(GRACE *drinks a cup of water.*)

HIDEO: Now that Grace is here, I think I'd better go to sleep. Goodnight.

ROSE: Good night Hideo.

(GRACE *moves to fire.*)

GRACE: Ahh, I needed that. The fire feels good. Did Hideo start it?

ROSE: Un-huh.

(*Pause.*)

GRACE: So what were you two talking about?

ROSE: Nothing in particular. His plans, what he'd like to do.

GRACE: Not the newspaper again . . .

ROSE: No.

(*Pause.* ROSE *moves to* GRACE.)

ROSE: He wants to move to L.A., did you know that?

GRACE: He told you?

(*Beat.*)

ROSE: He thinks there might be more opportunities there.

GRACE: There are plenty of opportunities right here. On this farm. If he doesn't like that, there are plenty of other things he can do in town. I'm not leaving here.

(CHIZ *comes strolling down the stairs.*)

CHIZ: We got anything to eat? I'm starving . . . (*Begins looking through boxes.* ROSE *moves away from* GRACE.) Food, food . . .

ROSE: Did we wake you up?

CHIZ: Had to convince Bola to move to the middle room.

GRACE: How'd you do that?

CHIZ: With my thighs. (*Rummaging, finds something.*) Crackers.

(ROSE *and* GRACE *sit on opposite ends of the room.*)

ROSE (*aside*): Don't ask her anything else.

CHIZ (*walking towards them*): I have to feed them. They get hungry.

(*Pause.*)

ACT ONE, SCENE TWO

CHIZ: I'm thinking about going to the country club on Saturday. Anybody want to come? Just like old times with Papa.

GRACE: Sure they'll let you in?

CHIZ: Why wouldn't they? Papa was a member. We played tennis there almost every day in the summers.

GRACE: A lot's happened. Things aren't the same.

CHIZ: So? Does that mean we have to stop living like we want to? They put us away because we were too Japanese. You know that. Think they would have done that if we'd all gone out and joined their clubs, gone to parties with them, became one of them?

(CHIZ *opens crackers, begins to eat them ravenously.*)

GRACE: That's what we did.

CHIZ: I know, but the other Nisei and Issei—they all stick together like a bunch of scared rabbits—go to the same church, go to the same social clubs, eat Japanese food, celebrate Japanese holidays, still speak the language, even have Japanese school so their kids can speak Japanese. Are you crazy? After what happened—my kids are only going to speak English. They're going to play with Caucasian kids, go to an all-white Christian church and celebrate every American holiday with a vengeance. *(Beat)* Oh, and I got rid of their Japanese middle names.

GRACE: How did you do that?

CHIZ: I un-named them.

(CHIZ *sits.*)

GRACE: Why?

(GRACE *joins* CHIZ. ROSE *moves away from* CHIZ *and* GRACE.)

ROSE: Papa would be mad Chiz.

CHIZ: He'd be happy. He'd know what I was doing. Hell, he's the one who was so pro-American. "America is good this, America is good that" . . .

ROSE: He also loved Japan . . .

GRACE: Papa loved Japan and America.

CHIZ: Maybe that was Papa's problem. You can't have it both ways. Maybe Papa should have made up his mind and kept his mouth shut.

[handwritten margin note, right side:] Chiz thinks that the way for them to be accepted by complete American's is to get rid of all Japanese mannerisms, customs, etc.

[handwritten note, bottom:] Chiz has given up trying to preserve her Japanese culture to preserve her social social status & personal well-being

GRACE: Chiz!

CHIZ: I'm not trying to make you mad.

GRACE: You do what you want, Chiz. I haven't any better idea than Papa about what's going on.

(GRACE *gets up and moves to the kitchen.*)

CHIZ *(muttering, rising)*: Criminy sakes, bite my head off.

(ROSE *sits away from* GRACE *and* CHIZ.)

GRACE *(hearing and turning back, faces* CHIZ): Why are you so ashamed of being Japanese?

CHIZ: I'm not.

GRACE: Yes, you are.

CHIZ: No, I'm not.

GRACE: Yes, yes, you are. Being Japanese was never good enough for you. You've always had to have white friends—be around them, have them like you.

CHIZ: I'm not ashamed of being Japanese Grace. I'm not. It's just . . . I just don't want it to get in the way of us being American.

(GRACE *stares at* CHIZ *for a beat.*)

GRACE: We should all go to bed. We have a lot of work ahead of us.

(GRACE *exits. The two sisters exchange looks.*)

(*Dim to darkness.*)

[handwritten margin note:] Problem / Being A hyphenated American — Chiz feels she has to choose between the two cultures

Scene Three

Five days later. Several photos of young men are tacked up on the cupboard. HIDEO *is in front of several packages he's finishing wrapping.* ROSE *struggles to bring in a bucket of water from outside. She's preparing lunch on the wood-burning stove.*

HIDEO *(noticing)*: Want some help?

ROSE: No, no, no—that's all right, Hideo . . .

(HIDEO *takes the bucket from her.*)

ROSE *(watching him)*: I hate having to bring water in all the time.

HIDEO: Right here, fine?

ROSE *(nodding)*: Un-huh. When can we use the well again?

ACT ONE, SCENE THREE

(HIDEO *returns to his packages as* ROSE *goes to check the pot on the stove.*)

HIDEO (*returning*): Bola and I went up to look at the water tower. The windmill's fine, the gears need a little oil. But the storage tank—water had been sitting up there for who knows how long. We drained and scrubbed it out. We just have to wait till it dries and cures.

ROSE (*checking the pot, looks over at the packages*): People gave so many things, and nice things. I could use some of those shirts, they're like brand new, huh?

HIDEO: We have enough for another shipment right now.

(ROSE *goes to porch to call* GRACE.)

ROSE: Grace! Come on in. Lunch is almost ready! (*Turn to* HIDEO.) So you taking those all in?

HIDEO: When Bola comes back with the car. We're all gathering at the Buddhist Church to organize the shipping. This goes to my uncle in Yamanashi-ken and this to your cousins and my sister-in-law's family in Hiroshima. And the rest will go to the orphanage in Tokyo.

ROSE: I feel sorry for all the families staying at the church— sleeping on the floor of the social hall.

HIDEO: <u>We're lucky we have this place to come back to.</u> ←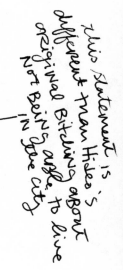

this statement is different than Hideo's original bitching about not being able to live in gone city

(GRACE *enters.* HIDEO *starts to move the packages to the front porch.*)

GRACE: Well, we got some of the tractors working—a couple of the Massey-Harrises and the John Deere. Mr. Mabalot is a genius with engines. I don't know where Hideo found him, but he's just what we need. He goes out and gets spare parts from some place, I don't want to ask him where. Hmm, smells good.

ROSE: It's not much.

GRACE: Those the vegetables that Bola dug up?

ROSE: Un-huh. I added them to the canned tomatoes we found.

GRACE: Can we still eat them, after all this time?

ROSE: Taste. The asparagus was no good, it had gone wild. But I think the onions are okay.

(GRACE *tastes.*)

GRACE: Still growing in our garden after all this time. Bola's something, isn't he?

ROSE: He's tenacious, huh? He just puts his nose in there till he gets what he's after. I think he likes digging around in the mud.

(HIDEO *reenters.*)

HIDEO: I'm just moving these out front. They'll be easier to load.

ROSE: Want some help?

HIDEO: No, no . . .

GRACE: How's the baby?

ROSE: Oops, I better check.

(ROSE *wipes hands and exits.* GRACE *starts taking off her shoes.* HIDEO *reenters.*)

HIDEO: Is there enough equipment to begin turning the soil?

GRACE: We should know in a day or so. Mr. Mabalot's a good worker. Think he'll stay on? We need some foremen.

HIDEO: He's Filipino.

GRACE: So?

HIDEO: So, nothing.

(HIDEO *takes the last load out as* ROSE *enters from the back.*)

ROSE: Sleeping like a little princess. Little Esther's such an easy baby. Not like Keiko's boy, next door in the barracks.

GRACE: He was okay once they could bring real milk in from outside.

ROSE: I didn't think I'd ever sleep, the walls were so thin.

(GRACE *starts to read the* Stockton Record.)

GRACE: It was Keiko and her husband that kept me awake . . .

ROSE: Oh, yeah . . . You ever think about adopting? Hideo was saying there are so many orphaned babies in Japan now.

GRACE: No.

ROSE: I would if I could. You need a husband, though.

GRACE: You can never tell where those babies come from.

ROSE: They're still babies.

GRACE: Mmm . . .

ROSE: Do you ever think that when you adopt, that it was somehow fated? And you got the baby you were supposed to have all along?

ACT ONE, SCENE THREE

GRACE: That's a nice fairy tale, Rose. *(HIDEO returns.)* I'm glad we're finding you a husband.
> *(HIDEO hears GRACE'S last sentence and responds to it.)*

HIDEO: Oh, that's right. Today's the big day, huh? What time is the fellow coming by?

ROSE: Three thirty.

HIDEO: Mrs. Okubo works fast.

GRACE: She wants our money. She says he comes from a very good family in Sacramento, quite wealthy. He was just hired as an accountant at a firm that handles the larger farming accounts. The way she talked about him, he seems like a great catch, huh.

ROSE: He's probably four-foot-eleven.

GRACE: Rose . . .

ROSE: Well, he might be. You notice Mrs. Okubo never said how tall he was.
> *(HIDEO goes to the photos on the cupboard.)*

HIDEO: Which one is he?

GRACE: That one . . .

HIDEO: So you going out or just sit around here and chat?

ROSE: No, we're going into town.
> *(GRACE hands HIDEO a piece of paper. We hear a car drive up.)*

GRACE: It's all set, the whole itinerary. Mrs. Okubo may be expensive, but she is thorough.

ROSE: We're going to watch the girl's basketball team play Sacramento at church—his sister's on the team. Grace used to play. She was pretty good.

GRACE: It was no big deal . . .

ROSE: The Stockton Busy Bees.
> *(CHIZ and BOLA enter. BOLA looks all disheveled.)*

GRACE: My god, what happened?

ROSE: Bola.

CHIZ: The Hawai'ian Hurricane was after another title.

BOLA: Come on, the guy deserved it. And if he didn't, then the other guys did.

HIDEO: You okay?

BOLA: Yeah, yeah . . .
> *(CHIZ looks out the window.)*

CHIZ: I expect the police any minute. How's the baby?

ROSE: She's been sleeping the whole time. I had to change her diaper once.

(CHIZ *goes to the back.*)

BOLA: Can I get some water? Rose?

ROSE (*going to get it*): Sure.

HIDEO: You got into a fight?

(BOLA *sits and* ROSE *hands him the water, which he guzzles down.*)

BOLA: You know how I've been having trouble finding office space to rent? Well, this one I called before I went. I didn't want to waste my time.

CHIZ: That's not where it happened.

BOLA: I'm trying to set the story up. On the phone—"Fine, fine, come on down—we have several offices available." The guy takes one look at me and I can tell. "Sorry we already rented the offices." So what can I do? Just the way he avoided looking me in the eye, you can tell . . .

(CHIZ *enters.*)

CHIZ: He's imagining it. If they didn't want to rent to you because you're Japanese, they'd just tell you. Why would they have to lie Bola? So then we go over to the country club. Bola's really steamed by now—because of what's just happened. But the manager—remember Larry?—he lets us right in. No problem. "Come on in Miss Chiz, sorry to hear about your father." I thought everything was fine, I was talking to people, they all asked about Papa. And then I hear this commotion. And there's Bola rolling around the floor with Mr. Bellingham, the president of the club. He hit Mr. Bellingham.

BOLA: I didn't hit him. (*Beat*) Okay, I hit him. But he was swinging back and so were all his friends.

CHIZ: Everybody's screaming and yelling, tables being knocked over—it was so embarrassing.

BOLA: Certain things I'm sensitive about. All of you know this. I don't make it a big secret. So I'm talking to Mr. and Mrs. Sanders and the discussion turns to how the Japanese Americans had their own fighting units. I guess they felt they had to bring it up since I was standing there. But, you know, they're nice

[Handwritten margin note: Bola couldn't rent office space because he was Japanese, so he got in a fight]

old fogies. Then out of nowhere, Mr. Bellingham pipes up about he's not sure whether it was a good idea as we were at war with Japan. He's not even part of the conversation. And his cronies are agreeing with him.

CHIZ: They were not agreeing with him—

BOLA: So I said, did he have the same feelings about Italian Americans or German Americans who fought in the war. Did he and his friends feel that was not a good idea? He said that was different. I asked why. He got flustered and turned away and began talking to the man next to him. Like if he ignored me I'd quietly go away. But I'm a Buddhahead, guess he never met one before, used to all you Kotonks on the mainland. But Buddhaheads don't like being treated like that—I just keep asking him why, he keeps ignoring me, I keep asking, he keeps ignoring—everybody's getting very uncomfortable, it's getting tense. But being a Buddhahead I say, "What the hell," and just keep putting my face in his. Finally, he says he doesn't like my attitude. That I should be grateful that we were still allowed into the country club. And that there was just something about us—not like the Italians and Germans, who were "okay," I guess—that made us different. And that an American G.I. could never tell when we might switch our allegiance to the enemy. That the difference was we couldn't be trusted.

CHIZ: Bola . . .

BOLA: That they were sneaky. Look at Pearl Harbor . . . My little brother, Jun-chan, died in this war. Along with all the other Buddhahead boys from the Islands, he spilled his blood so that those *haole* Texans could live. Jun-chan along with the rest of the 100th Battalion knew they were being served up like cannon fodder. They all knew, they weren't stupid. Going up to rescue a small battalion of soldiers trapped behind enemy lines. They didn't send any of the other units who were available. How could they sacrifice more soldiers than were being saved? Didn't make sense. But the 100th and the 442nd—the all-Japanese American units. Hey, they're expendable, let's send them. And they did and they went. Shig dies, Tak dies, George loses his leg, Paul loses his arm. They did it. To prove they were

(handwritten margin notes:) exhibition extreme pride

(handwritten margin notes:) reflecting the common feeling that the Japanese that were inscrutable & unreadable to the torturers

loyal Americans. And they proved it with their blood. So. Japanese American soldiers—Kotonks and Island boys gave up their lives. Eight hundred casualties to save two hundred *haole* boys' asses. And he says to me Japanese Americans can't be trusted. That we're sneaky. That they couldn't be counted on by the other American soldiers. He says that to me. To my face . . .

HIDEO: And then you hit him.

CHIZ: No he hit everybody. I think it's a Hawai'ian thing.

BOLA: No, no, they grabbed me. His friends, tried to pull me away. Hey, don't touch me, never touch me, especially if I'm pissed off.

CHIZ: Then he hit everybody.

BOLA: Then I hit everybody. I was fighting for my life, I had to defend myself—hey, they were trying to bust my ass. And they were big *haole* guys, this much taller than me—I knock 'em to their knees, and then I'm taller than they are. "Hello, Shorty."

CHIZ: Well. We won't be going back there again.

GRACE: You're lucky you didn't end up in jail.

HIDEO *(laughing, shaking his head)*: Or the hospital . . .

GRACE: I told you, didn't I?

BOLA *(to* HIDEO*)*: What?

(HIDEO *stares at* BOLA *for a beat.)*

HIDEO: Why are you so upset about what they say now?

BOLA: What do you mean?

HIDEO: You never heard what they were saying before?

BOLA: No, what are you talking about?

HIDEO: About the Japs and the 5th Column? About getting them off the West Coast? About herding them into Internment camps? These are the very same folks saying the very same thing. Why didn't you care about what they said then? Why didn't you hit somebody when it mattered? *(Beat)* No one cares what I think, anyway.

(HIDEO *turns and exits.* ROSE *is upset.)*

GRACE: Rose?

BOLA *(noticing)*: I'm sorry Rose. I didn't mean to talk about the 442nd boys.

ACT ONE, SCENE FOUR

CHIZ: He talks too much. You all right?

ROSE: I'm fine, I'm fine. I thought the last part of the story was funny. The part about, "Hello, Shorty."

GRACE: Chiz, I think you should look at the cut above Bola's eye.

BOLA: I'm okay, I got some bandages in my bag . . .

GRACE *(to* ROSE*)*: You better start getting ready. Take a bath. *(Announcing)* Rose's date is coming over at 3:30 to pick her up—

ROSE *(muttering)*: Oh, Grace . . .

GRACE: —so if you're going to show your face make sure it's clean. Otherwise, stay in the back until they leave.

    *(*CHIZ *moves to the photos.)*

CHIZ: Which one is it?

    *(*GRACE *points it out and they both inspect it.)*
    (Dim to darkness.)

Scene Four

Evening. BOLA *and* CHIZ *are playing rummy.* BOLA *has a bandage over his eye.* GRACE *is knitting.* HIDEO *is writing a letter to his brother.*

CHIZ: I thought he looked kind of young for Rose. Didn't any of you think so?

    *(*CHIZ *touches* BOLA'S *bandage to make sure it's on.)*

BOLA: How old is Rose—twenty-eight?

GRACE: Twenty-six.

BOLA: No spring chicken.

HIDEO: She's not old.

BOLA: So, we get the professor's attention. How old was Grace when you two got married?

GRACE: Bola, mind your own business.

CHIZ: Grace, didn't you think he looked kind of young?

GRACE: No, not particularly. He was kind of short, though. I know Rose prefers them on the tall side.

BOLA: She's gonna have to start considering those old maid type guys that live at home with their mamas.

CHIZ: Bola.

BOLA: I'm just kidding.

CHIZ: There are plenty of single men out there for Rose. She's still young, very pretty . . .

GRACE: And a Matsumoto.

CHIZ: And a Matsumoto, yes. And besides he's getting two beautiful sisters-in-law.

BOLA: Let's take a vote. Who says this guy is the one Rose chooses? No hands. Okay, who says he at least gets another date? No hands . . . oh, Chiz, you think so? I thought you said he was too young for Rose.

CHIZ: I liked his haircut and he drove a nice car.

GRACE: Let's just let her make her own decision. She's old enough for that.

(They hear a car drive up. CHIZ *and* GRACE *quickly get up and run to the window to peek out.* BOLA *figures he might as well look, too.* HIDEO *goes over to the fire and pokes at it.)*

CHIZ: He turned off the engine. They're staying in the car to talk.

BOLA: Or something else. Ooh, it's a Buick Unlimited.

CHIZ: No, they're getting out.

GRACE: Oh, what a gentleman, he's opening the door for her.

BOLA: See, that makes no sense to me—he's got to run all the way around just to open her door?

CHIZ: They're out. And, oh-oh . . .

BOLA: She's not letting him walk her to the door.

GRACE: Look how short he is compared to her.

CHIZ: They're shaking hands.

GRACE: Doesn't look good.

(They all quickly run and seat themselves as ROSE *hurries in.)*

ROSE *(moving)*: I hate having to hold going to the bathroom . . .

(She rushes past them into the back.)

CHIZ: I never ate, either.

BOLA: Oh, come on.

CHIZ: I was very dainty when I went out on a date.

BOLA: You ate more than my big brother—he stopped and watched you.

CHIZ: So I was a little hungry . . .

ACT ONE, SCENE FOUR

BOLA: How many desserts did you have?

CHIZ: I only had three servings, the *lilikoi* pie was very light.

BOLA: And then . . .

CHIZ: And then what?

BOLA: And then you ate the rest of the *lau lau.*

CHIZ: That's not a dessert.

BOLA: Then the *manapua* . . .

CHIZ: You always exaggerate.

(ROSE *returns and seats herself. Everyone watches her.*)

ROSE (*picking up a magazine*): Boy, thought I was going to burst.
   (*Pause.*)

GRACE: How was the evening?

ROSE: Hmm.

CHIZ: You going to see him again?

ROSE: He's very nice, but . . . I don't think so. GRACE, would you
   let Mrs. Okubo know?

GRACE: I'll talk to her when we go into town.

CHIZ: Knowing Mrs. Okubo, she'll be out here first thing in the
   morning.

GRACE: You want to see somebody else?

ROSE: I'm not good at this, Grace, I'm not.

GRACE: At least you meet boys who come from the same background. We know something about their families.

CHIZ: Otherwise, you get stuck with some poor, uneducated
   farmer whose family is full of disease and misfortune.

GRACE: Chiz . . .

CHIZ: I'm just trying to help her.

ROSE: All right. Why not.

   (ROSE *notices* HIDEO'S *handwriting and moves over to look.*)

ROSE: I wish I could write Japanese like that.

HIDEO: I've forgotten a lot. If you don't use it every day, you start
   to forget characters.

ROSE: What is that character?

HIDEO: *Kusuri.*

ROSE: Medicine.

HIDEO: Uh-huh. The top part of the character is *kusa*, plant. And
   the bottom half means enjoyment. "Plant enjoyment."

BOLA: Professor, who you writing?

HIDEO: My brother.

BOLA: Which one?

HIDEO: Tokyo.

BOLA *(to* ROSE*)*: You can read that?

ROSE *(shaking her head)*: I didn't like Japanese school.

GRACE: Papa let you skip it.

CHIZ: He let you get away with everything.

GRACE: Spoiled you rotten.

BOLA: We had a chicken back home who used to do just like what
Hideo's doing.

> *(He paws his feet.)*

HIDEO *(to everyone)*: I think I'll finish my letter upstairs.
Goodnight.

ROSE: Goodnight.

> *(Everyone says goodnight.* HIDEO *exits.)*

BOLA: Doesn't he ever loosen up? The guy's too serious.

GRACE: He's worried about his brother's family back in Hiroshima. They live on the outskirts but he's worried about how
much radiation they were exposed to. He couldn't get any of
the medicines they requested.

> *(*CHIZ *gets up to look at the photos on the cupboard.)*

CHIZ *(noticing)*: Hey, this guy's pretty cute.

ROSE *(pretending to not hear)*: Say, did anyone see them drilling
out where the Hershams' property meets ours? Just south of
the lake? We took the back way out going to town and you
can see them hauling all the equipment in.

GRACE: Mr. Hersham just refuses to give up. He probably talked
Pacific Gas into digging out there now. He's determined to find
gas on his land.

BOLA: Maybe we should get them to look on our land.

GRACE: Papa let them drill all over and they couldn't find anything. We should let Mr. Hersham know we're back.

CHIZ *(to* BOLA*)*: You and Papa would go duck hunting with Mr.
Hersham—remember?—and bring home sacks of ducks. And
we'd all have to help out pulling feathers and it'd get into everything, like it was snowing—your hair, your mouth.

ACT ONE, SCENE FOUR

ROSE: Let's invite Uncle Hersham over for dinner. Like we used to, when we came out on weekends. He and Papa'd come back from hunting, Mama would cook all the ducks up . . .

GRACE: Boy they were tasty. The way Mama cooked them, stuffed with apples and onion . . .

BOLA: Whatever happened to your father's guns? He had a double barrel 12-gauge and a smaller 16-gauge, I think.

ROSE: Didn't he hide them somewhere right after we heard about Pearl Harbor?

GRACE: That's right . . . somewhere in one of the bungalows, I think . . . where the workers stayed.

BOLA: Hey, let's go out back and look for them.

CHIZ: Bola, it's the middle of the night out there.

BOLA: I'll take the flashlight.

CHIZ: Bola, let's look in the morning . . .

BOLA: We can go hunt some duck or pheasant.
    (BOLA *exits.*)

CHIZ: Once he gets something into his head . . .

GRACE: So he was that boring, huh?

ROSE *(nodding)*: Un-huh. Didn't you think he was kind of short?

GRACE: I guess—a little, maybe.

ROSE: He had a nice car, though.

CHIZ *(to GRACE)*: See.

ROSE: Grace?

GRACE: Yes?
    (ROSE *doesn't speak.*)

GRACE: Rose?

ROSE: How was it when you and Hideo got together?

GRACE: What do you mean?

ROSE: You're marriage was arranged, wasn't it?

GRACE: Well, not really.

CHIZ: Yes, it was.

GRACE: It wasn't arranged. We were introduced.

CHIZ: *Introduced*, euphemism for arranged.

ROSE: Well, how did you feel about Hideo then? When you first met him?

CHIZ: Papa liked him so she did, too.

GRACE: Chiz. *(To* ROSE*)* People get together for different reasons, Rose. It isn't only just about you. It's the two of you. It's about the two families—

ROSE: But, I mean, you didn't have feelings for Hideo? When you got married?

GRACE: Rose, we didn't just meet, shake hands, then turn and walk down the aisle together. We saw each other for six months before we decided. Now. I don't want to talk about this anymore.

CHIZ: She had her chance.

GRACE: Enough, already.

*(*ROSE *turns her attention to* CHIZ.*)*

ROSE: You and Bola were lovebirds, though.

(Silence. ROSE *looks at* CHIZ *and* GRACE. CHIZ *looks at* GRACE.*)*

GRACE: Yes, Chiz, why don't you tell her *your* story? Hmm?

(Pause.)

CHIZ: Okay. All right. She's old enough, huh.

GRACE: It's your shame, not mine.

ROSE: What? *(Silence, looks from* CHIZ *to* GRACE.*)* What?!

GRACE: Chiz?

CHIZ: We had to get married. I was knocked up. Walking down the aisle I was four-and-a-half months along.

*(*ROSE *is speechless.)*

GRACE: That's why it was good Bola had his internship in St. Louis. She could leave and discreetly have the baby out there. Remember when I went back to visit them? It wasn't to help out a pregnant Chiz, it was to help out with the baby.

ROSE: And Papa knew?

CHIZ: Did Papa know? Whoa . . .

GRACE: Let's just say if Bola wasn't a doctor, Chiz would now be a Buddhist nun and Bola would be dead.

CHIZ: Bola handled it pretty well, though. Papa could crush you if you weren't tough enough. Bola surprised me how tough he was.

GRACE: I think Papa was impressed with him too. Papa made him sit down and drink with him—this huge bottle of *saké*. They had to talk, man-to-man. We found them, or we heard them, Papa in his underwear—

CHIZ: Bola was stark naked.

GRACE: —singing outside Chiz's window.

CHIZ: Papa couldn't sing on key—but boy, could he sing loud.
(Laughter. GRACE and CHIZ sing "China Nights." They quiet down and stare at the fire. CHIZ moves behind GRACE and begins to take her hair down. There is a familiarity to this gesture, as if they had done this together as children.)

CHIZ: Papa loved your hair.

GRACE: Chiz.

ROSE: I think it's beautiful.

CHIZ: He wouldn't let you cut it. It reminded him of Mama. *(Beat)* It was so much work to wash it. She only did it once a week. Remember?

GRACE: Un-huh . . .

GRACE: She kept it tied up in a bun. During her bath she would take it down. I used to help her. It was so long. It seemed to go on forever. A black, shiny river. She would lean over, pulling the hair across her shoulder and hold it out in front of her. I would pour the water from the bucket over her head, then work my way down. *(Beat)* Sometimes I would catch Papa peeking in and watching us.
(CHIZ continues with GRACE'S hair in silence. ROSE watches.)

CHIZ: You remember that night in Camp? When Papa died.
(GRACE doesn't respond.)

ROSE: Why, Chiz?

CHIZ: We were all at the dance at the canteen. Casey Nakamura's Big Band playing. You and Hideo were even dancing.

GRACE: Papa's gone. Let's move on with our lives.

CHIZ: Keiko told me she saw him walking along the outer fence. She was coming home early from the dance. She said she called to him but he didn't answer. What was he doing out there?

GRACE: It was snowing. He lost his way. He was an old man.
(Silence.)

ROSE: I thought winter was over. The Utsumis' garden was blooming. Everyone in Camp was in good spirits. Why did it snow? Such an odd thing to happen. In the middle of spring, it snows . . .
>   (CHIZ *strokes* GRACE'S *long hair.* ROSE *watches them.*)
>   (*Dim to darkness.*)

Scene Five

Day. We hear the sounds of radio music of the era. Lights up on ROSE *dancing with the baby. A man approaches the front door and knocks.* ROSE *turns off the music and answers the door with the baby. A handsome young man in his mid-to-late twenties stands there holding a package. More pictures of prospective husbands on the wall.*

ROSE: Yes?
>   (HENRY *Sakai stares at* ROSE *for a moment.*)

HENRY: Rose? It is Rose, isn't it?

ROSE: Yes.

HENRY: I'm Henry. Henry Sakai.
>   (ROSE *doesn't recognize him.*)

ROSE: Excuse me?

HENRY: My family used to work for your father—picking, driving tractor, sorting.

ROSE: I'm sorry, I . . .

HENRY: Then we leased a few acres from your father and started growing on our own. We used to all play together as kids.
>   (*Pause.*)

ROSE: There were three boys?

HENRY (*nodding*): Un-huh.

ROSE: And you were the middle one . . .

HENRY: No, that was Takashi—I'm the youngest, Henry.

ROSE (*gradually remembering*): Oh, oh, the small one. Your mother shaved your head, you were bald or something?

HENRY: Just one summer—I had ringworms.

Handwritten margin notes:
Enter Henry Sakai
— his family leased land from Rose's father before the war
after [?] mottie now

ACT ONE, SCENE FIVE

ROSE: Oh yeah, yeah—and you had a stocking cap on your head, too. My sisters kept teasing you.

HENRY: Yeah, they were pretty awful.

ROSE: "How come you're wearing stockings on your head?" That's right, I remember you—the crybaby with the bald head.

HENRY *(embarrassed)*: Yup, that's me.

ROSE: Come in, come in . . .

HENRY: Just for a moment, I don't want to disturb you or anything.

ROSE: No, no—would you like some tea?

HENRY: No, no, really . . .

ROSE: No trouble at all—let me put the baby to sleep.

(ROSE *exits with the baby.* HENRY *looks at all the pictures on the cupboard.* ROSE *returns and starts heating up a pot of water.*)

ROSE: The bottle ought to keep her quiet.

HENRY: I hoped you'd remember me. You just remembered too much. How many kids do you have?

ROSE: Oh—no, no, it's my sister Chiz's baby. Remember Chiz?

HENRY: She was the tomboy one, right? She beat me up once.

ROSE: Her baby. You're living where now?

HENRY: Watsonville—well, we were in Poston.

ROSE: Everyone around here went to Rohwer. *(Beat)* So are you here visiting?

HENRY: Uh-huh—What are these?

ROSE *(laughing)*: They're trying to marry me off. I'm being introduced to all the eligible men in the area. Mainly anyone with money.

HENRY: Who painted the mustache on this one?

ROSE *(sheepishly)*: I did.

HENRY *(remembering the question)*: Oh, I'm visiting relatives here, out in Manteca? They got recruited out of Camp by Driscoll Farms looking for workers. The Hayashino family?

ROSE: I don't think we know them.

HENRY: They didn't have anywhere really to go, and Driscoll got them out early and gave them housing and a plot of land to farm.

ROSE: Yes, I heard that.

(*Pause.*)

HENRY: You've grown up so much. You used to be this little girl, always hiding behind Grace. And when I'd try to talk to you, you wouldn't say anything.

ROSE: I was scared, you were the ringworm boy.

HENRY: Please, just one summer, just one summer.

ROSE: How is your family? Your mother and father?

HENRY: They're fine. Getting older but my father still works in the fields. A friend of the family, Mr. Martini, held the farm for us so when we got back from Poston, it was the same as when we left. Actually in better shape. And he saved the money the farm was making for us. Mr. Martini's been like a second father. Especially since I've taken over the farm.

ROSE: Oh the tea . . .

(ROSE *goes and pours the hot water into a teapot.* HENRY *sits.*)

HENRY: It's nice you can come back to your farm. A lot of people lost everything when they left, like my cousins—sold their farms for dirt cheap to those buzzards hovering around.

ROSE: Well, that's the way we lost our house in town. And as you can see the fellow my father leased the farm to didn't take the best care of it. But we're all determined to make a go of it again. Especially Grace.

HENRY: How is Grace?

ROSE: She's doing fine. She and her husband Hideo are out trying to recruit workers for the upcoming season. Here's your tea.

HENRY: Oh, thank you, thank you, this is nice . . .

ROSE: It just feels strange coming back to the farm. It's not the same without Papa.

HENRY: Yes, I was sorry to hear that.

(GRACE *and* HIDEO *enter the back anteroom and take off their shoes.* HENRY *stands.* GRACE *and* HIDEO *enter.*)

GRACE: I just hope they can do the work.

HIDEO: I was surprised how many Japanese were available.

GRACE: They have to do this kind of work for now. You think they'll keep it up once they get back on their feet?

(GRACE *and* HIDEO *notice* HENRY.)

ROSE: Grace, remember the Sakais? This is Henry, the youngest brother. Remember, the "ringworm" boy?

ACT ONE, SCENE FIVE

GRACE: Oh yes, yes, good to see you.

HENRY: Nice to see you, too.

GRACE: It's been so long, you've really grown up. This is my husband, Hideo. Hideo, Henry Sakai. His brothers and all of us sisters used to play together. Well, sit, sit, I'll get some teacups for us.

(The baby cries.)

ROSE: Sorry. *(She exits.)*

GRACE *(to HENRY)*: Chiz's baby.

(GRACE gets some teacups while HIDEO sits. HENRY remains standing.)

HENRY *(holding the package)*: Actually, it's not much, but this is from my mother and father.

(Offers it to HIDEO, who stands and takes it. No one is quite sure why this is being offered.)

GRACE: What is this for?

HENRY: I came to pay respects to you and your family on behalf of my family. Your father was very kind to my father. When he left here to go off on his own, your father lent him the extra money he needed to buy his farm. No one else would lend him the money. My mother and father are too old to make this trip so I came for them. My parents wanted you to have this gift. They felt very indebted to your father. My father said that Togo Matsumoto helped build the Nippon hospital and the Buddhist church. He would always say your father was a great man.

(Silence.)

GRACE: Well, I don't know what to say.

HIDEO: Please thank your parents on behalf of the Matsumoto family.

GRACE: Yes, yes, please thank them. They're much too kind.

(BOLA and CHIZ burst in holding a gunnysack.)

BOLA: The hunters return victorious! A couple mallards, a pintail and one small teal.

CHIZ: I'm not cleaning them.

BOLA: I said I will. Show 'em what else you got.

(CHIZ reaches in and pulls out a pheasant.)

CHIZ: A pheasant! I shot it driving back. I saw it hiding in one of the fields right off the levee. "Stop," I yelled.

(Acts out bringing up gun and shooting.)

CHIZ: Bang! Right out of the car window. Pretty good, huh?

BOLA: It was easy—pheasants fly like this . . .

(Moves his "wings" very slowly and moves in a straight line.)

BOLA: . . . slow and in a straight line. Now ducks fly like this . . .

(He flaps his arms very quickly. BOLA *notices* HENRY *and stops.)*

CHIZ: Oh hello, didn't notice you. Nice to meet you, I'm Chiz.

BOLA: Bola . . .

ROSE: And this is the "ringworm" boy.

HENRY: Rose . . .

*(*CHIZ *moves closer to get a better look.)*

CHIZ *(recognizing him)*: Hey, Henry! You're all grown up now! I used to pick on him.

BOLA *(sizing* HENRY *up)*: Not any more.

CHIZ: Stay for dinner. We're having duck and pheasant. The more the merrier. Bola's cleaning them! Is the baby upstairs? Excuse me.

*(*CHIZ *exits.)*

BOLA *(gathering up the gunnysack and exiting)*: I'll start pulling the feathers on these out back.

GRACE *(to* HENRY*)*: Would you like to? Dinner won't be for a while but you're welcome to stay.

HENRY: No, no, I couldn't impose on you folks . . .

ROSE: Yes, why don't you stay? We're having our neighbor over. Please?

HENRY: No, really, I feel like I'm—

*(*CHIZ *enters.)*

CHIZ: How's Takashi and that big, athletic brother of yours, Tetsu?

HENRY: Takashi is in Chicago, he's an engineer now, married, has kids. Tetsu. *(Beat)* We think he died during the firebombing of Tokyo.

CHIZ: Oh, I'm sorry to hear that.

ROSE: I'm so sorry, Henry.

HENRY: He was over there trying to start an export business when the war broke out. He got stuck there. I guess his whole neighborhood was burned to the ground. We assume he died.

(HENRY approaches GRACE and hands her something.)

I thought you might like to have this back. Your basketball medal. It was in his room with some of his other mementos.

GRACE: Thank you.

HENRY: Well, I really should be going. Thank you for your hospitality.

(Starts to exit.)

HENRY *(to ROSE)*: It was nice seeing you again.

ROSE: Nice seeing you again, too.

HIDEO: Nice meeting you.

CHIZ: Tell your mother and father we said hello.

HENRY: Good-bye.

(HENRY exits. GRACE is silent.)

GRACE: I think I'll take a walk. *(She exits out the front door.)*

(CHIZ joins ROSE.)

ROSE: What was that all about?

CHIZ: Grace used to go around with Henry's brother Tetsu.

(HIDEO walks through the French doors and watches GRACE walking in the fields. CHIZ and ROSE see HIDEO watching GRACE.)

CHIZ: Grace and Tetsu wanted to get married. The son of a poor tenant farmer marrying Togo Matsumoto's eldest daughter? *(Shaking head)* Un-uh. Papa said, "No." So Grace, being the good and obedient daughter, told Tetsu she couldn't marry him. A few years later Papa arranged the marriage with Hideo and Grace did what she was supposed to do.

(GRACE lit in pool of light. HIDEO watches her in half-light. Everyone else dims to darkness.)

(GRACE looks down at her medal. Dim to darkness.)

Scene Six

Evening. The aroma of roasted duck fills the house. ROSE is getting the table ready and GRACE is in the kitchen. BOLA stands by the win-

dow, practicing with the shotgun. CHIZ *is reading a magazine.* HIDEO *is out back working. Knock at the door.*

GRACE *(off, from kitchen)*: Chiz! Can you get it?

CHIZ: Bola?

BOLA *(practicing with the shotgun, ignores the request)*: I don't know how your old man did it.

ROSE: I'll get it.

GRACE *(off)*: Rose, can you help me in here . . .

ROSE: Okay, just a moment . . .

CHIZ *(to* GRACE*)*: I can help.

    (ROSE *answers the door.* MR. HERSHAM *arrives, holding a bag.)*

ROSE: Uncle Hersham!

HERSHAM: Hello, Rose.

ROSE: Come in, come in . . .

    (HERSHAM *hesitates for a beat.)*

ROSE: Come in, don't stand out there.

    (HERSHAM *enters.* CHIZ *approaches him.)*

CHIZ *(shaking his hand)*: Mr. Hersham.

HERSHAM: Hello, Chiz.

CHIZ: How are you? It's been so long. Where is Mrs. Hersham?

HERSHAM: She couldn't make it.

    (Beat.)

CHIZ: It's too bad the boys aren't here, you won't recognize them, they're big now. They're visiting Bola's sister in L.A.

    (BOLA *approaches.)*

BOLA *(shaking* HERSHAM'S *hand)*: We got another one, too. A little girl. I'm a baby machine.

HERSHAM: How are you, Bola?

BOLA: Good, good. You gained some weight.

GRACE *(entering)*: I need some help taking the ducks out of the stove—

CHIZ: Look who's here.

GRACE: Mr. Hersham . . .

HERSHAM: Hello Grace.

GRACE: You're a little early but that's okay. The ducks are done.

ACT ONE, SCENE SIX

ROSE: We weren't sure if you'd found the invitation or not. The house was all dark, I slipped it under the door.

GRACE: We just got our phone hooked up.

HERSHAM: I brought this. Canadian Club. The kind your father liked.

(Offers the bag of whiskey. BOLA *takes it.)*

GRACE: Sit, sit . . .

BOLA: Yeah, sit down, Joe. How's the farm doing?

HERSHAM *(moves but doesn't sit)*: Better, much better. I don't know if you heard, but I managed to turn things around.

CHIZ: Maybe Mr. Hersham can give us a hand.

BOLA: I'll say. You see our fields? And you should see the equipment.

GRACE: We'll do just fine. Rose, why don't you get a glass for Mr. Hersham?

BOLA: Good idea. For everyone.

*(ROSE *moves to the kitchen.* BOLA *takes the bottle out of the box and begins to open it.)*

BOLA: Hey, we got some nice ducks and we were only out there for a few hours. Out by Bacon Island. We gotta go.

HERSHAM *(nodding)*: Un-huh.

GRACE: Where's Mrs. Hersham?

HERSHAM: Jeanette's down in Bishop visiting her family on the ranch. She can hobnob with her family's society friends.

*(HIDEO *enters from out back.)*

BOLA *(to* HIDEO*)*: Hey, Professor—maybe Joe can help us figure out what to put in this season.

*(HIDEO *shakes* HERSHAM'S *hand.)*

HERSHAM: Hideo.

HIDEO: It's a mess.

*(ROSE *returns with glasses.* BOLA *begins to pour.)*

BOLA: Joe? Hideo?

*(HIDEO *shakes his head.)*

GRACE: None for me.

ROSE: Me either.

BOLA: Then who's going to drink besides Joe and me?

CHIZ: Me.

BOLA *(to others)*: Come on, this is a big deal. We haven't seen Joe since we left.

HERSHAM: I saw Grace and Rose when I visited you folks out in Arkansas.

BOLA: Yeah, but you leave without saying hello to Chiz and me.

HERSHAM: I had a business meeting in Kansas City. *(Pause)* When I saw where they put you all. It made me sick.

(Long, awkward pause.)

BOLA *(quietly)*: Let's drink. Come on, all of us.

(BOLA pours glasses for everyone.)

GRACE: A little . . .

ROSE: Just a little for me, too . . .

(BOLA finishes pouring. Lifts his glass.)

BOLA *(toasting)*: To good neighbors.

(They lift their glasses.)

ALL: *Kampai.*

HERSHAM *(lagging slightly)*: *Kampai.*

(They all drink. The flavor's a bit strong for GRACE and ROSE.)

HERSHAM: Haven't said that in a while.

GRACE: That was awful . . .

BOLA: What do you mean, this is good whisky . . .

GRACE *(remembering)*: Oh, the ducks. Rose, help me in the kitchen.

CHIZ: I can help, too.

HERSHAM: Saw that car out there, is that yours?

BOLA: We had to borrow it. What a jalopy.

(As CHIZ follows them to the kitchen, she sees BOLA pouring another shot for himself and HERSHAM.)

CHIZ: Bola . . .

BOLA: Just a little bit more . . . *(To HERSHAM)* I want to ask you something . . .

(They move to the window; BOLA picks up the shotgun.)

BOLA: When you went hunting with Togo? He could get off two shots real fast—bang, bang. Did he do some trick with his trigger finger or something?

HERSHAM: Nah, not that I could tell.

ACT ONE, SCENE SIX

BOLA: 'Cause I'd just be bringing up my gun . . .

HERSHAM: And he'd bring down his bird . . .

BOLA: Yeah, and your bird, too. Greedy son-of-a-gun.

HERSHAM: Yeah, he'd do that, huh?

> (GRACE *and* ROSE *enter with two platters of roasted ducks.* CHIZ *trails with a bowl of rice.*)

CHIZ: Food, food . . .

GRACE *(noticing* BOLA*)*: Please put that gun away.

BOLA: I'm just asking Joe something.

GRACE: I don't want you shooting that thing in the house.

BOLA: That was your father's idea, not mine. *(To* HERSHAM*)* He saw a pheasant outside, shot it from right here.

GRACE: Nearly broke all the glass in the house.

BOLA: Than he finished off his drink.

HIDEO *(seating himself)*: Umm, smells good.

ROSE: Sit where you always sit, Uncle Hersham.

BOLA: Joe, let's eat—come on, come on . . .

HERSHAM: This is such bad business. You all having to move out. Go to that place.

ROSE: We're all back now. We're all home.

> (BOLA *and* CHIZ *seat themselves while* GRACE *and* ROSE *help to lay things out.* HERSHAM *has moved over to the* obutsudan.*)*
> (HERSHAM *stands before the shrine looking at the photos. He bows his head and says a silent prayer. Turns back to the others who are watching him.*)

HERSHAM: Your Papa was a good friend. Seeing you all here, the food, everything . . . It's like Togo is still with us. Drink in one hand, telling me how I can't shoot worth a lick.

> *(Pause.)*

HERSHAM: When I left Hooker, Oklahoma. To come out here? My Pa wouldn't come with me. Wouldn't give up his land. Said it'd taken too much of his blood and sweat, it was part of his body. "What's a man worth if he give it up so easily?" He was like your father that way. That was 'thirty-one. Then it didn't rain for four years. When I went to get him and bring him back here, Pa was dead. I buried him there. On his land. He knew he couldn't beat the drought. He knew. But he never gave it up.

(Long silence.)

GRACE: Mr. Hersham?

HERSHAM: He didn't tell you, did he?

(Pause.)

GRACE: Tell us what?

HERSHAM: He said he would tell you.

GRACE: What? Tell us what?

(Pause.)

HERSHAM: Your father sold the place. He sold the land, this house, everything.

GRACE: What?

HIDEO: When did this happen?

HERSHAM: When I visited you in Camp, remember?

GRACE: Yes, but he never mentioned it to us, he never mentioned it once.

HIDEO: He sold it to you then?

HERSHAM: No, no, I didn't buy it. The Bank of San Joaquin bought it. I just brought the offer. I was out that way. So they asked me to act on their behalf and bring it.

GRACE *(moving towards* HERSHAM*)*: Bank of San Joaquin?—I don't believe it. I don't believe it!

HERSHAM: This is such bad business.

GRACE: But why would he do it? Why sell it to a bank, he didn't have a loan out, I would have known. And why would he keep it a secret from us? Huh? Why?

HIDEO: Please Grace . . .

HERSHAM: I don't know Grace.

GRACE: I would have had to sign for any sale. Papa wasn't a citizen.

CHIZ: It's not his fault, Grace.

HERSHAM: He told me he would tell you.

CHIZ: That's all right, Mr. Hersham.

GRACE: I don't understand.

HIDEO *(helping* GRACE *sit)*: Why don't you sit. Come on, Grace.

(Awkward silence.)

HERSHAM: When I found your note I didn't know what was going on. I should be going. Is there anything I can do?

(No response.)

ACT ONE, SCENE SIX

(Baby cries.)

BOLA: I'll go check on her.

HERSHAM: They probably didn't tell you there's some money at the Bank of San Joaquin. From the sale of the farm and land. *(Pause)* Well . . .

HIDEO: Thank you, Joe.

(HIDEO *goes out on the porch with* MR. HERSHAM. *Everyone else sits in stunned silence.* MR. HERSHAM *exits.)*

CHIZ: Papa sold this place? Why?

GRACE: He did not sell this place, no. I don't believe it. Papa would never sell this place. Never.

(Silence. BOLA *enters with the baby)*

(Dim to darkness.)

[END OF ACT ONE]

ACT TWO

Scene One

Two days later. Daytime. CHIZ *and baby sleeping in the back.* ROSE *returning from the back with an empty bottle.* BOLA *cleaning the two shotguns.*

ROSE: I finally got little Esther to sleep. It's like she knows. Chiz is out like a light.
>   (ROSE *crosses to join* BOLA.)

ROSE: They're still not back?

BOLA: Un-uh.

ROSE: I've never seen Grace like this. She hasn't slept for two days.

BOLA: They're going to find it's all legal, recorded and according to the law.

ROSE: At least Hideo went with her this time.

BOLA: The bank's not going to do something stupid. All the records are just disorganized because of the war. For whatever reason, your father decided to sell and not tell Grace.
>   (*Pause.*)

ROSE: Remember when Papa was roughed up in Camp? By those pro-Japan loyalists?

BOLA: Bunch of punk Tojo-lovers. They were Hideo's buddies.

ROSE: They were not Hideo's buddies.

BOLA: He attended their meetings, sympathized with their cause. And then says he had nothing to do with the beating.
>   (ROSE *shrugs.*)

ROSE: All I know is after that Papa didn't seem the same. Did you notice?

BOLA: He seemed a little quieter, but that's all. I mean, you can't blame him, everything was changing. He could hardly stand up like he used to at all the community meetings and say going

[handwritten margin note:] their attitudes were changed due to their Father's change in attitude. His voice was weakening — They definitely noticed

46   Sisters Matsumoto

into the camps was the right thing to do. That we'd be let out as soon as the government realized its mistake. A lot of people listened to him, because of who he was. Three years down the road, we're all still rotting in the camps. Your father had a reason to be quiet.

ROSE: He wouldn't eat with us at the mess hall. He just sat by the window, looking out.

(Knock at the door. ROSE *answers it. It's* HENRY.*)*

HENRY: Hello, Rose.

ROSE: Henry?

HENRY: Hello, Bola.

BOLA *(getting up)*: You're still here?

HENRY: Un-huh, few more days.

BOLA: Good to see you.

HENRY: Can I come in?

ROSE: Sure, sure . . .

*(*HENRY *enters.)*

BOLA: Well, I'm going to put these guns away.

*(*BOLA *exits.)*

HENRY: Oh, I brought you tomatoes from my cousins' farm.

ROSE: Thank you.

*(*ROSE *takes them to the kitchen and puts water on the stove. She returns, sits, and motions to* HENRY, *who sits also.)*

ROSE: I'm heating some water for tea. I didn't think I'd see you anymore.

HENRY: I was supposed to go back today, but I thought I'd stay a couple more days.

(Awkward pause.)

HENRY: I brought something to show you. I haven't shown it to too many people. I tried it out over at my cousins' farm.

*(*HENRY *goes out to the porch and brings in a kind of vacuum cleaner attached to a lawnmower engine.)*

HENRY: I invented it. I like making up things to help around the farm. This used to be my mother's vacuum cleaner.

ROSE: I hope she wasn't still using it.

HENRY: Oh no, no, I bought her a new one. Now we've been having a lot of trouble with two-spotted mites on the strawberries. They live on the underside of leaves. Kind of reddish in color. And the normal way to treat that is to spray DDT on the plants. The problem is that DDT is just poison basically and I don't care to put that on the berries 'cause you end up eating some of it. So I was trying to think of a way to get the two-spotted mites off that wouldn't poison the strawberries. So I invented this . . .

(Pulls a cord to start up the gas-powered engine. We hear the loud whine of the motor along with a sucking sound. He approaches ROSE *and runs the head along her arms.* ROSE *finds this funny.)*

HENRY: See, you just go from plant to plant and vacuum the leaves. I made a new head to accommodate the leaves and adapted the suction so that it would pull the mites off but not damage the plants.

ROSE: Does it work?

(Turns it off.)

HENRY: Oh, it works. It's just a little slow compared to spraying. I set aside about a quarter of an acre to experiment with. No DDT, just the old "two-spotted mite-eater." See if I can harvest a whole crop of strawberries that's poison free. I'm not even pumping methyl bromide gas into the ground to kill the cyclamen mite. My Mom's helping me vacuum the plants. She thinks it's funny. But my Dad . . .

ROSE: Taking over the farm, that's a big responsibility.

HENRY: Tets and Takashi weren't interested so Dad gave it to me. The market's kind of competitive—lot of new growers. But Mr. Martini kept most of our customers and I'm trying to do some things a little different. Like my "two-spotted mite-eater." See if I can find a market that no one has thought of yet.

ROSE: I hope you do it, Henry.

*(*CHIZ *comes out from the back room still groggy.* HENRY *stands up.* CHIZ *goes to the sink and wets her face. Stretches her right shoulder.)*

CHIZ: Boy, I could use a cup of coffee. What a night. Esther crying. Grace pacing around till all hours. *(Noticing* HENRY*)* Henry. I thought you left.

ACT TWO, SCENE ONE

HENRY: Just stopped by to drop off some tomatoes from my cousins.

CHIZ: I just had this dream. We were kids again. We were all helping Mama cook those huge pots of rice for the workers. She was smiling and she had two *shamojis*, one in each hand, scooping out just-cooked rice onto those bamboo platters, all hot and steamy. And Papa on his tractor, singing at the top of his lungs. *(Pause)* Funny the things you think of . . . *(Pause)* What's that?

ROSE: The "two-spotted mite-eater." It sucks the mites right off the strawberry plants.

CHIZ *(thinking)*: Why don't you just use DDT?

ROSE: Because it's not healthy for you.

HENRY: I'm trying to grow healthy fruits and vegetables that people can eat without putting poisons in their bodies.

(CHIZ looks at HENRY.)

CHIZ: First ringworms and now two-spotted mites. *(Beat)* Just kidding, just kidding.

ROSE: Sit down, Henry, I'll fix the tea. Chiz, You want coffee, I'll make it?

CHIZ: No, no, tea's fine.

(Pause.)

(CHIZ and HENRY settle into the seats.)

HENRY: How are you?

CHIZ: Truth? Crummy. *(Beat)* Did you tell him about the farm?

ROSE: I wasn't sure if it's something we wanted to talk about yet.

CHIZ: Might as well. With Grace running around in town, he'll hear about it sooner or later.

HENRY: Hear what?

ROSE: We don't own the farm anymore.

CHIZ: Papa sold it. He didn't even tell us.

HENRY: He sold the farm?

ROSE: Un-huh . . .

(GRACE and HIDEO come in. GRACE sits down exhausted.)

CHIZ: What'd you find out?

HIDEO: It's all legal. It's been sold.

GRACE: I remember now. Papa gave me a bunch of papers to sign.

When Mr. Hersham was visiting. I should have known something was funny. Papa kept pushing me: *hayaku, hayaku.*

HIDEO: We have to get out by this weekend. They want to start tearing things down.

GRACE: Oh, hi, Henry.

ROSE: If you didn't know what you were signing, is the sale legal?

CHIZ: Who do you think they'll believe in court? The bank or some Japs that just got out of prison?

GRACE: Please don't use that word, Chiz.

HENRY: Maybe I should be going . . .

ROSE: No, no . . . maybe we can go for a drive?

HENRY: You sure it's okay?

ROSE: We'll be back soon. There's some hot water for tea if you want it.

(ROSE *pulls* HENRY *along and they exit.*)

GRACE: I'm going upstairs for a while.

(CHIZ *and* HIDEO *are left alone with* HENRY'S *invention.* CHIZ *and* HIDEO *stare at it.*)

CHIZ: It's called a "two-spotted mite-eater."

HIDEO: Oh.

(*Dim to darkness.*)

Scene Two

ROSE *and* HENRY *outside. Silence.*

ROSE: Everything seems to be falling apart.

HENRY: You all right?

ROSE (*nodding*): Un-huh. (*Beat*) How fast does that truck of yours go?

HENRY: It's kind of old, just a Ford pickup. I don't know.

(*Pause.*)

ROSE: Henry, are you poor?

(*Pause.*)

HENRY: We don't have much money. But we're not poor.

ACT TWO, SCENE THREE

> (ROSE *looks at* HENRY.)

ROSE: Henry Sakai. I like you.

> (HENRY *is flustered but enjoying this.*)

HENRY *(motioning offstage towards the truck)*: Shall we find out?

ROSE: Yes, let's find out . . .

> (HENRY *pulls* ROSE *along.*)
>
> (*Cross-fade.*)

Scene Three

BOLA *at the balcony looking out. Drink of whisky in his hand.* BOLA *drinking but not drunk. Bottle on the table.* HIDEO *packing boxes to send to Japan.*

BOLA *(looking out window)*: I'm going to miss this place. I love to hunt duck here. Don't have that back in Kauai—mountain goat, boar, small birds, but not ducks like here. This delta region has just about everything. But the people here . . . *(Pause, recovering.)*

BOLA: I had some fun times going out with the old man, though. Togo Matsumoto was a character, just like my old man. Togo always told you right to your face what he was thinking. You two never much got along, huh?

> (HIDEO *doesn't respond.* BOLA *looks back at* HIDEO.)

BOLA: So what do you think of this whole mess?

HIDEO *(shrugs)*: I don't know.

BOLA: Guess we just have to do it on our own now, that's all. Can't rely on the wives' money anymore. That's fine—didn't need it before, don't need it now. I'll make money for us. You, too, if you need it. I'm not stingy.

HIDEO: We'll do just fine once I get the newspaper going.

> (*Pause.*)

BOLA: So the newspaper's been decided on, huh? I guess you don't have to listen to Grace anymore. You must be very happy now.

> (HIDEO *decides to ignore* BOLA.)

BOLA: Well, I mean, they've lost the farm. You don't have to pretend you like taking orders from the rich wife.

HIDEO: Maybe you've had enough to drink.

BOLA: No, no, I'm just getting started, Professor. I know you look down your nose at me. The Tokyo University graduate who had to marry down in order to marry up. That's funny, huh. You have to marry a rich, uneducated peasant's daughter in order to move up in social standing here. Now that's a success story. Here's to you, Professor.

(BOLA *raises his drink to* HIDEO. *Downs it.*)

HIDEO: You think because I don't talk all the time, I'm looking down at you. Maybe it's got nothing to do with you. Maybe my silence is not silence at all but an angry shout I have to keep locked inside. I was a good son. I did what my parents asked me to do. Should I indulge myself, talk about my feelings, tell you what I think of you? Just open my mouth and yak away? Should I, Bola? Or should I just keep silent?

(HIDEO *reaches across, takes* BOLA'S *glass, pours a shot, and downs it in one gulp.*)

HIDEO: Now excuse me, I have work to do.

(HIDEO *turns away from* BOLA *and returns to packing boxes.* BOLA *exits, sees* CHIZ.)

CHIZ: Bola, I thought I'd show Esther the farm one last time. Come on.

(BOLA *joins her. They exit.*)
(*Cross-fade.*)

Scene Four

HIDEO *is wrapping up packages to send to Japan.* GRACE *enters.*

GRACE: What are you doing?

HIDEO (*looks up, sees* GRACE, *then goes back to packing*): There're still no medicines in Japan, there's a shortage of clothing— nothing's changed over there.

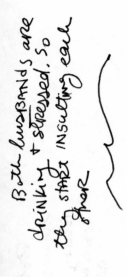

Both husbands are drinking + stressed. So they start insulting each other

ACT TWO, SCENE FOUR

GRACE: We just lost everything and here you are worried about the people over in Japan? What about us?

HIDEO: What about us?

GRACE: What do we do now? Huh? What are we supposed to do?

HIDEO: Why are you asking me? You never asked my opinion before.

GRACE: You're my husband, aren't you?

(HIDEO *stares at her, then goes back to packing.*)

GRACE: Why are you always thinking about Japan? You and your Kibei friends. "Japan is great," waving flags and shouting "Banzai!" With my Papa being such an important figure in Camp—do you know how that made me look?

HIDEO: So what should I do? Pretend I was happy they put us in Camp like your father? Japan never did that to me. What was I supposed to do? Huh?

GRACE: You could have fought. You could have finally shown some guts like Rose's fiancé and Bola's brother.

HIDEO: This country doesn't give a damn whether they lived or died.

GRACE: They died for something. Why do you think they let us out, huh? Why?

HIDEO: Because they had to.

GRACE: What do you mean, "they had to"?

HIDEO: They let us out because they had to. The court cases challenging the camps? They knew there was no way they could keep us locked up much longer. Hell, they had to create trumped up charges to get us into camps in the first place. The war was pretty much decided and what were they going to do with all of us? Soon there would be thousands and thousands of us pouring out into an America that had been whipped into such a state of Jap-hating who knows what might happen?—they'd have all this blood on their hands. How to reverse public sentiment? Then it comes to them. Let's make up an all-Japanese American fighting unit, let them go out, get killed defending the country and voila, instant war heroes. American war heroes. Serve them up like—what did Bola call 'em—cannon fodder, who cares. Then the country would open its arms and welcome us back.

Sisters Matsumoto

[handwritten marginalia:] Grace feels helpless & feels like Hideo doesn't support America at all. She sort of blames him for making the family "look" unpatriotic at Camp

[handwritten marginalia:] Hideo points out that U.S. cares 0. For their lives—they just want to come across as equitable to others

53

You think that it made a difference to this country—that Rose's fiancé and Bola's brother died for something? They died for a PR stunt to save the government's ass.

> (ROSE *enters, taking a scarf off her head after the ride. She overhears the last part of* HIDEO'S *conversation.*)

ROSE: Is that what they died for?

HIDEO: Rose . . .

ROSE: Did they die just for that?

HIDEO: It's what I believe.

> (*Long pause.*)

ROSE: You sound just like the pro-Japan loyalists back in Camp.

HIDEO: I'm sorry, Rose.

ROSE: Did you have anything to do with my Papa's beating?

HIDEO: No.

ROSE: But you knew who did it?

HIDEO: Yes.

ROSE: And you didn't say anything? How could you do that? You helped take Papa to the infirmary. You sat with me, all night watching over him.

HIDEO: Yes.

ROSE: And you don't say anything. I used to admire you.

HIDEO: I'm still the same person.

ROSE: I'm not. I've changed. Everything's changed.

GRACE: Rose.

> (ROSE *runs out.* GRACE *stands there looking at* HIDEO.)

HIDEO: You knew?

GRACE: I suspected.

HIDEO: All this time you knew?

> (*Pause.*)

GRACE: Why did you marry me?

> (HIDEO *doesn't respond.*)

GRACE: When Papa wanted something he wouldn't stop until he had it. Education, the one thing he didn't have and you did. I always said yes to Papa. How come you said "yes," Hideo?

> (*Long pause.*)

ACT TWO, SCENE FIVE

HIDEO: My family was in debt.
GRACE: That's it? Money?
   (Pause.)
GRACE: And now that the money's gone?
   (HIDEO *is silent. Dim to darkness.*)

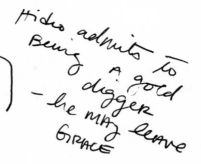

[Handwritten note: Hideo admits to Being a gold digger — he may leave Grace]

Scene Five

BOLA *and* CHIZ *walking in the fields.* CHIZ *holds the baby.*

BOLA: I don't know . . . Hideo . . . Maybe I'm taking it out on him, but sometimes I get the feeling he thinks he's better than me.
CHIZ: Don't let him bother you.
BOLA: Maybe if I'd gone to some high-tone place like Tokyo University I could find an office to rent.
CHIZ: That's not the reason, Bola.
BOLA: Yeah, I know. *(Pause)* This just isn't what I had in mind. You know? I had something else planned. My whole family sacrificed just so I could become a doctor. I'm supposed to have a practice, a home, my kids with me.
CHIZ: I know, I know honey . . .
BOLA: Instead, I get shipped off to some swamp in Arkansas. I'm told to start cutting people open with no medicines, no facilities and no trained staff—working sixteen-hour days—hell, I don't even know if I killed somebody.
CHIZ: You did a wonderful job. Everyone knows how hard you and the rest of the people in the infirmary worked. Besides, if someone had died, we would have heard about it.
BOLA: Oh, funny.
   (Baby cries.)
BOLA: I'm starting to wonder if leaving the boys in L.A. was a good idea.
CHIZ: Los Angeles is still safer.
BOLA: What about the White Star Sodaworks?

CHIZ: Look at here. Some men beat up the Kaneshiro boy in town—he was just walking along Washington Street. And they still don't know who shot the farmer in Lodi.

(Checking the baby.)

CHIZ: I have to ask around to see if the schools are okay. If any kids so much as touch a hair on our boys' heads, I'll break their necks.

(Pause.)

CHIZ: Did I ever tell you 'bout the time I heard the corn? I was playing hide and seek with Grace and the Sakai boys and it was around dusk and the sun was going down. I ran into the cornfields, crouched down and closed my eyes. I always thought if I closed my eyes, I was harder to find. Then I started to hear this funny sound. A crackling noise, like someone was crumpling up paper. Only it was pleasant. And it was coming from all around me. This wonderful, crispy, soothing sound. I knew if I opened my eyes it would go away so I kept my eyes closed and I listened and listened. When I finally did open them it was dark and everyone was gone. I got scared that I might get into trouble and ran home as fast as I could. That night, as I lay in bed, I began to hear the sound again. Ever so faintly, carried on the wind that passed over the fields and blew into my room. And I knew what the sound was. It was the corn growing.

(Pause.)

CHIZ: I wanted our kids to grow up here like my sisters and I did. Playing out here in the fields, getting their ears and hair filled with this spongy, black peat. Now I guess we just have to do it differently.

(Cross-fade.)

Scene Six

Next day. Dusk. The last day in the house. They must leave in the morning.

ACT TWO, SCENE SIX

ROSE *is moving furniture out of the way and covering it with white sheets again.* GRACE *is intensely wiping the dust off of things.* HIDEO *enters the house.* ROSE *turns away from him.*

HIDEO *(to* GRACE*)*: Mr. Mabalot took care of the rest of the workers and I want to pay him a week's extra salary. He'll stay on for a couple more days and take care of any loose ends. As far as the equipment, I'm assuming the bank will take care of it. Let them make all the arrangements.

GRACE: Is Bola back yet?

ROSE: Where'd he go?

GRACE: I don't know, he said he had to get some things. Did Chiz go, too?

ROSE: I don't think so. Maybe she's upstairs with the baby.

*(*HIDEO, *ignored, exits.* GRACE *is aware of* ROSE'S *coolness toward* HIDEO.*)*

GRACE: Rose?

*(*ROSE *doesn't answer.)*

GRACE: You and Hideo—you all right?

ROSE: I'm not a child anymore, Grace. I can take care of myself.

*(*ROSE *moves away and continues working.* GRACE *watches her for a beat.* CHIZ *enters wearing a tight sweater. Her bust is now big and pointy. She holds two badminton racquets.)*

GRACE: Why are we cleaning up? We're leaving tomorrow. No one's going to move in after us.

CHIZ: It's the Japanese thing to do. Mama always said you must never leave a place unclean. And I finally found these.

GRACE *(noticing)*: My god . . .

ROSE: What'd you do to your bust?

CHIZ *(modeling)*: Like 'em? The Betty Grable model. Got 'em in a specialty shop in St. Louis, just before we had the baby. I was depressed about my figure so I wanted to treat myself, something to look forward to. We're all so depressed now. I thought I'd try 'em out again. *(Posing)* Badminton, anyone?

GRACE: I don't know what to say . . .

*(*GRACE *looks at* ROSE *for help.)*

ROSE: They're . . . they're big. And . . . pointy.

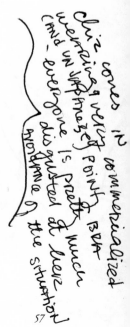

Chiz comes in wearing weird pointy BRA — everyone is pretty disgusted at their commercialized un Japanese response to the situation

Sisters Matsumoto   57

CHIZ: Didn't you always want bigger breasts like all the white girls in school?

GRACE: No. I think you look ridiculous.

ROSE *(coming closer to examine)*: That's amazing. Is it padding?

CHIZ: Yeah, but it's also got a wire under-meshing. I have a blonde wig upstairs, too.

ROSE: You do?

(ROSE and CHIZ start to run up the stairs. BOLA and HENRY enter. BOLA carries a paper bag.)

BOLA: That goddamn car finally died. If Henry hadn't come along, I would have had to walk the last two miles.

ROSE *(from the top of the stairs)*: Hi Henry.

HENRY: I thought I could help out. Moving things. My truck.

GRACE: Thanks.

BOLA: Since it's our last night here, I thought we should celebrate. *Saké*!

(Brings out a large bottle of saké. Everyone looks to GRACE, who motions to do whatever they want. BOLA starts opening a bottle and pouring. GRACE returns to her wiping. CHIZ poses at the top of the stairs.)

BOLA *(noticing CHIZ's bust)*: Whoa. . . . You gonna introduce me to your two friends?

HENRY: Don't we need to heat it up?

BOLA: Nah, who told you that? Room temperature is best.

(CHIZ and ROSE enter the bedroom.)

BOLA: Especially when you're in a hurry. Can you drive us into town tomorrow morning?

HENRY: Un-huh, no problem.

(CHIZ pokes her head out.)

CHIZ: Didn't you buy anything to eat, Bola?

BOLA *(pulling it out of bag)*: *Poi*! The store owner's Hawai'ian. He gave it to me.

CHIZ: Nothing else? Just *poi* and *saké*?

BOLA: We got lottsa food here, look in the icebox. We gotta eat everything up or just throw it away.

HENRY *(nodding)*: This is good this way.

ACT TWO, SCENE SIX

BOLA: See, I told you. Ice cold on a hot day is good, too. Want to try some *poi*?

(*HENRY tries some* poi. HIDEO *enters.* BOLA *walks over to* HIDEO *with a cup and bottle.*)

BOLA (*hands him the cup*): Good *saké*. Got it for you, Professor. (BOLA *offers the cup. They look at each other for a beat, then* HIDEO *extends his glass out.* BOLA *pours.*)

(CHIZ *and* ROSE *hurry down.* CHIZ *is wearing the blonde wig now.*)

BOLA: Whoa! Looks like Veronica Lake. I'm doing pretty good. A toast. Everybody get a glass? Come on. Come on.

(CHIZ *holds a record album.* CHIZ *hurries to put the album on the phonograph as* ROSE *grabs two filled glasses for them. The music starts.*)

BOLA: Everybody ready now?

ROSE: Grace?

(*They all notice* GRACE *lingering by the* obutsudan.)

CHIZ: Grace?

GRACE: Let's burn things.

(*Pause.*)

CHIZ: What?

(ROSE *turns off the music.*)

GRACE: I want to burn things. (*Silence*) Like Papa did when the FBI started taking people away. Some people buried their Japanese things, Papa had a bonfire.

CHIZ: I don't know, Grace. Hideo?

HIDEO: Why burn things now?

GRACE: I don't want strangers walking through the house touching our things.

HIDEO: Yes, but isn't that a little—

GRACE (*adamantly*): I want to burn things.

(*Long silence.*)

CHIZ: What kinds of things?

GRACE: Things that you don't want to be attached to. Things that you want to let go of. Last time they forced us to leave, what did we do? Huh? We trusted people to look after our

things and look what they did to us. That's not going to happen again. This time, they're not going to do that to us.
(Pause.)

HIDEO: I guess it's all right . . .

CHIZ: Everything we want to save we've set aside. All the stuff in the warehouse is ruined or stolen. They're tearing it all down. Let's burn things.
(CHIZ looks to the others.)
(Beat.)

BOLA *(looking around)*: Okay? *(Everyone nods, hesitantly.)* Okay. What kind of fire are we talking about?

GRACE: A big one. A bonfire. Like Papa's. Out front. So they can see it from the frontage road.

BOLA: A big fire, toss all kinds of things into it?

GRACE: Yes.

ROSE: Anything, Grace?

GRACE: Anything.

CHIZ: Things you don't want to be attached to, things you want to let go of . . .
(For a moment, they look around.)

HENRY: I've got some kerosene in my truck that'll start your fire.
(GRACE puts on record.)

BOLA: There's some wood right here.
(He hands a bucket of wood to HENRY. HENRY exits.)

ROSE: Oh, I know.
(She grabs the photos off the mantle, and exits.)
(GRACE disappears upstairs. CHIZ rummages through boxes and begins to gather things in her arms.)

CHIZ: Stale crackers, canned beans, Spam—

BOLA: You're not going to throw away the Spam.

CHIZ: I ate these kinds of things in Camp, I never want to eat them again.

BOLA *(going over and taking the Spam)*: Whoa, whoa, but Spam goes good with anything.

HIDEO *(starting to pull up a floorboard)*: I always hated this one. It creaked every time I walked on it. *(Pulling up on the floorboard)* Bola?

ACT TWO, SCENE SEVEN

BOLA *(seeing what* HIDEO*'s doing)*: Hey, all right, Professor!
> *(*BOLA *stuffs the cans in his pockets and they begin to yank on the board.* BOLA *and* HIDEO *let out "kiyais" as they do it.)*

BOLA: YAAAH!

HIDEO: EEEYAAH! The warehouse. Where the kids wrote all over the walls.

BOLA: I whitewashed it.

HIDEO: I want to burn the boards anyway.
> *(*BOLA *and* HIDEO *exit. Ad lib, "yoisho," as they throw the boards on the fire. Dim to darkness.)*

Scene Seven

A crackling light comes in through the front windows and open door. The sound of fire can be heard, then "In the Mood" playing loudly on the phonograph, as lights come up. CHIZ *enters from outside, wearing the blonde wig and wiping her hands together.*

CHIZ *(exiting up the stairs)*: So much for badminton.
> *(*GRACE *comes down from the stairs carrying a load of dresses and exits out the door as* BOLA *and* HIDEO *enter looking for more things to burn. Everyone is in an excited, festive state. Faces and clothes smudged with soot.)*
>
> *(*GRACE *exits.)*

ROSE *(off)*: Oh, that stinks!
> *(*ROSE *and* HENRY *stumble in laughing, their faces covered in soot.)*

ROSE: Why'd you do that?

HENRY: It's the only thing I had to throw in.

ROSE *(to* BOLA *and* HIDEO*)*: He threw in a spare tire.

HENRY: It's burning like crazy!
> *(The music is too infectious and* ROSE *grabs* HENRY *and they start dancing.)*

BOLA: Hey! Fred and Ginger! Grab those chairs. Hey. I figure if you're gonna have a bonfire, you better have a bonfire!

(ROSE and HENRY exit, carrying two chairs. Ad lib reaction to the smell of the tires.)

(HIDEO and BOLA start to exit.)

HIDEO: Hey, too bad we don't have a pig!

BOLA: Hey, maybe we sneak over to Hersham's and grab one of his!

(Offstage the group shouts as they toss wood into the fire, "yoisho!" GRACE stumbles in and stands for a moment in a daze. CHIZ comes down the stairs carrying a few items, including a small box.)

GRACE *(noticing)*: What is all that?

CHIZ: It's just odds and ends, from Camp—just the kinds of things we should be burning . . .

GRACE: Aren't those Papa's?

CHIZ: Yeah, but . . .

GRACE: No wait, let me see.

(Laughter outside.)

BOLA *(off)*: Chiz! Get on out here!

ROSE *(off)*: Grace, come on! You're missing the fire!

CHIZ: Okay, okay. Grace?

(CHIZ exits. More "yoishos" heard as the two chairs are thrown on the fire. GRACE seats herself and begins to look through the box. She finds Papa's spectacles and looks at them fondly. She then notices a letter. She picks it up and begins to read it. She stops and looks up, thinking. GRACE exits upstairs.)

(CHIZ, ROSE and HENRY come stumbling in followed by BOLA and HIDEO.)

CHIZ *(looking around)*: Grace, you gotta come out and see this now. Grace?

ROSE: We'd have a huge bonfire before the Big Game at Berkeley— lit up the sky . . .

HIDEO: What else is there to burn? The porch!

BOLA: Good idea!

ROSE *(going to the phonograph)*: I want to dance more . . . Henry?

HIDEO: The railing, everything.

BOLA: Professor, whoa.

(A car is heard pulling up. ROSE proceeds to put a record on. HENRY joins HIDEO.)

ACT TWO, SCENE SEVEN

HIDEO (*looking out the door*): Hey Joe.

> (HIDEO *holds the door open.* HERSHAM *rushes in.*)

HERSHAM: I saw the fire. Everyone all right?

BOLA: Joe. Everything's fine. No problem.

ROSE (*grabbing* HENRY *and dancing*): Hi, Uncle Hersham. This is Henry. Henry Sakai.

HIDEO and BOLA: EEYYAHH!

HERSHAM (*confused*): Are you sure everything's all right?

HIDEO: They're going to bulldoze it all down.

HIDEO and BOLA: EEYYAHH!

CHIZ: So we thought, you know . . .

All: Burn things!

CHIZ: Mr. Hersham? I know you and Jeannette like to dance.

HERSHAM: Well . . .

> (CHIZ *takes* HERSHAM *and they start to dance.*)

CHIZ: Not bad . . .

HIDEO: Anyone seen Grace?

BOLA: Hey, Joe, you got anything you want to burn? One of your pigs?

CHIZ: Bola.

BOLA: Taste gooood. Roast pork. Maybe do some kahlua pig.

HERSHAM (*stopping*): No, no. I didn't bring a pig. I brought something else for you. It's for your family. A Buick Road Master. I knew the other car wasn't working too good. It's right outside. Take a look. Come on. Take a look.

> (*Confused silence.*)

CHIZ: You're giving us a car?

HENRY: Top of the line.

ROSE: But why?

HERSHAM: I wanted to.

CHIZ: Yeah, but a car . . .

ROSE: I don't think we can accept this . . .

> (*They notice* GRACE *coming down the stairs. She's cut all her hair off. Everyone is shocked.*)

GRACE: It's for us?

CHIZ: Grace?

ROSE: Grace? Your hair? What did you do?

[handwritten margin note:] The point of forgiveness ←

[handwritten margin note:] brave cut her hair. she had long hair, like her mother's that had been admired

GRACE: The idea was to get rid of things. Things you didn't want to be attached to anymore. Well? *(Pause)* A car—it's rather extravagant, isn't it?

HERSHAM: No, no, not at all.

(Awkward pause.)

GRACE: It's as if you feel guilty about something.

HERSHAM: Grace, are you sure everything's all right?

GRACE *(holds up the letter)*: Mr. Hersham. I found this letter. It was sent to my father in Camp. It's from Mr. Daugherty, Papa's stockbroker. He writes that he heard a funny rumor going around involving Papa and made some phone calls. He found out that after Papa sold the property to the Bank of San Joaquin, a week later, title was transferred to Pacific Gas.

(Silence.)

HIDEO: What? . . .

GRACE *(to* HIDEO*)*: If we'd made them search through all the files we'd have found records of the transfer. *(To* HERSHAM*)* Did you know about that?

HERSHAM: Not at the time, no.

GRACE: They discovered gas on our land, didn't they? And you knew it when you visited us in Camp. And you worked with Pacific Gas and the Bank of San Joaquin to help them steal it from my father.

HERSHAM: No, I didn't know about the transfer to Pacific Gas, then. Later I learned they'd transferred title.

GRACE: Why would the bank send you to get my father to sell? Doesn't it seem odd? Didn't you wonder what was in it for them?

HERSHAM: I didn't know the bank's board were heavy stockholders in Pacific Gas.

GRACE: What was in it for you, Mr. Hersham?

HERSHAM: My farm was in trouble, okay? You all knew that. Hell, everybody knew it. They were going to take it away from me. Then they asked me to take this offer to Togo. I knew the land was stripped out, your father wouldn't want to come back to that. And if he tried to sell it on the open market—hell, look what happened to the other Japanese farmers when they tried to sell.

ACT TWO, SCENE SEVEN

GRACE: What did you get out of it?

HERSHAM: They knew your father'd never sell to them and that's why they asked me, and it didn't matter what they wanted, I knew I could help your father out.

GRACE: What did you get out of it!

HERSHAM: They took care of my outstanding debts. All of them.

BOLA *(muttering)*: That's how you managed to turn things around . . .

HIDEO: And you didn't know about the deal between the bank and Pacific Gas?

HERSHAM: Not at the time. No.

GRACE: How could you not know?

HERSHAM: Your father thanked me. When I explained what that boy had done to the farm. How things had changed, everything had changed, your father thanked me—

GRACE: Mr. Hersham, Mr. Hersham, couldn't you tell? He wasn't the same man. His whole community had turned on him, everyone had turned on him, he was a broken man Mr. Hersham, couldn't you see it? *(Beat)* Get out.

HERSHAM: Grace, it was the only thing to do. It was the only thing I could do.

GRACE: Get out, Mr. Hersham.

HERSHAM: I tried to help him. Think anybody else would? Hell no, it's war time. People hate the Japanese. But I helped him because we were friends, because your father was a good man and he always treated me fairly.

BOLA: So you lie and cheat him out of his land.

HERSHAM: No, I tried to help him—

BOLA: You helped yourself just like everybody else—

HERSHAM: I stuck my neck out—*(Continues.)*

BOLA *(overlapping)*: You're worse, 'cause you don't even have the guts to say what you really think.

HERSHAM *(continues)*: —for you people and almost got it cut off. *(Beat.)*

HERSHAM: Your people are over there killing our boys. American boys. Hey, the camps, this farm, all that's happened to you— whose fault is this whole thing, anyway? Who started this whole

thing in the first place? Was it me? Was it the Bank of San Joaquin? Was it Pacific Gas? No. Ask yourselves, really ask your-selves. If the Japs hadn't bombed Pearl Harbor, would you be in the mess you're in today?
> *(Silence.)*

ROSE: Mr. Hersham. We are Americans. (BOLA *picks up the shotgun.*)

BOLA *(holding it)*: Take your car, take your ass and get the hell off our land.
> *(MR. HERSHAM looks at them for a beat, then turns and leaves. BOLA cracks the barrel, loading shells as he goes out on the front porch. We hear the engine starting and the car driving away.)*

HIDEO: Bola?

GRACE: Oh, no . . .

CHIZ: Bola, don't do anything stupid—
> *(We hear two loud shotgun blasts. Silence. BOLA walks back in. They all stare at him.)*

BOLA *(shrugging)*: I missed.
> *(BOLA moves into the room and sits down. CHIZ goes to GRACE.)*

CHIZ *(touching)*: Oh, your beautiful hair!
> *(GRACE and CHIZ embrace. For a moment everyone is quiet. GRACE walks out on the front porch.)*

ROSE *(getting up)*: I better go check on her.

HIDEO: Rose, let me do it?
> *(HIDEO grabs GRACE'S sweater and goes outside.)*
> *(Cross-fade.)*

Scene Eight

GRACE *stands looking out into the night at their land.* HIDEO *enters and puts the sweater around her shoulders.*

HIDEO: It's pretty cold.
> *(GRACE nods.)*

ACT TWO, SCENE EIGHT

HIDEO: You want to be by yourself?

GRACE *(shaking her head)*: Un-uh.

> *(They stand looking out.)*

GRACE: He was too ashamed to let me know he was selling the land.

HIDEO: He was a proud man.

GRACE: And then to get that letter . . .

> *(Pause.)*

HIDEO: Maybe he was a little too proud.

> (GRACE *turns to* HIDEO.)

HIDEO: The letter was dated eight months ago. Your father got lost in the snowstorm about eight months ago.

> *(Silence.)*

GRACE: I'm tired of being proud all the time. I can't be my father's daughter anymore.

HIDEO: There's nothing wrong with being proud, Grace. Sometimes you just can't be proud all by yourself.

> *(Pause.)*

HIDEO: In the beginning. Us? I was the obedient son. At times, I wondered if the price was too high.

GRACE: Was it?

HIDEO: Let me be proud with you. And I'll know that my place is here.

> *(Pause.)*

GRACE: I always liked your way with words. Remember your lecture, Papa and I attended? "Twentieth-Century Japanese Novelists."

HIDEO: "You make peace with yourself when the individuality you were born with arrives where it belongs."

GRACE: Natsume Soseki.

> *(They quietly laugh.)*

HIDEO: You and your father were there to get a good look at me. Your father fell asleep right in the middle and snored so loudly I almost had to stop.

> *(They laugh. Calm down.)*

GRACE: Hideo?

HIDEO: Hmm?

GRACE: I don't know what to do.
> *(Pause.)*

HIDEO: Maybe if we're proud together we can figure something out.
> *(Crossfade.)*

Scene Nine

A little later. Lights up on the living room. HENRY *and* ROSE *playing cards.* CHIZ *and* BOLA *at the table looking through a box.* HIDEO *is off to the side on the floor looking through another box.* HIDEO *finds a paper and brings it over to* CHIZ *and* BOLA *at the table. They all begin to read it.* GRACE *enters from the back, wiping her face with a towel.* ROSE *notices her.* GRACE *joins the others at the table.*

GRACE: Did you find it?

HIDEO *(looking at the paper)*: Thirty-five thousand.

BOLA: Thirty-five thousand for this whole place—acreage, buildings, equipment?

HIDEO: That's it.

GRACE *(shaking her head)*: Papa . . .
> *(Looking around.)*

GRACE: I don't know what we can do. If we divide that up amongst us, it's not going to be enough to help any of us individually—buy houses, set up our businesses . . .

ROSE: We have the money from the sale of the house in town. If we put that together with the thirty-five thousand—

GRACE: No, no—that money's for your own families for absolute emergencies. Besides—for what we had to sell it—there's not much.

HIDEO: Then we should use the thirty-five thousand from the farm on something to help all of us.

CHIZ: Yeah, but what?

GRACE: I don't know . . . Hideo?
> *(Pause.* BOLA *tries to lighten the mood.)*

ACT TWO, SCENE NINE

BOLA: Hey, I know, let's place a bet on my brudda's racehorse, Buddha Buggy. Thirty-five thousand on the nose.

CHIZ: Bola, not now.

BOLA: I'm just trying to lighten things up—don't get your coconuts all in a bunch.

GRACE: Why don't we talk about this later when we get settled at the church.

HENRY: My brother Takashi? He wrote me that some of the Japanese who got out from the camps early couldn't find places to stay. So some of them chipped in together and bought boarding houses. This is out in Chicago? That way, they at least had their own place to stay and they could rent to other Japanese who were coming out. It's something I toyed with. If the farm didn't work out.

GRACE: I don't know . . .

HIDEO *(thinking)*: In the thirties, your father got together with some other Issei and started the Nippon Hospital. Because the white hospitals wouldn't treat them . . .

GRACE: Yeah?

HIDEO: What if we bought our own place? Like Henry was saying?

GRACE: A boarding house?

HIDEO: Old Man Sato's selling his place. Remember, I saw the sign.

BOLA: Yeah . . .

CHIZ: The Europa Hotel?

HIDEO: Why don't we consider buying it?

CHIZ: It's on the edge of skid row.

GRACE: Hideo . . .

HIDEO: They're still some Japanese businesses there.

ROSE *(pointedly)*: It's not the best area, Hideo.
 (Awkward beat.)

GRACE: Let's think of something else.

BOLA: Togo stayed there.

HIDEO: Un-huh . . .

GRACE: That was the only place they could stay in those days.

CHIZ: I'm not going to let my kids run around there. Broken wine bottles . . .

BOLA: Yeah, but do we have a choice? In case anyone's forgotten, we're all sleeping on the floor of the Buddhist church tomorrow night.

GRACE: Papa had a shooting gallery there. Next door to the hotel.

(Surprised beat.)

ROSE: The Europa Hotel?

GRACE: Un-huh. Mama made him sell it, she thought it was too dangerous for a baby.

BOLA: Ahhh, that's where Togo learned to shoot.

CHIZ: Papa had a shooting gallery? In skid row?

GRACE: It wasn't skid row then Chiz. Just a run-down section of town.

HIDEO: We can live in the rooms for free.

HENRY: If you own the hotel, you can use the other rooms for anything you want. You don't have to use them just for people to live in.

BOLA: Maybe I can set up my practice there for the time being.

HIDEO *(to GRACE)*: We can knock out a wall between two of the rooms and he'll have enough space.

GRACE: What about the rest of us?

HIDEO: We could set up a pharmacy downstairs. In the empty storefront. Rose?

(No response.)

HIDEO: We can hire another pharmacist to work with Rose until she feels comfortable on her own. We have a little money to refurbish and stock it—

(Pause.)

ROSE: I can run the pharmacy by myself.

HIDEO: Of course, of course you can. I've always known you'd stand on your own two feet one day.

CHIZ: Yeah, but skid row . . .

GRACE: Chiz. Papa and Mama lived there. For the time being, we can live there, too.

(Beat.)

HIDEO *(to CHIZ)*: And since you like bossing people around, you can run the hotel.

BOLA: He made a joke.

GRACE: Hideo? We should we call Mr. Sato.

ACT TWO, SCENE TEN

HIDEO: Tonight?

GRACE: Tonight.

GRACE: Rose, brew up a pot of strong coffee. Oh, see what's in the icebox, maybe make some sandwiches or something. It's going to be a long night.

ROSE: Henry, come help me.

> (ROSE *and* HENRY *go into the kitchen.*)

BOLA: Hey, and no hanky-panky in there.

CHIZ: I'm not bossy, am I?

HIDEO: Bola, we should talk about what we want from Old Man Sato. We should be sure there are rooms to make into your office. See if the storefront is usable.

BOLA *(back to* CHIZ, *hiding his smile)*: You're not bossy, Chiz.
> (*The family moves into action. Dim to darkness.*)

Scene Ten

Lights up. Hours later, still dark outside. House lit in half-light. Cups of coffee all around, a plate with a few sandwiches left on it. We see in semi-silhouetted action HIDEO *on the phone and* GRACE *watching him.* CHIZ *has the baby and is standing by the window looking out at something.* BOLA *is seated, sipping coffee and also watching* HIDEO.

> *Not hanging up,* HIDEO *sets the receiver down and comes back to confer with* GRACE. CHIZ *turns to watch and* BOLA *stands expectantly.* HIDEO *looks to* GRACE. *A beat. Then* GRACE *nods.* HIDEO *goes back to the phone to continue the negotiations with Old Man Sato.*
> *Cross-fade to* HENRY *and* ROSE *out in the fields, looking at the stars.* HENRY *is eating a sandwich and sipping coffee. He shares the coffee with* ROSE.

ROSE: God, the stars are beautiful out here. It's one of the things I missed most living in town. I used to sneak out here at night with a blanket. Just sit by myself looking at the stars. *(Silence. They look at the sky.)* I don't think about the future anymore.

Have dreams. Things I want to have. Things I want to do. I have a hard enough time accepting the past. *(Beat)* You still have dreams, don't you?

HENRY: Yes.

ROSE: Your farm?

HENRY: Un-huh. I'm going to make it into something. Make it prosper again.

ROSE: It's going to be hard. Not like it was before the war. They don't like us now.

HENRY: They never liked us. You just didn't notice it. You didn't have to. My father taught me to make the most out of things. No matter what's there or not there. You have to adapt. That's why I invent things, try new techniques, Rose. Tomorrow's going to be different, whether we like it or not. It doesn't have to be bad.

(Pause.)

ROSE: I had a fiancé. I met him in Camp. He died over in Italy. A lot of boys did. But when he died, I promised myself two things. One, that I would never forget him. Never. The other, that I would never let myself feel like that about any boy ever again. It's too painful. I promised myself those two things. Do you understand?

HENRY: What I know is that nothing's given to you. Nothing's promised to you. You have to go out and earn it with hard work and more hard work. That's all you can do, that's all anyone can do and that's what I plan to do. Every day of my life. Till I get what I want.

ROSE: I bet you will. I bet you will.

(Dim to darkness on the young couple.)

(Cross-fade to inside the house. Lights are brought up to full. CHIZ *is standing by the window looking out.* GRACE *is pacing, watching* HIDEO'S *phone conversation.* BOLA *is seated again, sipping coffee and watching* HIDEO. GRACE *notices* CHIZ *and goes to see what she's looking at.* GRACE *and* CHIZ *look out the window together at* ROSE *and* HENRY.*)*

CHIZ: We won't need Mrs. Okubo's services anymore.

GRACE: I don't think the two of them even know it yet.

ACT TWO, SCENE TEN

CHIZ: I think they do.

GRACE: Hmm. *(Beat)* Mrs. Okubo's going to be disappointed.

CHIZ: No bonus.

(GRACE hears HIDEO on the phone and goes over to check.)

HIDEO: . . . good, good. We'll be there tomorrow. Right, right, I mean today. And we apologize for calling so many times in the middle of the night. Right, right—the price, how much we could offer—and we had to make a decision tonight. You know the Matsumotos. Yes, just like the father. Okay, bye. Done.

(HIDEO hangs up and nods to GRACE. She breathes a sigh of relief.)

GRACE: I think we should celebrate.

HIDEO: I'll get Rose and Henry.

(GRACE goes to the kitchen. HIDEO goes outside and discovers ROSE and HENRY embracing.)

ROSE *(shaking)*: It's freezing out here.

HENRY: The temperature must have dropped ten degrees in the last few minutes.

ROSE: Beautiful, though. Clouds rolling in.

(They all re-enter the house. GRACE re-enters from the kitchen with a tray holding a bottle of saké and cups.)

GRACE: He accepted. *(Looking at HIDEO)* It took a bit of negotiating.

(Silence. No one knows what to say.)

BOLA: Well. I finally get a place to practice.

CHIZ: The Europa Hotel . . .

BOLA: I think GRACE has the right idea. We should toast.

(Saké is poured and glasses given out.)

GRACE: Henry?

(BOLA checks to see that everyone has their saké.)

BOLA: To the Sisters Matsumoto.

The Men *(quietly)*: *Kampai.*

(The sisters accept the toast and the men drink.)

GRACE: To Papa, Mama, and this house.

All: *Kampai.*

(They all drink. Begin to gather up the glasses.)

BOLA: So you figured out what kind of business you want to do?

HIDEO: I'd still like to start the newspaper.
   (Silence.)
HIDEO: I have some new ideas. I'll print it in Japanese and English.
   (Pause.)
GRACE: Okay. We'll see.
BOLA: Hey, this is good. Every morning, I can get up. I pat the
   kids' heads. Chiz hands me my cup of coffee as I'm walking
   out the door. *(Takes a deep breath)* Ahh, the Europa Hotel. I
   stroll down the hall, grab the paper—hot off the presses—set-
   tle into my office, put my feet up . . .
   (Mimes bringing up a paper to read, shocked.)
BOLA: What the hell, it's in Japanese . . .
   (Turns to the next page.)
BOLA: Ah yes, I can read this . . .
GRACE *(breaking the moment)*: Well. We better finish packing . . .
   *(BOLA starts to go upstairs to get the suitcases. Others begin to
   start their separate duties. GRACE and HIDEO continue to look
   at each other.)*
BOLA: Henry?
   *(HENRY joins BOLA up the stairs. HIDEO moves into the back to
   begin packing. GRACE moves out onto the porch. ROSE and CHIZ
   join her.)*
GRACE *(to her sisters)*: It'll be all right. Whatever happens. We'll
   be all right.
ROSE *(noticing)*: The sun's beginning to rise.
   *(The three sisters stare out at the dawn breaking over the land
   that was once theirs. HENRY, BOLA and HIDEO have come back
   into the house and remain in half-light in the background watch-
   ing them.)*
ROSE: I was thinking about Papa again.
CHIZ: I was too.
GRACE: Maybe we can bring him back. When things get back to
   normal.
CHIZ: It's so beautiful.
ROSE: I want us always to remember it. Just like this.
GRACE: I'll remember.
   (Snow begins to fall.)

ACT TWO, SCENE TEN

GRACE: My god, it's starting to snow . . .
 (The sisters look out and marvel.)
 (Dim to darkness.)

[END OF PLAY]

The Wind Cries Mary

With new ending, July 2003. Loosely adapted from Ibsen's *Hedda Gabbler*

The Wind Cries Mary had its world premiere at the San Jose Repertory Theatre in 2002.

ARTISTIC DIRECTOR: Timothy Near

DIRECTOR: Eric Simonson

CAST —
Eiko Hanabi: Tess Lina
Miles Katayama: Stan Egi
Raymond Pemberthy: Thomas Vincent Kelly
Rachel Auwinger/Cohen: Allison Sie
Dr. Frank Nakada: Sab Shimono
Auntie Gladys: Joy Carlin

Set Design: Kent Dorsey
Sound Design: Jeff Mockus

Front of Theater Program
The unformed language of articulation for this new world . . . the still unshaped face of the new America. We stand so silently. With our breaths held and minds empty, staring out over the abyss. Waiting. Waiting to be filled with the new knowledge . . .
—M. Katayama & E. Hanabi, *The Thought Unknown*

Mental illness as a pathology of liberty . . . does no good to treat patient alone . . . must treat the cultural and political context also . . .
—Frantz Fanon

I'm a walking, talking, living, loving puppet . . .
—Oldham & Penn song, "I'm Your Puppet."

When you are you, you see things as they are . . .
—D.T. Suzuki

It's a man's world . . .
—James Brown

Pre-show Lobby and House Music
The Who: "My Generation" from the *Live at Leeds* album
The Kinks: "Well Respected Man"
Rolling Stones: "Spider to the Fly"
The Byrds: "Eight Miles High"
Quicksilver Messenger Service: "Who Do You Love?"
Grateful Dead: "Anthem In the Sun"
Bob Dylan: "Subterranean Homesick Blues"
Paul Butterfield: "East West"

Preface

In 1968, demonstrations against American involvement in Vietnam took place on campuses across the country. These demonstrations in turn intersected with the growing unrest of *minority* students who sought equal entitlement and representation at college institutions. At campuses like San Francisco State College, young Japanese, Chinese, Filipino, and Korean Oriental American students, inspired by the emergence of Black Movement issues, had renamed themselves Asian American and had begun to merge their developing identity politics with a broader analysis of the war in Vietnam as part of a global anti-Asian campaign. The Asian American, African American and Chicano students at San Francisco State and other institutions were now referring to their united front of minorities as the Third World. This would be the beginnings of a push that would lead to the eventual establishment of Ethnic Studies departments. Within these there would be a component devoted exclusively to an *Asian American perspective*. Such a beast had never existed anywhere before. Ever. Segments of the Asian American populace, especially those in the age range of twenty-five to thirty-five, were caught in the midst of America's changing consciousness of identity, leaving them unsure as to whether they were *Oriental* or *Asian American*. This play is loosely based on those historical events as well as on events that took place at U.C. Santa Cruz, U.C. Los Angeles, and other campuses.

Acknowledgments

This play was commissioned by the San Jose Repertory Theater. Support provided by the California Civil Liberties Public Education Fund.

Author's thanks to Diane Takei, Timothy Near, Eric Simonson, Tom Bryant, John McCluggage, Tom Tompkins, Jacqueline Kim, Eric Steinberg, Chay Yew, and Diane Matsuda. Special thanks to Carl Mulert and the Joyce Ketay Agency.

Front of Script

Somewhere a Queen is weeping . . .
—Jimi Hendrix

Characters

EIKO HANABI/PEMBERTHY
MILES KATAYAMA
RAYMOND PEMBERTHY
DR. FRANK NAKADA
RACHEL AUWINGER/COHEN
AUNTIE GLADYS

Time

1968

Note: As much as possible, I've tried to avoid a sense of parody of the sixties in language and tone. Thus, it's important to downplay styles of the era in costuming and hair.

Place

San Francisco

ACT ONE

Morning. "Not So Sweet Martha Lorraine," the studio version by Country Joe & the Fish, comes up and plays for a minute. Then news sound bites reporting American troop activity in Vietnam are gradually brought in. These news reports continue all through the play, giving a continual sense of growing U.S. involvement, rising death toll, and escalating unrest on college campuses. These reported activities and events should compress several years into the course of the play's brief time frame.

> *As lights dim, the music swells to a high volume, holds, then fades away as the lights come up. The news is now emanating from the TV at a low volume.*
>
> *The Pemberthy house. Moving boxes are laid about. A large stereo console. Color TV is on. Upstage there's an obutsudan (Buddhist shrine) with a photo of Mr. Duke Hanabi prominently displayed next to it.*
>
> *We hear the news about the war in Vietnam going on in the background.*
>
> RAYMOND PEMBERTHY, *twenty-nine, stands in front of the stereo Hi-Fi putting a record on. He wears a kimono loosely thrown over his clothes.*
>
> RAYMOND *carefully takes the record out of the jacket, making sure he doesn't touch the LP's surface. Then he wipes it with the dust cloth, sets it on the arm, and clicks the lever full-turn to make the record drop onto the turntable. It's the We Five's, "You Were On My Mind." He stands and listens for a moment, nodding his head. He has no rhythm. He goes over to the kitchen, bobbing awkwardly to the beat.*
>
> *On one of the kitchen table's chairs, he notices a moving box marked "EIKO." He sets it on the table, about to look inside, then changes his mind. He remembers what he was going to do, goes to the counter, and excitedly opens a small, delicately wrapped*

package containing a canister of tea. He opens it and sprinkles leaves into a teapot. He turns the stove burner on under a pot filled with water. Then he takes out a serving tray and prepares to serve tea to EIKO *in their bedroom.*
Knock at the door. RAYMOND *stops, goes to answer it. A woman in her mid-fifties stands at the door. She is overweight and dressed in the clothes of an office worker, except with a more stylish, yet unmistakably tacky flair to them. She wears a headband. She holds a large candy box and a folded piece of paper.*

RAYMOND *(surprised and happy)*: Auntie Gladys, how good to see you!

AUNTIE GLADYS: Welcome home, Raymond . . .

RAYMOND: Come in, come—

AUNTIE GLADYS *(handing him the box)*: Chocolate bonbons, large size, usually $3.50 a box but I bought three and got a discount so I paid only $2.99 for each. Payless. Got stamps, too. And this was on the porch in front of the door . . . *(Hands him the folded note)* It's from Rachel Auwinger. Apologizing and saying that she came by but realized it was too early and she'll come by later.

RAYMOND *(hands now full)*: Oh yes, Rachel Auwinger . . .

AUNTIE GLADYS: "You do remember me, don't you, Raymond?" she writes. Of course I remember her, you used to date her. Pretty girl, a bit mousy for my tastes and flat as a pancake. She could be a boy, for all I know. Auntie Vicky—*(looks sad and shakes her head indicating things don't look good)*—keeps a stiff upper lip and as long as *General Hospital* stays on the air, she's just dandy. Oh, and she insists we now watch *Bonanza*.

RAYMOND *(looking at the note)*: My goodness, hadn't thought of her in a long time, she always smelled so fresh—

*(*RAYMOND *fixes on her headband.)*

AUNTIE GLADYS *(noticing)*: You like?

(She goes straight to the stereo, turns it off without a word, and immediately moves to the TV.)

AUNTIE GLADYS *(shutting it off, referring to the war news)*: They oughta just drop one big bomb on 'em like we did before. I

Sab Shimono as Dr. Nakada and Tess Lina as Eiko in *The Wind Cries Mary*, San Jose Repertory Theatre, 2002

Photo by Tom Chargin, courtesy San Jose Repertory Theatre

Tess Lina in *The Wind Cries Mary*, San Jose Repertory Theatre

hope it's not too early, I just had to come by and see how you were. You look tired, dear, you been getting enough rest?

RAYMOND: I'm fine, all the traveling, that's all.

AUNTIE GLADYS: The bride?

RAYMOND: Eiko's still sleeping, I was going to bring her some special tea.

AUNTIE GLADYS: Still in bed, at this hour? My goodness, she *is* a princess . . .

RAYMOND: Jet lag, you know . . .

AUNTIE *(looking around)*: Jeez Louise, they just left everything all over. I told the movers which rooms to put the boxes in. I put away most things but what I wasn't sure about I left in their boxes, I know how particular she is. I didn't know you read *Playboy Magazine*?

RAYMOND: What's with the—

(Motioning to her head.)

AUNTIE GLADYS: What do you think, all the kids on campus are wearing them now and well, I know how stylish Eiko is and I wanted to, you know, let her know your auntie has some style in her, too . . .

RAYMOND: Ahh, you don't have to worry about that Auntie, you're always stylish in my eyes.

*(*AUNTIE GLADYS *goes over and smooches* RAYMOND*.)*

AUNTIE GLADYS: Oh, you're too sweet to me—aren't you going to open it?

RAYMOND: What? Oh, okay.

AUNTIE GLADYS: These are special, have nuts inside along with the nougat. *(Looking around at the house, impressed)* My . . .

RAYMOND: You know, we wanted to both thank you for helping with the move, Eiko was in such a hurry to leave on the honeymoon . . .

AUNTIE GLADYS: She gets a bee in her bonnet, it seems nothing can stop her no matter who has to pick up after her. Comes from being an only child and spoiled by her rich daddy. I'm glad you weren't raised that way.

*(*AUNTIE GLADYS *walks around the house, opening the curtains.)*

RAYMOND: Japan was quite illuminating, the gender roles are fas-

cinating. On the surface, yes, it appears the woman is subservient to the man, which I might say—off the record, of
course, lest the libbies bite my head off—was a refreshing
thought compared to American male-female dynamic. But in
fact a simple system of division of labor has been developed
such that the woman alone raises the child—the father, the
salaryman, absent, being forced to work all day and then drink
till all hours—and is, the woman that is, in the end the true
steward and progenitor of cultural mores. And—this is
interesting—thus the unsung motor of its fledgling economic
boom, the child taking on an overdeveloped sense of depend-
ency on the mother, and in turn, as an adult, transferring this
filial allegiance on to the *zaibatsu*, or big corporations, which
become the new surrogate mother-parent—known to house,
feed and at times even arrange marriages for their children as
it were—guaranteeing the continuum of social and economic
order, the zeitgeist of Japan, an eerie hybrid of family values
and filial allegiance to the company god. One could argue it's
a woman's world.

(AUNTIE GLADYS *has ended up in front of the photo by the*
obutsudan.)

AUNTIE GLADYS: This him?

RAYMOND: Her father, the one and only, Duke Hanabi.

AUNTIE GLADYS (*shaking her head*): Looks like he just got off the
boat.

RAYMOND: The shrine was the first thing Eiko wanted unpacked.
(Beat) Oh, and especially thank you for helping out with the,
you know . . .

AUNTIE GLADYS: Oh, you never mind, anything for my little
Raymond and his new bride.

RAYMOND: I finally told Eiko about Dr. Nakada helping us.

AUNTIE GLADYS: He did all the work. I didn't have to do anything. *(Looking around)* It is a bit overwhelming, though. I
never woulda imagined you living in a place quite like this . . .

RAYMOND: Nice?

AUNTIE GLADYS: Large.

RAYMOND: You like it?

AUNTIE GLADYS: Very big.

RAYMOND: She saw it and fell in love with it. So I did, too.

*(*RAYMOND *has brought over the box of candies and holds it to allow* AUNTIE GLADYS *to take another bonbon, but she takes the whole box.* RAYMOND *smiles and goes back to the kitchen to pour the hot water into the teapot.)*

AUNTIE GLADYS: To tell you the truth, I'm still amazed she married you. Nothing against you Raymond but it's not like she didn't have the pick of the litter. Auntie Vicky—

(Looks sad and shakes her head, then goes right back to the conversation)—and I talked about this. I mean, her type

usually don't go for someone with your paycheck, they usually like one of those country club types . . .

RAYMOND *(taking the tea tray up the stairs to the bedroom)*: Not once I get the teaching position and Dr. Nakada said it's in the bag . . .

AUNTIE GLADYS *(not noticing he's left, eating bonbons all through this speech)*: Only Oriental. You know they do have 'em in Hawai'i I read. Oriental Rockefellers. Her father was one, not in Hawai'i, here I mean. The girls in the office heard stories about him, he was quite the character. Heard he liked the Mamie Van Doren type, if you know what I mean, and what the "hello" does she see in that baseball player, what's his name . . . Dr. Nakada knew him, the father, guess they did some business together. He said the father lost everything 'cause when he drank it made him stupid. Bo Belinsky! But while she was growing up? Like a little Oriental princess. Such a short courtship, too. I can tell you now we did wonder if there was a bun in the oven, if you know what I mean—

*(*RAYMOND *reappears, coming down the stairs after dropping off the tea.)*

RAYMOND: What's that about the oven?

AUNTIE GLADYS *(without missing a beat)*: —No thanks, I have to watch my figure—which, well, still woulda surprised us, me in particular 'cause, well, you never really dated girls that much and these things take a little know-how and you never really showed much of any know-how in those areas. 'Course maybe we're to blame, me and your Auntie Vicky—*(Shakes her head sadly)*—cause we're just not good talking about those things—your father, our brother—he would've been good at it, too good at it actually. But maybe it's okay because, well, let's face it, she *is* more sophisticated than you, if you know what I mean.

(EIKO *appears on the stairs, unseen by* RAYMOND *or* AUNTIE GLADYS, *and observes.* RAYMOND *busies himself in the kitchen area.)*

AUNTIE GLADYS: There are those rumors, especially about getting kicked out of college, you know, the boy in the dorm room thing? And a particularly disgusting rumor the boy was colored. But still we were all surprised when you two got together seeing as who she is and seeing as who you are. But then it's not like you don't have anything to offer 'cause after all you're, I mean, let's be honest, you're Caucasian and she's not and I think it balances things out, you know. Then there's—me and Auntie Vicky *(shakes her head)* talked about this—the baby—which we hope to hear some news about soon—to think about, being half Oriental and all.

(EIKO *withdraws up the stairs.)*

AUNTIE GLADYS: Still, we want to support you and you come saying you need to have this house so what should you do, so I ask around the office and Dr. Nakada, who's pretty high up in the Business School and sort of my boss 'cause I do work in that department's office, he offers to handle it and since he knew her father and well . . .

RAYMOND: Would you like some tea, also?

AUNTIE GLADYS: I used my own money on the down.

RAYMOND: What?

AUNTIE: My nest egg. For your house.

RAYMOND: I thought Dr. Nakada was arranging a loan through folks he knew.

AUNTIE GLADYS: Yes, but it wasn't enough and there was also the size of those monthly mortgage payments, we both thought it just might be too big . . .

RAYMOND: Your savings, Auntie?

AUNTIE GLADYS: Yes.

RAYMOND: But that's all you have. You're living off it.

AUNTIE GLADYS: You're my brother's son, I couldn't do less. And who knows, maybe if I need to, if things work out that way, you know with Auntie Vicky—*(she shakes her head very sadly)*—I could, you know, if I got lonely and needed a place to stay . . .

RAYMOND *(understanding)*: Oh, yes, yes, of course, wouldn't that be so nice . . .

AUNTIE GLADYS *(getting excited)*: Especially when we start to hear the pitter-patter of little feet, you're going to need some help.

RAYMOND: Oh, Auntie, I do love you, but I worry, that was all you had.

AUNTIE GLADYS: Dr. Nakada said it wouldn't be a problem, what with you getting the teaching position, a large raise in salary, and I heard that Eiko was quite the chemistry whiz, I'm sure she can get a job at the college—

(EIKO HANABI *enters down the stairs, twenty-nine, striking, carries herself with a sense of breeding and class.*)

EIKO: Who's getting a job?

RAYMOND: Oh, you're up. I thought you'd stay in bed for a bit longer.

EIKO: I don't drink barley tea. Hello Gladys, what brings you over so early? Make some coffee for all of us, Raymond.

RAYMOND: But we're having . . .

(EIKO *walks pass the box of candies directly over to the curtains that* AUNTIE GLADYS *had opened and proceeds to close them.*)

AUNTIE GLADYS: My, but you're looking stunning as always. Did you get the dress over there?

RAYMOND: Auntie couldn't wait to see us and say hello. Find out how our trip was.

EIKO: I got this in New York last season, Saks. It was awful, the Orient, I hated it.

RAYMOND *(keeping the conversation light)*: We stayed up all night watching *The Invisible Man*—Claude Raines, I always get him mixed up with Adolphe Menjou . . .

EIKO: Funny, the *man*, you could see him even when he was invisible . . . *(Noticing the box of candies and picking it up)* Oh, look, one of the movers left these cheap candies.

ACT ONE

RAYMOND: Eiko.

EIKO: Hmm?

AUNTIE GLADYS: They aren't cheap. I bought them on sale but they aren't cheap.

RAYMOND: Auntie brought them, they're really very good.

AUNTIE GLADYS: Just because it's Payless, doesn't mean they're cheap.

EIKO: Oh, I'm sorry. I don't eat these types of candies so I don't know.

AUNTIE GLADYS: Some of us happen to know the value of a dollar. I know Raymond does.

RAYMOND: Try one. Please?

EIKO: Of course, maybe later. *(To* AUNTIE GLADYS*)* I am sorry . . .
 (EIKO *spots the storage box with her name on the kitchen table.)*

EIKO: I need my coffee first.
 (EIKO *quickly crosses over and sets the box inside the back room and closes the French doors.)*

RAYMOND: Auntie, you were having tea, weren't you? Or did you want coffee?

AUNTIE GLADYS: Sure, sure, whatever we're having, dear. What are we having?

RAYMOND: Eiko, I thought you'd like the tea. Remember, we bought it from that nice little farmer near your father's village.

EIKO *(moving to counter)*: *You* bought it.

RAYMOND *(to* AUNTIE GLADYS*)*: It's called *mugi cha*, made from barley.

AUNTIE GLADYS *(impressed)*: Oh, my, that sounds exotic. I guess I'm one of the family, now.

RAYMOND: Come on, Eiko.

EIKO *(getting out instant coffee for herself)*: That's why my father left there, so his daughter wouldn't have to drink *peasant's* tea.
 (AUNTIE GLADYS *stares at her tea and puts it down.)*

RAYMOND: Everybody drinks it now. Especially during the summers, chilled. Honey, I'll make your coffee . . .
 (RAYMOND *leads* EIKO *over to the sofa.)*

RAYMOND: Go, go, sit down and visit with Auntie, I'll make it for you.

(EIKO and AUNTIE GLADYS *sit down across from each other. Awkward silence.)*

AUNTIE GLADYS: So we have a doctor in the house now.

EIKO: Excuse me?

RAYMOND: She means me, now that I have my doctorate.

EIKO: Oh, that kind of doctor. I thought you meant a real doctor.

AUNTIE GLADYS: You're still called a doctor, aren't you? They call you doctor, right?

RAYMOND: Well, yes, of course.

EIKO: I just meant not like a medical doctor, that's all.

AUNTIE GLADYS: A doctor's a doctor, my nephew's a doctor.

RAYMOND: I'm a doctor, Auntie.

AUNTIE GLADYS: I know you're a doctor.

EIKO: Just not a medical doctor.

(Pause. AUNTIE GLADYS *holds out the box of candy to* EIKO *who pretends not to see it, casually looking away.* AUNTIE GLADYS *doesn't move it. It sits out there.* EIKO *will have nothing to do with it.* AUNTIE GLADYS *gets up and stands beside* EIKO, *holding the candy in front of her nose. Finally,* EIKO *takes one and stares at it.)*

AUNTIE GLADYS: Yes, yes, come on now, you can do it . . .

RAYMOND: Auntie, maybe you shouldn't . . .

EIKO: That's all right, Raymond.

*(EIKO *takes a very small bite.)*

AUNTIE GLADYS: Over the lips and through the gums, look out stomach, here it comes . . .

EIKO *(to* RAYMOND*)*: You had an interesting childhood, I take it.

AUNTIE GLADYS *(making an announcement, with emphasis to* EIKO*)*: We watch *Bonanza* now!

*(EIKO *and* RAYMOND *stare at her.)*

AUNTIE GLADYS *(moving back to her seat)*: Oh, I heard some news about that dreadful friend of yours, ex-friend of yours, what's his name, the one that went nuts and they had to kick him off the faculty . . .

RAYMOND: You mean, Miles Katayama?

AUNTIE GLADYS: Un-huh, that one. They were talking about him in the president's office. He wrote some new book or some-

thing. Elsie in the office told me, they have a copy over at the
Sociology Department.

EIKO: Miles Katayama?

AUNTIE GLADYS *(nodding)*: Un-huh.

RAYMOND: He has a book out? Really? I find that hard to
believe.

AUNTIE GLADYS: I saw the book jacket, you should see his
photo. He looked as silly as ever—hair in a ponytail, and that
Chinaman's moustache—what do they call it . . .

RAYMOND: Auntie, you don't say "Chinaman."

EIKO: I think it's more correct to say "Chink."

RAYMOND: I didn't know he was writing again.

AUNTIE GLADYS: Then what do you call someone from China—
"Hey, you!"? *(Muttering)* Besides, we watch *Bonanza* now . . .

RAYMOND *(to* EIKO*)*: You know Miles, don't you?

EIKO: A little, from the old days.

AUNTIE GLADYS: Terrible fellow—drugs, student strikes, getting
arrested—he hit a policeman, you know that.

> *(*RAYMOND *brings coffee over for* EIKO*.)*

RAYMOND: He didn't hit a policeman, he resisted arrest.

AUNTIE GLADYS: Oh, like they're different . . .

> *(*RAYMOND *and* AUNTIE GLADYS *sit in silence, munching on*
> *candies.* EIKO *sips her coffee, lost in thought.)*

AUNTIE GLADYS: Fu Manchu!

> *(*AUNTIE GLADYS *giggles self-consciously.* RAYMOND *and* AUNTIE
> GLADYS *return to munching on chocolates.)*

AUNTIE GLADYS *(noticing, to* EIKO*)*: You got a little fat.

EIKO: Excuse me?

RAYMOND: She filled out a bit, huh. More of her to hold onto now.

AUNTIE GLADYS: More in the face, the cheeks. Like a chipmunk.

EIKO: I don't think so . . .

RAYMOND *(noticing)*: You are getting a little tummy . . .

EIKO: I am not.

AUNTIE GLADYS *(wondering)*: Oh, really?

EIKO *(getting up and moving to the counter)*: You always make my
coffee too weak—it's the style of the cut, the material drapes
funny and can give that impression . . .

AUNTIE GLADYS *(cheering up)*: Oh, well, yes, of course.

EIKO: I'm not gaining weight.

RAYMOND: I don't mind, I always thought you were kinda skinny.

AUNTIE GLADYS *(announcing)*: And besides your book is going to be a much bigger hit than that communist agitator, Mr. "Hey, you"!

(Getting up suddenly with renewed vigor) Well, I better be getting back to the office. I'm going to stop by and see Auntie Vicky first. The girls are covering for me and I'm already late. We're trying to get our work done before the demonstration starts.

RAYMOND: You be careful.

AUNTIE GLADYS: And who knows how long we could get stuck in the building—police, tear gas, my goodness. And you deary, you should get as much rest as you can. Well, you know what I mean . . .

EIKO: No, I don't know what you mean.

RAYMOND: You have to leave already?

AUNTIE GLADYS *(touching her headband, in* EIKO'S *direction)*: All the kids are wearing them on campus, especially the ones who take drugs.

RAYMOND *(playfully scolding)*: Auntie, you hippie . . .

AUNTIE GLADYS *(to* EIKO*)*: You should get one. *(To* RAYMOND*)* I'm sure you two want to be alone. Make sure she gets plenty of rest and drinks lots of milk.

> *(*RAYMOND *escorts* AUNTIE GLADYS *to the door and sees her out.* EIKO *is upset and mad. She takes the box of chocolates and stuffs it into the garbage, using her foot to bash it down violently.* RAYMOND *enters and heads over to the stereo.* EIKO *moves to the counter to add more instant coffee to her cup.)*

RAYMOND: What was Auntie talking about, rambling on and on like that?

EIKO: Four spoonfuls, I've told you before, I like it strong . . .
> *(*RAYMOND *puts on the band We Five again. Starts to dance, very badly, towards* EIKO.*)*

RAYMOND: See, the thing about the We Five is it's the bridge to today's music. Being an old folkie, it allows me to understand the music the kids are listening to these days. *(Dancing, sort of)* See, I know how to be groovy. *(Trying to get* EIKO *to dance)* "Kimono my house, I'll show you my koto" . . .

> (EIKO *ignores him. She goes to the stereo, turns up the volume, and stands next to it, sipping her coffee and listening.* RAYMOND *wonders what's going on.)*

RAYMOND *(yelling over)*: What are you doing?

EIKO: This is killing me!

RAYMOND *(shouting)*: What?

EIKO: It's killing me!

RAYMOND: What?

EIKO: It's killing—

> (RAYMOND *lifts the needle off the record.)*

EIKO: . . . me.

RAYMOND: What's killing you?

EIKO: It's too early to be playing that kind of music.

RAYMOND: It's never too early to play rock 'n roll.

EIKO: The We Five is not rock and roll.

RAYMOND: Yes, it is. I got it from one of my students, he has hair down to his shoulders.

EIKO: Jimi Hendrix is rock and roll.

RAYMOND: Negro people do not play rock 'n roll. He's an anomaly. Even the Motown folks won't claim him as one of theirs. I read in Rolling Stone his stepmother is Japanese, up in Seattle. I wonder what nationality Ben Fong-Torres is? How do you know about Jimi Hendrix?

EIKO: You'd be amazed at what I know.

RAYMOND: And that's what I love. I never know what you're going to surprise me with next. There's only one thing.

EIKO: What?

RAYMOND: If you could call Auntie Gladys, *Auntie* Gladys.

EIKO: Why? She's not my aunt.

RAYMOND: Yes, but I know it'd make her so happy to hear you say it.

EIKO: Her happiness was your concern. *My* happiness is your concern now. You're married to me, aren't you?

RAYMOND: Yes, I know that, honey, but—okay, all right. What would you like to hear . . .

(RAYMOND *goes to the stereo and looks through the albums.*)

EIKO (*referring to the coffee she's sipping*): Ahhh, that's more like it. The first cup you made was like water. I like coffee that bites back, let's you know it's there. Four spoonfuls, four spoonfuls.

(RAYMOND *puts on Erik Satie's "Trois Gymnopedie."*)

RAYMOND: How's that? Better?

EIKO: Don't ever take me to Japan again. I hate the toilets, I hate the baths, I hate the food, I especially hate anything raw, I hate the crowdedness, I hate how everything is so small, I hate that they can't speak English, I hate even more that they can't *understand* English. I hate the way the women all cater to the men. And I hate how they all stare at me like I'm some kind of freak because I look like I'm Japanese but I act American and there's a very good reason for it because I *am* American, goddamnit!

RAYMOND: Okay . . .

EIKO: There's one thing I want you to know.

RAYMOND: Yes, honey?

EIKO: I'd rather kill myself than get fat.

(RAYMOND'S *not sure how to take this. Turns off the stereo and changes the topic.*)

RAYMOND (*referring to the house*): What do you think of it? Is it what you thought it would be? I'm a little overwhelmed to tell you the truth.

EIKO: I wished to God you hadn't used Nakada to get the loan. What am I supposed to do here all day long?

RAYMOND (*under his breath*): Hopefully not get fat.

EIKO: What?

RAYMOND: Hopefully get unpacked. Auntie Gladys said he offered to help—was only too happy to help.

(EIKO *walks around looking at the place. She goes through the French doors into the back and hits a single note on the piano four times. She holds the sustain and it lingers.*)

EIKO (*off*): If I'm going to use this one for now, it needs to be tuned.

(*Note lingers in the air for a long moment. Doorbell rings.* RAYMOND *goes to answer it.* EIKO *releases the note and reenters the room, going to the* obutsudan. *Touches her father's picture.* RAYMOND *enters with* RACHEL AUWINGER, *twenty-seven, very pretty in a girlish fashion, though now with a bust. Nervous, a bit high-strung. She carries a knapsack and looks slightly hippie-esque, but not overdone.)*

RACHEL: I was worried you wouldn't remember me.

RAYMOND: This is a surprise. *(To* EIKO*)* This is Rachel Auwinger, an old friend of mine. *(Leaning in)* Is it still Auwinger?

RACHEL: Cohen, now.

RAYMOND *(announcing)*: Cohen now, Rachel Cohen.

RACHEL: Hello Miss Hanabi. I came by earlier but I realized you were probably still sleeping so I left a note under the door—I signed it Auwinger so if you did remember me, you'd remember me—and walked around the neighborhood till now.

*(*RAYMOND *pulls the note out of his pocket and waves it around self-consciously.)*

RAYMOND: Yes, we got it. *(Leaning in to* RACHEL*)* It's Mrs. Pemberthy now.

RACHEL: Oh, yes, I heard, that's right, that's right, I'm sorry, Mrs. Pemberthy. I'm so used to thinking of you as Eiko Hanabi, that's how everyone knew you. You probably don't remember me—I was two years behind you at Japanese language school.

EIKO: I didn't attend very long.

RACHEL: You used to make me eat dirt.

RAYMOND: Sit, sit. What exactly did you want to see us about?

RACHEL *(sincere)*: It's good to see you again Raymond. The years have been good to you.

RAYMOND: Yes, well . . . I almost didn't recognize you, you've . . . You look great . . .

(Awkward beat. He looks back at EIKO*.)*

RACHEL: I live up north now. Just outside of Portland Oregon? I didn't mean to come to you folks but he mentioned he used to know you *(to* EIKO*)* and since I didn't know who to turn to I looked up *(to* RAYMOND*)* your name under information and got your address and came over here. It was under new listings.

*(*RAYMOND *and* EIKO *are not sure who she's referring to.)*

RACHEL *(realizing)*: Oh, you don't know who I'm talking about, I'm sorry, yes, it's Miles Katayama, you know him right? I just

know he's going to get into trouble, I know it, so I had to come
down here and find him.

EIKO: Miles Katayama?

RACHEL: Yes, you do know him, don't you?

RAYMOND: We both know him. I taught an undergraduate
course with him at San Jose State.

EIKO: What's he doing in town?

RACHEL: Oh, he shouldn't have left our place. He thinks he's fine,
he's ready now that his book is about to come out. But he's
really not ready yet.

RAYMOND: Ready to what?

EIKO: How do you know Miles?

RACHEL: Oh—I'm sorry, yes, I haven't explained everything, I live
outside Portland—oh, I said that already—anyway, my husband teaches at Reed College, Lawrence Cohen, you may have
heard his name, he's kinda controversial—been experimenting
with some of Ronald Laing's theories, radical psychiatry?

RAYMOND: I think so . . .

EIKO: R.D., he's a Brit.

RACHEL: Actually it's a commune. We live there with five other
families from the college—all from the Psych Department,
mainly Abnormal. I met Miles at the commune, he's an
acquaintance of one of the wives, or girlfriends, they're not
really married but they have a baby—not Miles but his
acquaintance's boyfriend or husband—we think it's his baby,
or maybe my husband's, oh jesus, that's a whole other story—
anyway, he needed a place to stay.

EIKO: Miles?

RACHEL: Yes. He was a wreck. He was underground for a while
because of his anti-war activities. Quite frankly, he was hard
to understand, almost incoherent. Burned out, totally. But we
all could tell he was different so we let him stay. He tutored
the kids to pay for his keep. He's really quite brilliant. I realized that the moment I met him. So did my husband. I was
trying to help him get back on his feet, stay healthy, start writing again, but Larry convinced him to—

ACT ONE

RAYMOND: Your husband?

RACHEL: Yes, my husband, Lawrence, I call him Larry—he convinced Miles to take part in his research, a new experimental "blow out" treatment he's been developing with several others in the commune involving cohabitating for periods of time with schizophrenics who have been purposely taken off Thorazine so they're in full blown schizophrenic happy hour—

EIKO *(impatient to move the story along)*: The idea is to create a climate for the patient to have a guided benign and healthy mental breakdown. You're supposed to come out at the other end —if you come out—with a whole newly integrated consciousness about the world . . .

RAYMOND: Where did you learn—

RACHEL: Yes, and Miles? Thrust into this room of full bloom psychoses? I mean he wanted to do it, volunteered—and it worked, scrambled his brain in a good way, but I nearly lost him, too. His mind is still fragile but then the last six months, he's been amazingly prolific. We were getting so much good work done.

EIKO: You say he's in town now?

RACHEL: What? Yes.

EIKO: Do you know where he is?

RACHEL: Yes, I found out where he's staying.

EIKO: Well, why don't we invite him over? And you can be here, also.

RACHEL: Oh, yes, that would be good.

RAYMOND: Why don't you just go over there and see him yourself?

(Pause.)

RACHEL: I don't think I could do that . . .

EIKO: She can't do that.

RAYMOND: Why not?

(EIKO *observes* RACHEL *as she addresses her.)*

EIKO: That's why you came over here, isn't it?

(RACHEL *is silent.)*

EIKO: You don't know a thing about women, Raymond.

RAYMOND: I thought that's what all this bra burning was about? So a woman doesn't have to be all quiet and demure, she can grab the club and go after the man herself?

EIKO: Bra burning doesn't accomplish anything. The men get more to ogle and the breasts just sag sooner. Now if you got rid of the breasts . . . Where's he staying?

RACHEL: At the York Hotel.

EIKO: Raymond, call there and invite him over tonight. *(To* RACHEL*)* How's that?

RACHEL: That'd be wonderful. Oh, I knew you could help.

RAYMOND: Now?

EIKO: Now.

RAYMOND: Tonight?

EIKO: Tonight.

RAYMOND *(leaving to the back room)*: Okay . . .

EIKO *(scooting him along)*: Yes, go, go . . .

> *(Once* RAYMOND *has left,* EIKO *pulls* RACHEL *over and makes her sit next to her on the couch.)*

EIKO: Come over here Rachel. Come on. I do remember you from Japanese school.

RACHEL: I got the feeling you didn't.

EIKO: I do now. I mean how many *happa* kids were there in the classes?

RACHEL: That's true.

EIKO: And I didn't make you eat dirt.

RACHEL: Yes, yes, you did 'cause I was half white—you all teased me. I haven't forgotten.

EIKO: No, I liked you Rachel.

RACHEL: Funny way of showing it.

EIKO: Really, I did.

RACHEL: Truth is I hated you.

EIKO: Oh.

RACHEL: Those were very confusing times for me. Didn't know if I wanted to be Japanese or Caucasian. Trouble was neither one wanted me.

> *(*EIKO *studies* RACHEL, *who's uncomfortable under her gaze.)*

EIKO: Does your husband know you're down here?

ACT ONE

RACHEL: Of course.

EIKO: He doesn't, does he?

RACHEL: Why would you say a thing like that?

EIKO: And you've been working with Miles? *Closely?*

> *(Awkward beat.)*

RACHEL: He says I'm his muse—

EIKO *(interrupts)*: His muse?

RACHEL: Un-huh, I've gotten him to trust himself again. To trust the world. He doesn't drink, smoke dope, take any chemicals anymore. He told me he'd be dead if it weren't for me.

EIKO: I see . . .

RACHEL: I just have to see him, make sure he's okay. He told me about some woman who nearly drove him mad. She's here. I worry he'll get mixed up with her again.

EIKO: Did he say who this person was?

RACHEL: I think it's a singer with one of the bands he used to hang out with. Do you know which one? He said she almost killed him.

EIKO: What else did he say?

RACHEL: That maybe that's what he wanted. That's why I'm so worried. *(Beat)* Mary. I think that's what he called her. Mary.

EIKO: Mary . . .

> *(EIKO is quiet for moment. Then turns her attention back to RACHEL.)*

EIKO: Those were difficult times for me, too—our time together in Japanese school. I bet you didn't know that I was born in Japan. Yamanashi area. My mother died when I was quite young and then after the war we came to the States—

RACHEL: I'm sorry about your mother, I didn't know.

EIKO: No, no, she would run after him like a skitterish mouse, waiting on him hand and foot, quite pitiful actually. Anyway, the point is I was secretly an FOB. When I made fun of others I was really making fun of myself. You hated me? I hated me more.

> *(EIKO watches her for a beat, then gets up.)*

EIKO: I believe the band you're referring to might be Mad River—I read they're playing at the Fillmore this weekend. I think Miles used to run into them at those anti-war benefits he was speaking at. They have a female singer that Miles knows.

RACHEL: I thought so. We have to help him. His work is getting so good but his state is delicate still, he can be a little paranoid. You should read his new paper. He's quite mad, he's doing it all longhand, page after page, like it's being dictated to him from some mysterious place. He's drawing from so many sources—". . . the apocalypse is here right now. The children, the insane and deformed of soul can see it as they live outside the boundaries of institutionalized consciousness. The worm needs to die first, all of it, and we must help it." He's got it all in his knapsack. I have all his notes in here—

*(*RAYMOND *enters.)*

RAYMOND: I left a message at the front desk. At least we know he's there.

RACHEL: When he comes over, maybe he can read some of it, his new paper? So you can hear what we've been doing?

RAYMOND: You mean the book?

EIKO: No, this is more recent, new stuff.

RAYMOND: Oh, I don't think he'd want anyone to hear his ideas before he's published them.

EIKO: Nonsense, we're all friends—you think he would? Ms. Muse to Miles?

RACHEL: Oh, he wouldn't mind, besides the ideas are so visionary most folks wouldn't know what to think anyway. "We must help the worm die"—

EIKO *(interrupts)*: Something along the lines of, "So the butterfly can be born." Mr. Katayama's very eclectic, isn't he—drawing from Alejandro Jodorowsky, Chilean filmmaker. Jodorowsky's command of English is limited so he mixes up worm for caterpiller—". . . you and I will be the first movements in the wings of the great butterfly."

(Awkward pause.)

EIKO: Well, there. We're all set.

RACHEL: Yes, this is wonderful. It might help him to stay on track. You could help him Raymond. You seem much more politic than he is. He doesn't know how to play the academic game.

ACT ONE

You've got such a sensible head on your shoulders. He seems
to offend people on purpose some times.

RAYMOND: Well, let's see what happens tonight. It's been a while
since I've seen him.

EIKO: Yes, now you must go and rest, you look weary.

RACHEL: I am. *(Beat)* It's really good to see you Raymond.

RAYMOND: And I, you.

(Doorbell rings.)

RAYMOND *(exiting)*: Jeez, what's going on—I'll get it.

EIKO: Where are you staying?

RACHEL: I'm crashing at the faculty guest housing.

*(EIKO leads RACHEL out as we hear RAYMOND letting DR.
NAKADA in. We hear them meeting in the hallway offstage.
RAYMOND and DR. NAKADA enter. DR. NAKADA is fifty-ish,
in good shape, thinks of himself as a ladies' man. A moustache,
sideburns and slightly long hair are his acknowledgement to the
changing styles.)*

RAYMOND: I wanted to thank you for helping out with the, you
know . . .

DR. NAKADA: Yes, umm, nice looking girl—she's half Oriental?

RAYMOND *(nodding)*: Un-huh, half Caucasian.

DR. NAKADA: What's her name again?

RAYMOND: Married to a Professor Lawrence Cohen, up at Reed
College—

DR. NAKADA: Lawrence Cohen . . . Ahh that one, the hippie psy-
chiatrist, got arrested a few years back—something about cavort-
ing around with young, naked girls—caused quite a stir. *(Looking
towards the door)* For such an old geezer, he's doing all right . . .

(Beat.)

DR. NAKADA: I'm actually glad I have you alone for a moment.

RAYMOND: What, is there a problem? The loan? Auntie said you
thought there was nothing to worry about.

DR. NAKADA: Well, yes and no.

RAYMOND: Yes and no?

DR. NAKADA: First off, as your informal financial advisor, you've
bitten off quite a bit, what with the house and now this
extended trip through Asia.

RAYMOND: It was our honeymoon.

DR. NAKADA: Yes, but given the monies you put into this place, I don't think it was all that prudent to compound your debt with such an extravagant trip.

RAYMOND: Eiko was so excited about traveling—

DR. NAKADA: I know how Eiko can be, you don't have to tell me, I knew the old man only too well. Now there's something else too.

RAYMOND: The "no" part?

DR. NAKADA: Did you know that Miles Katayama was back at the college?

RAYMOND: Yes, as a matter of fact.

DR. NAKADA: And that he has a book coming out, I believe with a major mainstream press?

(EIKO *enters.*)

RAYMOND: Not an academic press . . .

EIKO: Rachel mentioned it, the book part.

RAYMOND: That's probably why we didn't hear about it.

DR. NAKADA: Well it's getting a lot of attention. He sent advance copies all around and it's causing quite a stir. He's definitely gotten his act together—not only does he write but he knows how to promote, too.

EIKO: I'm sure it was Rachel who did it.

DR. NAKADA: The girl who just left?

RAYMOND: So what's the problem?

DR. NAKADA: The teaching position.

RAYMOND: The teaching position? You said it was a done deal, there was no other real competition . . .

(*Pause.*)

RAYMOND (*realizing*): Miles, that's why he's in town . . .

(DR. NAKADA *nods.*)

EIKO: He's applying for the same position?

DR. NAKADA: Apparently so.

RAYMOND: So he's going to get it?

DR. NAKADA: No, it doesn't mean he's going to get it but it's not a shoo-in for you anymore.

EIKO: Oh my. A competition.

ACT ONE

RAYMOND: What? This isn't a game Eiko.

DR. NAKADA: Well. I just wanted to let you folks know the situation so you can better plan in regards to any future expenditures. May I suggest you two have a meeting about this, get a handle on it. I better be going.

RAYMOND: I'll see you out.

EIKO: Dr. Nakada?

(NAKADA *stops.*)

EIKO: I understand we have you to thank for the loan on the house.
(*Beat.*)

DR. NAKADA: Yes, yes you do. (*Beat*) I do hope we'll be seeing you at the club now that you're back. Your father always cut a colorful figure there. I do say, we all could use another Hanabi there again.

RAYMOND: Pemberthy.

DR. NAKADA: Yes, well . . .

(RAYMOND *exits with* DR. NAKADA. EIKO *seems oddly giddy.*
RAYMOND *returns, distraught.*)

RAYMOND: This is not good. You don't think they'll really give the position to Miles? I mean, after all the trouble he's caused with his speeches and organizing and the way he left the college?

EIKO (*musing*): Raymond and Miles going for the same position.

RAYMOND: Eiko? I need this position so we can meet all our obligations.

EIKO: A little competitive spirit never hurt anyone.

RAYMOND: I'm going over to the department, see if I can get a sense of what the committee members are thinking.

EIKO: My fingers want to dance—(*She extends them out and wiggles them.*) I need my new piano. Where's my new piano? I want to tickle the ivories! And I can't play on that second-rate one in there.

RAYMOND: I don't know if we can do that right away.

(EIKO *kicks off her shoes and seats herself.*)

EIKO: We agreed. Raymond? There's a life style I'm introducing you to. A way of life you need to understand and become familiar with if you're going to be a good husband for me.

RAYMOND: Yes, we agreed. Still.

(EIKO extends her foot out to RAYMOND.)
EIKO: What am I? Raymond, what am I?
(Pause. RAYMOND takes her foot and kisses it.)
RAYMOND: You're my Japanese American Princess.
(EIKO smiles. RAYMOND exits.)
EIKO: And all Japanese American Princesses must learn to play
the piano. Not for fun but for achievement. Not for the love
of music but for survival of her species. She's up on a pedestal.
La-dee-dah . . .
*(She goes upstage to the obutsudan, opens a drawer and takes out
a pendant. She opens it and takes out two bright pink pills.)*
EIKO: And the wind cries Mary . . .
*(Fade to black. Rolling Stones' "19th Nervous Breakdown" comes
up. We hear the news regarding the Vietnam War and student
unrest brought up till they are overlapping each other.)*

ACT TWO

Later that afternoon. Music already playing softly on the stereo. Cream's "White Room."

> EIKO *brings in the moving box that she earlier had put away in the back room. She pauses, goes to the stereo, and turns it louder. She likes it loud. Then goes back to the box and opens it up. Looks at the contents.*
>
> *Takes out a few albums—Jimi Hendrix, The Beatles, Blue Cheer, It's A Beautiful Day, Country Joe & The Fish, The Kinks, Them. Picks up a lab beaker.*
>
> *We see a figure peer in from the back window. He watches her for a beat, then moves away.*
>
> EIKO *notices something buried beneath her things. She reaches in and touches it. She's about to take it out when she hears a noise coming from the back area and quickly closes the box. She hides next to the entrance to the living room, waiting for the person to enter.*
>
> *"White Room" continues to blare over the speakers.*
>
> *As* DR. NAKADA *pokes his head out,* EIKO *grabs him with a trained chokehold. They shout to be heard over the music.*

DR. NAKADA: Hey, hey, what are you doing?

EIKO *(not letting go)*: You shouldn't sneak into my house like that!

DR. NAKADA: Are you going to release me Emma Peel?

> *(*EIKO *starts to squeeze tighter.)*

DR. NAKADA: I came by to get Raymond—This is not funny, I can't breathe, Eiko! . . .

> *(*EIKO *lets go.* NAKADA *gasps for breath.)*

EIKO: If you're going to sneak in the back way, you need to ask permission.

DR. NAKADA: I had no idea you were so strong.

EIKO: It's technique, purely technique.

DR. NAKADA: Could have fooled me.

EIKO: And this music . . .

(EIKO *goes to stereo, turns up the volume even higher. Leans into it with her back to* NAKADA. *The music is raucous. She listens deeply to it, shaking her head frantically. Then she abruptly shuts it off. Silence.*)

EIKO: It affects me.

(*Breathing heavily, looks back at* DR. NAKADA.)

EIKO: My father wanted to make sure I could defend myself.

(DR. NAKADA *rubs his neck.*)

EIKO: It could've been much, much worse. I was just practicing.

DR. NAKADA: I won't forget this, Miss Hanabi.

EIKO: And I won't forget what you did to my father.

DR. NAKADA: I think we're both well aware he did it to himself. And where were you all during that time? Off gallivanting around in the Santa Cruz Mountains doing god knows what . . .

(*Pause.*)

EIKO: Would you like some water?

(NAKADA *straightens his clothes.*)

DR NAKADA: No. But how about something more interesting?

EIKO: There's no alcohol in the house. I think you know that.

DR. NAKADA: I meant something more interesting.

(*He casually takes out a thin, hand-rolled marijuana cigarette from his pocket and proceeds to light it.*)

EIKO (*noticing*): My . . .

DR. NAKADA (*offering it to* EIKO): It's amazing what you can buy in America.

EIKO: No thanks.

DR. NAKADA (*taking a puff*): Too bad. Maybe you really are more the Pat Boone type. I thought maybe I knew things about you . . .

EIKO: And if you did?

DR. NAKADA: Nothing. I'm just a person who likes to know things about people.

EIKO: So you can take advantage of them. Like you did my father.

DR. NAKADA: I did not take advantage of him, I merely spoke his name out loud so everyone could hear.

ACT TWO

EIKO: Duke Hanabi was a smart businessman, he founded the Nippon Bank of California—

DR. NAKADA: But in a previous life in Chicago they knew him as Sam Fujita, the infamous dealer of expensive Japanese wares who made his money by stealing antiques from—

EIKO *(overlapping)*: He was a shrewd and tough negotiator . . .

DR. NAKADA *(continuing)*: —the poor Japanese who were so desperate to get food and medicines after the war, they'd take pennies for their most treasured family heirlooms—

EIKO *(interrupts)*: All right, all right, enough already . . .

(NAKADA *watches her for a moment. She still looks disheveled and wild.*)

DR. NAKADA: You're bored, aren't you?

(Pause.)

EIKO: Maybe. Maybe not.

(Beat.)

DR. NAKADA: How was Japan? I understand they have the gall to speak only Japanese there. Personally I found it exceedingly rude of them.

EIKO: So did I.

DR. NAKADA: And how did Raymond like it? I bet he was in Oriental heaven.

EIKO: Oh, he loved it. Mr. Japanophile himself. He's even taken to wearing a kimono around the house. I don't have the heart to tell him those colors are for an old woman.

(They both find quiet humor in this.)

DR. NAKADA: Raymond's not a challenge. You need a challenge.

EIKO: A challenge means you have the opportunity to participate. And by participating, an opportunity to win.

DR. NAKADA: Or lose.

EIKO: That wouldn't be so bad. At least I'd be in the game.

DR. NAKADA: I like to win.

EIKO: You have that option. Being in the game is part of your entitlement as a man.

DR. NAKADA: Is that what you want, then? To be a man?

EIKO: I wouldn't mind being a man, the things you're free to do.

DR. NAKADA: And not to do.

EIKO: I just have no use for the penis.

(DR. NAKADA *licks his fingers and tamps out the lit end of the marijuana cigarette, puts it back in his coat pocket.*)

DR. NAKADA: You know where you learn the most about people?

EIKO: I'm sure you'll tell me.

DR. NAKADA: In bed.

EIKO: Does that line actually work?

DR. NAKADA: It's not a line, it's the truth. That's why it works.

EIKO: And how does Mrs. Nakada feel about all this truth telling?

DR. NAKADA: Ahh, the Missus.

EIKO: Pretty? Contemporary European Literature? Twenty years your junior?

DR. NAKADA: Amazingly still under the same roof. Still in the same bed.

EIKO: At the same time?

DR. NAKADA: At the same time.

EIKO: And with each other?

DR. NAKADA: We're mature adults. This is the sixties. We have an understanding.

EIKO: Ahhh. An *understanding*. Open marriage, the other professors' wives?

DR. NAKADA: It's been mutually pleasurable. I thought maybe we might have an understanding.

(*Beat.*)

DR. NAKADA: May I have permission to come in the back way?

(EIKO *watches him for a bit, as if assessing his sexuality.*)

EIKO: It's a good thing you don't really know me. I'd hate to be in your debt.

DR. NAKADA: I do know you. I just don't know *about* you. Not yet.

EIKO: What's that supposed to mean?

(NAKADA *moves over to the box he had seen her looking into from the window. He takes out an album and looks at it. A hand mirror. Then the beaker. He holds it up and examines it.*)

DR. NAKADA: You were a chemistry major, weren't you? Mixing up batches of brew. Quite promising, I'm told.

ACT TWO

(EIKO *takes the beaker and puts the box aside.*)

DR. NAKADA: "Why Raymond?" I thought to myself. He's so safe. No, he's not even safe. He's mediocre. She's not just trying to run away. She's trying to punish herself.

(DR. NAKADA *picks up the hand mirror and approaches* EIKO. *During the following the two move about in a kind of cat and mouse dance,* NAKADA *trying to corner* EIKO *and* EIKO *continually evading him. It has the quality of a dangerous game, mutually pleasurable but with cutting intent. They can be physically rough with each other.*)

EIKO: Not only a swinging professor but he reads minds, too?

DR. NAKADA: She's been with any and all the suitors—including that handsome, powerful Kennedy-esque boy—and in the end turned them all away. What does she want? What is she looking for?

EIKO: See, that's the thing about a woman having . . . *many* suitors. Professor Nakada? He's a man about town. Her? She's someone with a *problem.* That he wants to have an *understanding* with.

DR. NAKADA: She is beautiful, brilliant and, of course, knows it. And yet, her burden is that she also knows she doesn't fit in anywhere. What a cruel fate. Why was she given all this, if she can't really be free to enjoy the fruits of her plentiful gifts? Why?

EIKO: Hmm . . .

(DR. NAKADA *has maneuvered himself behind her and holds up the mirror so both their reflections are seen in it. She starts to move but he grips her arm.*)

DR. NAKADA: Because she *sees.* She truly sees her predicament. A few of us are given this horrible gift . . .

(EIKO *pushes him away forcefully. He renews his attack.*)

DR. NAKADA: And so. She chooses to live life like a bat, neither beast nor fowl. The sky is too high, though no one would guess she feels that way, after all she appears to glide so smoothly in that world. And below, the earth—it's the womb from whence she sprang. But that's a second-class world, so how can she live there.

EIKO (*sneering*): I see, above the *white* world and below the *yellow* world . . .

DR. NAKADA: With her secret festering. Loathing everyone and everything. But most of all, loathing herself. For how can you be free if what you want, you won't let yourself have, and what you don't want, you know you truly are.

EIKO: Ahh, so I settle for less than I want and for more of what I don't.

DR. NAKADA: That way, you lose on all fronts equitably. How egalitarian. Here she is—Mrs. Raymond Pemberthy. Not married to an Oriental, but not married to a real Caucasian man either.

EIKO: I guess you've found me out.

(EIKO *moves to the stereo to change the record.*)

DR. NAKADA: Perhaps one day it'll be different. A woman such as you will give herself permission to soar an arc of total and complete participation. But not right now. Not in 1968. Not for you. Welcome to the world of the bat.

(NAKADA *moves in close.*)

DR. NAKADA: See, we have much in common . . .

(EIKO *cranks up the stereo, Blue Cheer's "Summertime Blues."* NAKADA *pulls back, realizing he's been rebuffed.* EIKO *and* NAKADA *stand staring at each other from across the room while the wall of noise blares.*)

EIKO: You didn't have to tell everyone about my father!

DR. NAKADA: Oh, but I did!

EIKO: Once the Japanese American community found out who he was they pulled all their money out! He was ruined!

DR. NAKADA: He said Japanese Americans didn't know how to be real Americans. Look what happened—we all got locked up in camps and he's a rich man with his own bank!

EIKO: I know what you're up to arranging this loan behind my back!

DR. NAKADA: I paid the price to be the real American. I got locked up, not your father, not you, me! I paid the price!

EIKO: Maybe you got my father but you'll never get me, never—

(RAYMOND *bursts in and they stop. He goes over and shuts off the stereo, unsure of what's been going on.*)

DR. NAKADA: I came by to get you for the rally.

ACT TWO

RAYMOND: I thought someone was having a party, you could hear it down the street.

EIKO: Oh, hello Raymond.

RAYMOND *(noticing)*: Was someone smoking in here?

EIKO: I think outside, drifted in through the window . . .

RAYMOND: Is everything okay?

EIKO: Yes. Everything is fine.

RAYMOND: I just came from my Aunties' house and Auntie Vicky is not doing well.

EIKO: She's always not doing well.

RAYMOND: No, this time it's serious.

DR. NAKADA: I'm sorry to hear that Raymond.

RAYMOND: I stopped by Miles's hotel and he hasn't picked up his note at the front desk, so I don't know. I also had a chance to take a look at Miles's book, they had it on file at the Sociology office.

EIKO: And?

RAYMOND: I can see why it went through a mainstream press, it's not really an academic book. It's a kind of a rambling journal of his experiences over the last few years—the whole anti-war thing, psychedelics, the music scene, going underground—an insider's look.

EIKO: So it's not any good?

RAYMOND: No, no I didn't say that. It's just . . . different. Different and fascinating. Actually, from what I read, it's very good.

DR. NAKADA: Raymond, you should be careful. It means you'll have to lobby the other members of the hiring committee—

RAYMOND: After they read his work, I won't have much to worry about anyway.

EIKO: It's that good?

DR. NAKADA: You have a paper coming out, don't you?

RAYMOND: A sociological study of the late fifties—changing male and female rituals of the white middle class. Competition brings out the best . . .

DR. NAKADA: Ahh, a person who likes to get in there and muck around, not afraid of what they might find out about themselves.

EIKO: You're hardly making it interesting, Raymond.

RAYMOND: Everyone knew Miles was brilliant but no one thought he'd be able to write down what was going on inside his head—

EIKO: You underestimate yourself. You underestimate me. I am your wife and the competition has hardly begun.

RAYMOND *(looking at* NAKADA, *remembering)*: Oh, the administration's big counter rally we're supposed to go to.

DR. NAKADA: The president made it clear he wanted all faculty, and in Raymond's case, would-be faculty, to be there to support him.

RAYMOND: What if Miles comes by?

EIKO: I'll take care of him. Rachel's coming by if anything. And you said yourself he hadn't picked up the message yet.

RAYMOND: That's right. Yeah. But . . .

EIKO: But nothing, you boys should move along now, we don't want you to be late.

RAYMOND: Do I have to sit on the stage?

DR. NAKADA *(interrupting)*: It's still early, let's relax. What shall we do to ready ourselves?

(DR. NAKADA is about to take something out of his pocket when EIKO strides by. She goes straight to the TV and flicks it on, then moves away disinterested. Once again it's about the war in Vietnam, growing involvement and death toll, student unrest. However, world events that are also shaping this period should also be included here. NAKADA and RAYMOND each sit down reluctantly, as if this isn't what they want to be doing. They are quickly drawn in and watch as if in a kind of trance. EIKO refuses to look, with her back to the TV. They hold an informal freeze.

This should last for a full thirty seconds. Listening to the news about the war, student unrest, and world events. It should be sensorially assaulting—they enter into another zone, lighting shift with a rapid montage of images, exaggerated sounds and news that sums up that particular era in a thirty-second blitz. In some way, this break presages MILES'S *appearance.*

Knock at the door. Everything returns to normal. RAYMOND *would like an excuse to get away from the dismal news.)*

ACT TWO

RAYMOND: I'll get it!

> (RAYMOND *scoots out to the front door.* EIKO *turns around, watches TV for a beat, then goes to shut it off.*)

> (RAYMOND *walks in with* MILES KATAYAMA. MILES *has long wild hair and a quality of erratic genius. Dark sunglasses.*)

RAYMOND: Look who's here—and no moustache, too!

> (MILES *stops and looks at* EIKO *for a long beat.*)

MILES: Hello Eiko.

EIKO: Hello Mr. Katayama.

RAYMOND: This is quite a surprise. We weren't sure whether you got our message or not.

MILES: I phoned in and got them. I've been in meetings all day.

RAYMOND: This is Dr. Nakada, from the Business School.

> (*They shake hands.*)

DR. NAKADA: You do look familiar, have we met?

MILES: Probably seen each other around campus.

DR. NAKADA: What kinds of meetings?

> (*Beat.*)

MILES: Just meetings.

RAYMOND: Well, I understand you've come back with a bang. I mean, everyone's talking about your book.

MILES: It's not even out yet. And it's not all that interesting.

DR. NAKADA: Why all the false modesty? I hear you sent advance copies to all the major schools.

> (MILES *takes off his dark glasses. He appears not to know this but feels it's not important enough to address.*)

MILES: Hmm.

RAYMOND: You must be quite proud. I must tell you Miles, I didn't know if you'd ever write again. The circumstances, well, under which you left . . .

EIKO: What have you been doing these last few years?

MILES: Thinking. Going places. Visiting unknown countries.

DR. NAKADA: Such as?

MILES: Unfortunately, mostly just in my head, so they'd be of little interest to you. But that's all changed now. I've come back.

DR. NAKADA: Aren't you the least interested in all the happenings on campus? Students protests, anti-war demonstrations, all the Oriental students stirred up. I mean, it was your early activity that helped spawn it.

MILES: You give me too much credit. Besides, my interests are evolving. "Revolution comes from the barrel of a gun"?

DR. NAKADA: Chairman Mao . . .

MILES: More like the end of a man's dick.

RAYMOND: Hugh Hefner.

> (Silence.)

RAYMOND: Joking, joking. *(Beat)* Oh. Well. Congratulations on your book whenever it comes out. It's a great accomplishment for you.

MILES: The one I'm working on now is the important one. The first book, the one that's coming out, is a rehashing of things I've thought about for a while, I needed to lay the foundation for the new paper. *(To* RAYMOND*)* It's some of the stuff we talked about when we were teaching together—Fanon, colonialism, his theories on race—

RAYMOND *(remembering)*: Ah—ah—I still feel racial issues are merely one small component of who and what we are and are being vastly overemphasized in present-day politics—

MILES: Race, the great boogie man of the twentieth century.

EIKO: Do you really believe that Mr. Katayama?

MILES: The only illusion besides God that makes us kill with conviction and clear conscience.

RAYMOND: Then you agree now—this obsession with what is really only a social construct can only drive us further apart as a society . . .

EIKO: What about Fanon's theories on colonized women and their choice of mates?

MILES: I've had discourse in these matters . . .

EIKO: How it can lead to complicitous sexualization of the colonizer and desexualization of their own men?

MILES: I have put into action what I believe and opened a few eyes.

> (Beat.)

MILES *(to* EIKO*)*: "In all writing I love only what is written in blood" . . .

ACT TWO

EIKO: Nietzsche.

MILES *(answering* RAYMOND*)*: If illusion can kill, then race is real enough and must be investigated.

DR. NAKADA: So tell us more about this new paper of yours.

MILES: The one I'm writing now—it's where I begin to decipher the codes—you have to see through the ventriloquism of history, find the linkages. I'm creating a kind of emergency kit for today's living. It isn't meant as a scholarly endeavor but a call to commitment, not an act of writing but writing as an act. There is so little time, so little of us left. I'm trying to grab hold of it, this tiny bit of hope. That we might all get to live a life of uncompromising simple and large truths—a Miles Davis horn riff; a steamy, rich cup of Jamaican Blue Mountain—harvested without tyranny or exploitation; the silky, rhapsodic dimensions of another body that fit so perfectly with yours you no longer know the boundaries of your own flesh . . .

EIKO: A kind of *uber* recipe for liberated everyday living? A space of true spiritual, gender and racial democracy?

MILES: Yes . . . For one to eat, another need not go hungry. For one to reap, another need not be forced to bow to the other's will. Why can't we all eat! Why can't we all sleep under a roof and dream the dreams of a mind free!

EIKO: "You have made your way from worm to man."

MILES: Nietzsche.

EIKO: I hope to get a chance to read your new paper some day.

MILES: I've begun to incorporate preliterate, nonrational arguments, stuff I learned at the commune I've been living on—intuitive revolution, Zen-Zapata, shoot to vanish stuff—*(imitating a gunslinger)* Pow-pow-pow!

EIKO: You're referencing the movie *El Topo*, I take it?

MILES: Jodorowsky, the madman—guns and mysticism, his discussions of the entomological metamorphoses—

EIKO: I do find much of his film decadent, slightly misogynist, and at times, quite frankly, obscene—dwarves with no legs . . . Mr. Katayama, perhaps "much of you is still the worm."

MILES: I am not the worm. *(Beat)* It's as if I'm watching an organ-

ism grow. Before my eyes. Inside me. At times, my brain feels as if it has a fever . . .
> *(Doorbell rings.)*

EIKO: Raymond, get that.
> *(*RAYMOND *is hesitant but exits. Leaves* MILES *and* EIKO *looking at each other.* DR. NAKADA *stands off to the side observing them.)*

MILES *(leans in and whispers)*: Hello *Mary.*

EIKO: You mustn't call me that. It's Eiko Pemberthy now.

MILES: Mary, Mary, quite contrary.

EIKO *(out loud for show, moving away from* NAKADA*)*: *So Mr. Katayama, I see your work is influenced by the French Caribbean, Frantz Fanon. (Whispering)* Rachel said you were looking for some woman.

MILES *(following)*: Rachel? Rachel Cohen? She's here?

EIKO *(out loud)*: *But do his ideas have relevance to Anglo America?* *(Whispering)* Yes, she's here—she said this woman almost killed you. Is it true?

MILES *(out loud)*: *Mental illness as a pathology of liberty. (Whispering)* I heard it almost killed the woman.

EIKO *(whispering)*: Oh really? *(Out loud) So you must also examine the cultural and political context of the patient as well.* *(Whispering)* And what else did you hear?

MILES *(out loud)*: *Yes, sometimes it's the prevailing institutions themselves that must be treated. (Whispering)* I heard they had decided to find out just how deep they could get into each other's heads. They took large doses of this special LSD that they manufactured themselves—and when they got tired, they'd drop some bennies and start all over again. It must've lasted days, maybe weeks—

EIKO: Weeks? I think that's a bit of an exaggeration—

MILES: By the end they'd gone so deep into each other they had lost their individual identities, their separate selves—

EIKO *(overlapping)*: This sounds silly.

MILES: —The yin-yang had collapsed, no duality, there was only union.

EIKO: Union?

ACT TWO

MILES: Yes, though for some reason she resisted.

EIKO: Maybe it wasn't union for her. Not in the way he thought it was.

MILES: If two people love each other—

EIKO: It was but it wasn't—

MILES: It terrified her, she couldn't handle it, losing herself in another. She started provoking him, hurling despicable, vile insults at him—

EIKO *(overlapping)*: This is fucking ridiculous . . .

MILES: —which in turn made him do the same to her, making each of them hate each other with equal contempt—

EIKO: Maybe it was the only thing she could do to save herself, to differentiate their identities—

MILES: It set each one against the other.

EIKO: The psychic divisiveness created psychological division again. She saved their lives.

MILES: She saved herself . . .

(Silence. EIKO notices NAKADA watching.)

EIKO *(out loud)*: *And how do you like working with Professor Cohen, Mr. Katayama?*

MILES *(out loud)*: *An intellectual pickpocket.* (*Whispering*) And I can't believe you're with Raymond. It boggles the mind. I'm amazed there's anything left of him. You should've eaten him alive by now.

EIKO *(whispering)*: That's enough. He's a nice fellow.

MILES *(out loud)*: *Where do you think he got his new ideas?* (*Whispering*) He's a toad.

EIKO *(whispering)*: That's enough, I said.

MILES *(moving close to her)*: He's a toad.

(MILES *slips his hand beneath her dress.)*

EIKO *(weakly resisting, while he moves it slowly upwards)*: I like toads.

(Watching each other closely.)

MILES: There's a small South American frog. Bright yellow. It lives in the humid, tropical rain forest. The poison it excretes— *(Continues.)*

EIKO *(overlapping)*: Most amphibian skin toxins are complex nitrogenous compounds. There are much more dangerous poisons called neurotoxins—*(Continues.)*

MILES *(continues)*: —from its skin glands against predators has a bitter, peppery taste that induces vomiting . . .

EIKO: *(continues)*: —some of which can be introduced by the male during sexual activity—*Batrachotoxin,* is one such nerve toxin—known to . . . *stop the female's heart beating.*

(EIKO, *breathing heavily, pushes his hand away. She sees* NAKADA *watching them and moves away.* RAYMOND *enters with* RACHEL *who immediately rushes up to* MILES.)

RACHEL: Oh, Miles, I was so worried about you.

MILES: What are you doing here? Why aren't you up north?

RACHEL: Oh Miles, Miles, you left so suddenly, you didn't even say good-bye to the kids, they were so disappointed.

MILES: I was going to come back and visit as soon as I finished my business here.

RACHEL: Were you really?

MILES: How come you're here? Does Larry have some business down here?

RACHEL: I came down to take care of some business of my own.

MILES: Are the kids with you?

RACHEL: No.

EIKO: I think she was concerned about you.

(RACHEL *is silent.*)

MILES: I'm fine, I feel better than I have in a long time. *(To* RAYMOND*)* I'm not going after the teaching position. What with the new book I'm working on now, I don't think I'll have a problem getting a position with a prestigious university.

EIKO: Cocky, isn't he?

MILES *(glances at* EIKO*)*: It's the least I could do for you, Mrs. Pemberthy.

RAYMOND: Really? Miles, are you sure?

RACHEL: That gives us more time to work through the ideas we've been struggling with. Make sure they're exactly what you want to say. It'll be so exciting. We're creating something special.

EIKO: How big of you, Mr. Katayama. Isn't it Raymond?

ACT TWO

RAYMOND: Well, yes, I'm still a bit stunned. Relieved, I can tell you.

EIKO: Rachel was worried sick about you, that's why she came down, isn't it?

MILES: Is it?

RACHEL: Well . . .

EIKO: She didn't think you had the strength yet to avoid the temptations that awaited you here.

RACHEL: Eiko, that's not really what I was saying . . .

EIKO: Your tendency to be rather vulnerable to certain impulses given your fragile nature. After your adventures with Mr. Cohen's "blow out" therapy? You have a propensity to be—how did you put it? Oh, hell, why not just say it—paranoid?

RACHEL: Eiko . . .

MILES: Rachel?

EIKO: Certainly given the nature of your close working relationship, these are things you've openly discussed? Or at least, should have? *(To* MILES*)* You're upset? Why, considering how much she seems to be sacrificing for you—*(Continues.)*

RACHEL *(overlapping)*: It's not really a sacrifice, I want to do this, it's what I feel I should be doing.

EIKO *(continues)*: —the least you can do is listen to what she has to say. After all, it's for your own good, isn't it?

MILES: What, are you and Larry checking up on me now? How many times have I told you, I'm not going to fall back into my old ways, not this time.

DR. NAKADA: All this truth telling is making me long for some good ole civilized subterfuge.

EIKO: Lies?

DR. NAKADA: The revelation of truth can be a double-edged sword.

EIKO: Speaking of which . . .

    *(*EIKO *starts to exit.)*

RAYMOND: Honestly Eiko, you're not going to drag *that* out now, are you?

EIKO *(calling as she exits)*: When I get paranoid, my weapon of choice?

RAYMOND *(calling)*: Eiko, no . . .
(She ignores him, disappearing into the back room.)
RAYMOND: She gets something into her head . . .
(Awkward silence.)
RAYMOND: Well, Dr. Nakada, considering what Miles has told us this evening—*(to* MILES*)* and I am certainly in your debt now—maybe I should sit on the stage with the rest of you faculty folks after all. That is, if you are sitting on the stage with President Sommers?
DR. NAKADA: We still have time. This calls for a celebration. How about we loosen up a bit before we go over to the Admin's rally. Only lies please, only lies . . .
RAYMOND: I'm sorry, we don't have any alcohol here, Eiko doesn't like to have any around.
DR. NAKADA: I know, I know, Eiko made me aware of this earlier. Might I suggest something less debilitating.
(Pulls out a marijuana cigarette and lights it.)
RAYMOND: Oh my, oh my . . .
*(*NAKADA *puffs, then holds it out to* MILES. RAYMOND *goes over and discreetly closes the window, curtains.)*
RACHEL: I don't think Miles should.
MILES: No thanks.
(He offers it to RACHEL, *who shakes her head.)*
*(*EIKO *enters holding a small sword-knife.)*
EIKO: Some prefer pistols. Me? The *aikuchi*! My mother's mother's mother's . . .
RAYMOND: Oh, I thought it was on your father's side.
EIKO *(does a move)*: Not this. This is from the female side.
*(*EIKO *reaches over, takes the joint and inhales deeply. As if she's been doing it all her life.)*
RAYMOND: Oh my, oh my . . .
EIKO *(offers it to* RAYMOND*)*: Would you care to try some, dear?
RAYMOND: You never cease to . . . surprise me.
EIKO: Isn't that why you married me?
*(*RAYMOND *hesitates.)*
RAYMOND: I thought you didn't drink?
EIKO: I don't.

ACT TWO

RAYMOND: I know, I know but it's sort of the same thing, isn't it?

DR. NAKADA and EIKO: No.

EIKO: Besides my not drinking has nothing to do with me.

RAYMOND *(taking it)*: I've never done this before.

DR. NAKADA: I think it's pretty evident.

RAYMOND: Like this?

> *(Inhales like a doofus.)*

DR. NAKADA: Ahh, a natural . . .

> *(EIKO takes it from RAYMOND and offers it to MILES again. RACHEL pulls him away.)*

RACHEL: No, he doesn't want any.

DR. NAKADA: Let's play some billiards. *(To RAYMOND)* You any good?

RAYMOND: No.

DR. NAKADA: Perfect, neither am I. How about we wager a little something to make it interesting, say fifty cents a ball . . .

EIKO: Lies abound . . .

DR. NAKADA: They're more accommodating, aren't they?

RAYMOND: I think I feel something.

EIKO: It's your heart beginning to beat.

DR. NAKADA: Only lies, remember?

RAYMOND *(getting an idea, suddenly very excited)*: Hey, hey, hey—The We Five! Let's rock 'n roll!

EIKO *(under her breath)*: Oh, my god . . .

> *(RAYMOND runs over to the stereo and sees EIKO'S box. Looks inside and pulls out several albums.)*

RAYMOND: . . . The Kinks, Cream, Them, Country Joe, ah-hah—Jimi Hendrix . . . *(Calling back)* Eiko, you never cease to amaze me!

EIKO: That's why you love me, isn't it?

RAYMOND *(back to the albums)*: . . . Who's Blue Cheer? . . . The Beatles! *(Takes the record out)* Magical Mystery Tour, I loved that movie—Sam Houston Coliseum, third row, seat forty-four—you could see the spit flying!

> *(RAYMOND puts on the Beatles, "I Am the Walrus.")*
> *(Note: at the end of the actual song, it sounds as if there is a phrase being chanted over and over.)*

RAYMOND *(music starts, proclaims)*: I Am the Walrus!

> *(*RAYMOND *joins* NAKADA *in the back room to play billiards.* EIKO *approaches* RACHEL *and* MILES. MILES *is irritated with* RACHEL.*)*

EIKO: Belonged to my great-grandmother. A woman can be Samurai, too. They weren't allowed to use the bigger blade, though. Always the short end. Ain't it a bitch being a girl . . .

> *(Starts to demonstrate her skill with the blade.)*

EIKO: "You're such a nice *otonashii* Daddy's girl"—quiet, well-behaved, subservient. "But here in America, remember, you must speak up or you're ignored." But when I open my mouth and say what I think—"Oh no, I'm a castrating American bitch." The worst of the East mixed with the worst of the West . . .

> *(She slashes.)*

EIKO: Better to nod and smile. I haven't the faintest idea what he's saying—nod and smile, nod and smile . . .

> You want to marry me?
>
> Nod and smile . . .
>
> Buy me a house?
>
> Nod and smile . . .
>
> Give you babies?
>
> *(Slashes violently.)*

EIKO: It was also used to commit *ōjigi*, if you were captured by the enemy. Rather than let yourself be *defiled* by your *husband's rival*, you would kill yourself by doing thus . . .

> *(Demonstrates.)*

EIKO: . . . slashing your carotid artery and bleeding to death. But before you did that—this is interesting—you'd tie your legs together, because, god forbid, when you're thrashing around on the ground with blood pouring out of your neck, you should happen to *open your legs*. How indelicate.

MILES: Would you ever consider killing yourself?

EIKO: I've considered killing someone else.

RACHEL: I'm surprised you smoke. I didn't know you did things like that.

EIKO: I did it once a long time ago.

MILES: Why did you stop?

ACT TWO

EIKO: Well. Once upon a time, I met someone. And upon meeting him I felt I had met myself for the first time. He could see me, and I was cast in the bright light of day. I did not have to be unseen. I heard myself thinking my own thoughts, I spoke my own words, I fought for my territory, I argued my truths. I had never felt that way before. With any man. Especially an Oriental—I mean, Asian man. I was born. But in the end, maybe I was just nodding and smiling.

MILES: Is that what you think?

(RAYMOND *runs in with the joint.*)

RAYMOND *(holding the joint out to* MILES *and* RACHEL*)*: Dr. Nakada says we have to share.

EIKO: And wasting my time.

RAYMOND: Miles?

RACHEL: Oh no, Raymond, I don't think it's a good idea.

MILES: Rachel, I can speak for myself. No, not right now.

(EIKO *reaches for it and inhales deeply.*)

EIKO: If not now, when?

RAYMOND: Carpe Diem!

(RAYMOND *takes a hit and holds it out to* RACHEL.)

RACHEL: No, thanks, I'd better not.

MILES: Go on, Rachel. Go on, I can take care of myself.

EIKO: Go on Rachel.

RAYMOND: Yes, Rachel, go on.

(RACHEL *reluctantly takes a hit.*)

MILES: Is that what things have come to for you? Nodding and smiling and wasting your time?

RAYMOND: You could go to work.

EIKO *(affectionately)*: You could go to hell. But that's where you found me, so what's the fun in that, huh?

RAYMOND: You little devil, you . . .

EIKO *(taking the joint from* RACHEL*)*: I want another hit . . .

(EIKO *takes a puff and looks at* MILES *and* RACHEL. *She begins to circle, inspecting them while blowing smoke at* MILES.)

EIKO: Not like you two, though. Wasting time? No, more like *doing time*. From what Rachel has been saying—locked in your commune hive, busy as worker bees, Rachel buzzing around

Miles, taking care of him, bzzz-bzzz, collecting the honey, bzzz-bzzz, storing it in a safe place, bzzz-bzzz—

DR. NAKADA *(poking his head out)*: Hey, where is everybody!

(MILES *has had enough of* EIKO'S *taunts and snatches the marijuana cigarette from her.*)

RACHEL: Miles, what are you doing?

MILES *(pulling* RAYMOND*)*: Come on Raymond, let's show them how to really party . . .

(MILES *takes a hit as he begins to exit with* RAYMOND.)

RAYMOND: Right on!

RACHEL *(starting to follow)*: Miles . . .

MILES *(to* RACHEL*)*: Stay out here.

(MILES *and* RAYMOND *exit to the back billiards room.*)

DR. NAKADA *(off)*: All right, another victim!

MILES *(off)*: Let's do a supercharge!

DR. NAKADA *(off)*: Oh, my, my, he *has* decided to join the party.

RAYMOND *(off)*: Hey, Miles is smoking!

RACHEL: Why did you do that? You know it's not good for him.

EIKO: I did it for you.

RACHEL: I'm beginning to think you do everything for yourself.

EIKO: Oh, trust me, I've no interest in Miles. Besides, get too near him and I trust Rachel will sting me dead.

RACHEL: I don't understand you. First I think you want to help us, then it's quite obvious your intentions are anything but.

EIKO: And?

RACHEL: I don't think you even know what you want.

EIKO: Maybe the point is, I want nothing.

RACHEL: Nobody wants nothing.

EIKO: Dead people do.

(*The Beatles' song has gotten to the ending where in the background we hear the circular chant "Everybody smokes pot."* DR. NAKADA *and* RAYMOND *come out chanting along excitedly.*)

RAYMOND and DR. NAKADA *(chanting)*: . . . everybody smokes pot, everybody smokes pot—

DR. NAKADA: It's amazing, Raymond deciphered this—"everybody smokes pot, everybody smokes pot" . . .

ACT TWO

RAYMOND *(demonstrating, chanting enthusiastically)*: "Everybody smokes pot, everybody smokes pot . . .

DR. NAKADA: The Beatles have left a secret message and Raymond's discovered it!

RAYMOND: I'm brilliant! Finally, I'm brilliant!

(MILES strides out behind them, pontificating. RAYMOND continues to excitedly chant along with the record.)

MILES *(over the music)*: —Malcolm X? They killed him. Martin Luther King? They killed him. Bobby Kennedy? They killed him. Bobby Hutton? Dead, murdered, all killed. But look at us. *(To NAKADA and EIKO)* You and me. Buddhaheads. We're still standing, we're still here, we're not dead. Why?

DR. NAKADA: Because we never stick our necks out—we're the model minority!

MILES: Because we don't matter enough! We're not important enough! We're not *dangerous* enough to kill! We must be like our black and brown sisters and brothers who despite the cost of their actions, commit to action thus transforming their acts and themselves in the process. We must—*(Continues.)*

EIKO *(overlapping, under the fray)*: . . . blah, blah, blah, blah, blah . . .

MILES *(continues)*: —elevate our consciousnesses by whatever means and become dangerous!—*(Continues.)*

(RAYMOND and DR. NAKADA continue enthusiastically chanting along. They've dragged RACHEL away from MILES to join them.)

MILES *(continues)*: —Otherwise it's just theoretical, existing in the imaginary world where no one grows old and no one dies—

RAYMOND *(calling, excitedly)*: The suburbs!

MILES *(to EIKO)*: You merely play at life. Not—*(Continues.)*

EIKO *(overlapping)*: Blah, blah, blah, blah, blah . . .

MILES *(contiues)*: —participating. Nothing you do is of consequence. You're not dangerous. No love, no revolution. White Face. You.

(DR. NAKADA turns off the stereo.)

DR. NAKADA: Are we ready?

RAYMOND: We're ready! Fuckin' A we're ready! Bring on the student anti-war demonstrators! All power to the Administration! Fuck the students! Fuck Jane Fonda! Fuck Dr. Spock! Fuck Donna Reed! All power to the faculty!

MILES: I'm coming, too.

RACHEL: Oh, Miles, I don't think it's a good idea—

RAYMOND and DR. NAKADA: All right!

MILES: I can't miss this, the president speaking to hundreds of pissed-off black, brown and yellow students—And the "Asian American Students Alliance" might have a surprise in store, too. They've begun to see the connections, the bigger picture— it's not just here, it's about what they're doing to Asians all over the world—Self-immolating monks to the *manongs* fighting eviction at the I-Hotel, Hiroshima genocide to the immigrant holding cells at Angel Island. And besides, how could I miss watching Raymond fuck Donna Reed!

RAYMOND: The ground swell of support for—*(Continues.)*

EIKO *(overlapping and above the fray)*: Rachel, come over here. Observe, look look—liberated men off to join the revolution. And what is the position of women in the revolution? To quote Stokely Carmichael, "On their backs!" Yoo-hoo, men, would you like us to serve coffee now? Or how about some cookies and milk for the little warriors before they go off to battle! Would you like some free love now? We're ready to take up our positions for the revolution!

RAYMOND *(continues)*: —the faculty will be enormous. You'll see you, you commie-hippie, rabble-rouser—where's your god-damn Fu Manchu moustache! Dr. Lao puts you to shame and he's Tony Randall!

MILES: And you, you old right-wing, establishment John Birch butt fucker—we'll see what the students truly think of this out-dated, backwards institution of lower learning and what Third World students are capable of when they reclaim their pasts and see the true future!

DR. NAKADA: Lies only lies!

RAYMOND: Fuck Donna Reed!

DR. NAKADA: Me, too! And Jane Fonda, too! *Barbarella* was a great movie! Roger Vadim is God!

ACT TWO

(RACHEL *starts to gather her things.*)

MILES: You stay here.

RACHEL: I want to come.

DR. NAKADA: No girls allowed.

RACHEL: It's *woman.*

(NAKADA *and* RAYMOND *giggle like two schoolboys and start to exit.*)

MILES: I'll be back in a few hours. We can drive back up north tonight.

RACHEL: I'm not some little girl.

(MILES *starts to exit;* EIKO *grabs* RACHEL's *arm.*)

EIKO (*holding on to her*): I'll take care of her. You stay here with me.

RAYMOND (*calling from off*): Come on Miles, let's go!

(MILES *exits.*)

EIKO: Tell me all the sordid details when you animals get back!

RACHEL (*upset*): Don't you want to go with them?

(EIKO *watches her. Then lets her go.*)

EIKO: Okay. I won't stop you. Go.

RACHEL: All right, I will.

(RACHEL *starts to gather her things again.*)

EIKO (*suddenly she speaks forcefully*): But he doesn't want you to go, Rachel, he doesn't want you to go.

(*Beat, conciliatory.*)

EIKO: But go anyway, because that's what *you* want, right? Even if *he* doesn't. After all, it's for his own good. To keep him from fucking up, as it were.

(*Now ferocious, closing in on her.*)

EIKO: But isn't he going in the first place because you didn't trust him enough to take care of himself—"He's paranoid, he wants to die," you blathered on—so he got pissed off—and rightly so—and now he's out there and you're in here? So what are you waiting for! Rachel! What are you waiting for? Go! Go! Let's see if you can fuck it up again!

(RACHEL *breaks down crying.* EIKO *goes over to the stereo and puts on "Here Comes the Night" by Them. She goes and opens the curtains again. Moves back towards* RACHEL.)

EIKO: Do you know what a double bind is?

RACHEL: What?

(EIKO ignores her own question.)

EIKO: You must let him go. Little boys must be allowed to grow up. *(Beat)* He'll return, you'll see, all grown up in mysterious male ways that you or I will never be allowed to understand.

(EIKO notices something out the window.)

EIKO: Oh-oh, looks like a tear gas canister. Let the games begin . . .

(She begins to dance by herself to "Here Comes the Night." She's now holding the small sword.)

EIKO *(over the song)*: I'd go. But I don't want to. I want to stay at home *and* want to go. Does that make sense?

(Takes out the sword and whips it around, with skill and precision. It intimidates RACHEL. EIKO forces RACHEL to dance with her, while still holding the sword. They watch each other closely.)

EIKO *(over the music)*: When you can't act but you have to. When you can't scream but you need to. When you can't live but you're simply dying to . . .

(Points the knife at RACHEL'S neck.)

EIKO: Right there. That's where you cut . . .

(EIKO and RACHEL continue to dance.)

(Black out. News comes up overlapping and continues the commentary.)

Intermission

House Music Line-up during Intermission
Otis Redding: "Dock at the Bay"
Dan Hicks and His Hot Licks: "Canned Music"
Sopwith Camel: "Hello, Hello"
Beau Brummels: "Laugh, Laugh"
James & Bobby Purify: "I'm your Puppet"
Love: "My Little Red Book"
James Brown: "It's a Man's, Man's, Man's World"

ACT THREE

Early the next morning. As lights fade, James Brown's "It's a Man's, Man's World" is brought up. Dramatic strings begin the song, then into Brown's soulfully ironic chauvinist tribute to women: "It's a man's world, but it wouldn't be nothing, without a woman to love a man . . ." Then a slow fade as lights come up.

> RACHEL *sits up on the couch wrapped in a blanket, waiting.* EIKO'S *asleep on the couch snoring lightly. Phone rings in the back room.* EIKO *gets up and exits to the back to answer it.* EIKO *re-enters moments later.*

RACHEL: Was it Miles?

EIKO: No. How did you sleep?

RACHEL: Terrible. I only got a few hours.

EIKO: I slept quite well, thank you. Why don't you go sleep in my bed.

RACHEL: What if he comes?

EIKO: I'll wake you up—go, go.

> (RACHEL *exits into the back room.* EIKO *is about to put some hot water on when* RAYMOND *arrives.*)

RAYMOND: Eiko . . .

EIKO: Where are Miles and Dr. Nakada?

RAYMOND: They didn't come by?

EIKO: No.

RAYMOND: I don't know, we got separated. It's been such a strange night Eiko. I'm sorry I stayed out so late but one thing led to another . . .

EIKO: What happened?

RAYMOND: Well, the rally was a mess. It never really got started. The Black Students Union had brought in outside support. A contingent of students—the Asian American Students Alliance, I think that's what they call themselves—marched right up to the president at the podium with bullhorns, carrying banners—calling for his resignation, saying the university was doing research for a—what'd they say—a *racist* war, that America was killing Asian people—

EIKO: How did you get separated from Miles and Dr. Nakada?

RAYMOND: Well, when the students started to climb onto the stage, suddenly, out of nowhere, the riot police come storming in—then all hell broke loose. We tried to run away but the police were swinging at everything so Miles just opened the door to this van that was parked there and we all piled in. We surprised a guy and a girl who were in there. We locked the doors, pulled all the shades down and just waited. There was nothing else to do so Miles took his manuscript out from his knapsack and began reading. I'm not sure how long he read, if it was a few minutes or a few hours, they were smoking all this hash, but at one point he stopped, looked up and said it was dedicated to the one great love of his life. And I thought, this could be me talking about you. I mean, if I had written it. We waited till the tear gas cleared up and then we made a run for it. I was the last to leave. That's when we got separated. I looked for them but it was dark and people were still running every which way. I thought maybe they had come back here.

EIKO: I wonder where they went?

(RAYMOND *takes out a manila folder from inside his coat and holds it out.*)

RAYMOND: Look what I found. It's his new paper. Miles's. The one he read to us in the van. He left it behind. Luckily as I was leaving I noticed it. By the time I got outside they were gone.

EIKO: That's it?

(*No response.*)

EIKO: Raymond?

RAYMOND: There's something else, too.

EIKO: Yes?

RAYMOND: When Miles was reading it? I felt something quite. Quite, unsettling—ugly, actually. I don't know if I should tell you this. You might think other of me, if I do.

ACT THREE

EIKO *(getting excited)*: No, no, tell me, tell me Raymond.

RAYMOND: I don't think I want to—

EIKO *(almost out of control)*: Tell me! Tell me, Raymond!

(Shocked silence. RAYMOND *is affected by* EIKO'S *excited state.)*

RAYMOND: I felt. I felt all twisted inside because I wished. I wished it was me, not Miles, but me who had written this. I. I found myself envying him with a kind of hateful bitterness— *(Continues.)*

EIKO: Yes, yes . . .

RAYMOND *(continues)*:—because of what he was capable of doing, this seeming undisciplined braggard, pothead, and maybe I couldn't do it and I wanted to and he didn't deserve to—*(Continues.)*

EIKO: Yes . . .

RAYMOND *(continues)*: —it should have been me who . . .
(Silence.)

RAYMOND: It's really quite extraordinary. His paper. Wild assertions, at times erratic, and yet . . .

EIKO: Raymond? Did you really try to find Miles? After you found it?

RAYMOND: What do you mean?

EIKO: It doesn't matter, you're going to get the teaching position, remember?

RAYMOND: Well, yes . . .

EIKO: Here, give it to me.
*(*EIKO *takes the manuscript and tosses it on the chair.)*

RAYMOND: I have to return it to him, I'm sure he's going crazy if he knows it's gone.

EIKO: Is this the only copy?

RAYMOND: I think so.

EIKO: And no one knows you have it?

RAYMOND: No. *(Beat)* What a strange night.

EIKO: I have some other news, too. Your Auntie Vicky is very ill.

RAYMOND: When did you hear this?

EIKO: Just before you got here. Your Auntie Gladys called. You should hurry over there.

RAYMOND: She's dying?

EIKO: I believe so.

RAYMOND: Okay, okay, I better go. Did you want to come? It'd mean a lot to Auntie Gladys. And me, too.

EIKO: I really don't think I can handle it, I've been up all night worrying about you and I'm very much out of sorts. I think it's better you go ahead alone. Also, Rachel's sleeping in the back and just in case the rest of them show up . . .

RAYMOND: Okay, I'll call you later. Where are my things? And, let's see—where's the manuscript?

EIKO: I'll keep it until you get back. Now go, go, you have to hurry . . .

(RAYMOND'S *flustered.*)

RAYMOND: All right . . .

EIKO: Raymond? I'll take care of everything.

(As RAYMOND *exits, he stops and looks back.*)

RAYMOND: The stakes at which he was writing . . . Like blood pouring from a wound. I envied him not being white.

(RAYMOND *turns and exits.* EIKO *goes over and picks up the script.*)

EIKO: We stand so silently. With our breaths held and minds empty, staring out over the abyss. Waiting. Waiting to be filled with the new knowledge . . .

(EIKO *opens the script and begins to read it. Silence as she becomes absorbed. A knock on the front door. She starts.* EIKO *hurriedly puts the manuscript in a drawer and goes to see who it might be. She enters with* DR. NAKADA, *who looks quite disheveled.*)

DR. NAKADA: Is Raymond back?

EIKO: Yes—My goodness, Raymond didn't say how bad the strike was. Was anyone hurt?

DR. NAKADA: Oh, this wasn't at the rally. This happened afterwards with Miles. I mean, the rally wasn't a walk in the park. Miles was right, as soon as President Sommers started speaking—well, even before he started speaking—oh, it was a mess. Throwing things at him, at us—your husband talked me into sitting on stage, he's quite persuasive when he's stoned, by the way—and you should've seen the students, calling themselves the "Third World"—Negroes, Mexicans, Orientals. I thought they were going to kill us. And I recognized some of them from class—business students! And the Oriental students—I swear they were leading the damn thing—*(Imitating the students)* "The Vietnamese never called me Gook!" What happened to the quiet hardworking model minority? They had approached me a few months ago, wanted to know if I'd be their group's faculty sponsor. I told them maybe they'll change for Negroes but never Orientals. Yellow Power? What the hell is that? More like Yellow Stupid!

EIKO: What about afterwards with Miles?

DR. NAKADA: Oh, yeah, yeah. Anyway, the real trouble started after we got separated from Raymond. Well, actually we ditched him—he's really quite uncool. But Miles—my god, he turns into a raving lunatic, I loved it, I really loved it—he talks me into going over with a couple of the students to the Fillmore, catch the last set of this band he knows. We get over there and he drags me right up to the front of the stage—it's crazier than the riot at the school, only these kids are happy! And the girl, the singer that Miles knows? Beautiful girl, flaming red hair, no bra, see-through blouse—she's singing right to us—

EIKO *(impatiently)*: What happened, what happened?

DR. NAKADA: So we get backstage and it's another big party. This time it's nitrous oxide, a huge tank of it, filling up balloons, handing them out—

EIKO: Okay, okay . . .

DR. NAKADA: Everything's cool. We're all smoking, drinking, sucking up laughing gas—Miles is chatting with Katey, she's the singer—and, I'm, well, there's this naked girl, just sitting there, in front of me, meditating. But I can tell she's looking at me—

EIKO: Oh, for god's sake Frank, I don't want to hear about your sexual exploits!

DR. NAKADA: Okay, all right, then next thing I know Miles is getting crazy—tearing up the place, he's holding up his knapsack, ranting and raving someone took something out of it. Well, one thing led to another, people start swinging, screaming, the police come—I can hear Miles, "Fuck you pigs! Fuck you pigs!" *(Beat)* I don't think Miles has to worry about getting a job at State. Ever.

EIKO: Where is he now?

DR. NAKADA: In jail, I imagine. I have to make some phone calls to people, make sure my name is kept out of this. The last thing I need is to have my name attached to Miles and some violent, drug-induced orgy. I'm having nothing to do with that fellow from here on out. You'd better do the same, too, if you want to protect Raymond's teaching position. Have nothing to do with Miles. Especially now. If he comes by, don't talk to him, don't see him, you'll be implicated in this whole sordid mess.

EIKO: Why would I be implicated?

DR. NAKADA: I've been watching you two. There's more here than meets the eye. I can see it. I can smell it.

EIKO: You've a pretty vivid imagination.

DR. NAKADA: I have no imagination, I teach business, remember?

EIKO: Then you're guessing.

DR. NAKADA *(grabs her arm forcefully)*: Try me. *(Moves a finger from her neck down to her breast)* Besides, I have my own personal interests to protect here.

EIKO: You can be quite nasty, can't you.

DR. NAKADA: I told you I wouldn't forget. Your father underestimated me, too.

EIKO: I know how to defend myself, remember?

(During the following speech, NAKADA *holds* EIKO *with one hand and moves the other behind her neck.)*

DR. NAKADA: Ahh, that's right, *technique,* the secret language of the privileged, it makes them appear as if their feet don't touch the ground when they walk. I know how to take care of myself, too. I learned at a very special place. Camp Manzanar? For underprivileged Americans? Sent there just as my life and career were about to begin. My style may not be pretty but I know how to get by. Stay low on the radar, don't make waves and you'll be amazed how far they'll let you go. And not go. And I accept that from them—

ACT THREE

(During the rest of NAKADA'S *speech, he begins to push* EIKO'S *head down to his groin. She struggles to resist but he is too strong.)*

DR. NAKADA: —It's also allowed me to know and understand people like you, who think they're above all of it. It makes me know that if I'm to get any taste of the real thing, you're the closest I'll ever get to it, and if you knew how much I hated being cut off in the middle of my manhood, then you wouldn't be surprised as to how far I'd go to get that taste.

*(*NAKADA *releases* EIKO'S *head and she yanks it away.)*

EIKO: You vile, disgusting, little man.

*(*NAKADA *straightens his clothes.)*

DR. NAKADA: Now. I have to go and make sure I've nothing to do with this mess.

*(*NAKADA *crosses to leave by the back way.* EIKO *notices.)*

DR. NAKADA: Back door, front door, perhaps soon enough it won't matter.

(He exits. EIKO *stands there for a moment. Then remembers* RACHEL *is in the back and goes to check on her.*

MILES *enters through the front door without knocking. He looks haggard, disoriented. Sees* EIKO'S *box and goes over to it. Takes out a chemistry beaker and stares at it. Looks at the records. Pulls an album and puts on a song. Jimi Hendrix's "The Wind Cries Mary."*

EIKO *and* RACHEL *come out. They notice how he looks.)*

RACHEL: Miles? Are you okay?

MILES: No, no I'm not. Hello Eiko.

(He listens to the music.)

MILES: It's a nice song, isn't it?

EIKO: I hadn't heard it in a while.

RACHEL: What's wrong Miles?

MILES: Nothing. Everything. We can't see each other anymore. Or rather, I might want to but I don't think you will. Then again, maybe I won't want to see you either. Besides, I've decided to just say "Fuck it." After all, I can't really see anything anymore.

(Points to his eyes and makes them ridiculously big, giggles.)

RACHEL: What are you talking about?

MILES: My eyes. I haven't mentioned it because it seems too weird but it's as if I went to sleep and woke up with new eyes. I can see patterns and connections and just by closing my eyes I begin to connect the dots, something comes into being. A kind of living picture born of the simple act of *seeing*. Seeing with new eyes.

RACHEL: Yes, yes Miles, that's what we've been doing with your new book, together, and I don't see any reason why we can't continue to do that.

MILES: No, we can't.

RACHEL: Why not?

MILES: Go Rachel, go back to your husband, go back to your children, go back to whatever life it is you had because there is no more you and me, there is no more working together, there is no more new book, I'm not a revolutionary, I'm a fuck-up.

RACHEL: I don't understand.

MILES *(to* EIKO*)*: Did you ever want a baby?

    *(*RACHEL *is confused.)*

EIKO: No.

MILES *(back to* RACHEL*)*: I destroyed it.

RACHEL: What?

MILES: The new manuscript. Our work, what we've been doing together. I threw it away, I tore it up—*(Continues.)*

RACHEL *(overlapping)*: What are you saying?

MILES *(continues)*: —I burned it, I threw it in the garbage, I flushed it down the toilet, the manuscript, all the ideas, what I was thinking, inside my head, how it all fits together, how it all makes sense—

RACHEL: Why? Why? Why did you do that?

MILES: It's gone, I destroyed it, I killed it, I killed it!

    *(*RACHEL *stares for a beat, then runs off.* EIKO *turns off the stereo.)*

EIKO: You talk as if the manuscript was a child.

MILES: These past six months I've been on fire. I write it all down on whatever I can find—napkins, old envelopes, toilet paper— I'm writing, writing . . . And lo, finally I am change. Now I am revolution. And then I go for a walk down the street and

I lose the baby. I'm not change, I'm not revolution. I'm still just a fuck-up! That night? I would've preferred we died then and there. Folded into each other's lives so completely we disappeared. Poof. Perfect.

EIKO: I didn't get scared. I didn't run away. I said those vile despicable things to you because I really meant them. At the point of what you think was complete union, I was fighting with every ounce of my soul to resist. Was I to allow myself to be so overwhelmed by you, absorbed so completely into your identity that I was to be rendered virtually invisible?

MILES: We would disappear together.

EIKO: It's not the same thing for me. What if the worm dies and there is no butterfly yet to emerge? Maybe for the woman it's still unborn, a womb of swirling inchoate ideas and we want it to be there so much we pretend to see what is not there yet. Should I still kill the worm?

(Silence. MILES *stares at* EIKO, *then sits down, exhausted.)*

MILES: What else can I destroy? What else can I kill?

*(*EIKO *watches* MILES *for a long beat.)*

EIKO: Do you mean that? Do you really mean that Miles?

MILES: No book. No Rachel. No Mary.

(Pause.)

EIKO: There is so little time, there is so little left of us. What do you want? At this moment, what do you really want?

MILES: I want to be gone. Invisible. Perfectly disappeared. I want to be at the place you so hated and reviled. That's where I want to be.

*(*EIKO *watches him for a beat, then takes the pendant out from her blouse. She opens it and takes a pill out.)*

MILES: It's a Mary?

EIKO: The special batch I made. That we took that night.

(He reaches for it but she pulls her hand away, then goes to the windows and slams them open—we hear sirens echoing in the pre-dawn darkness.)

EIKO: Listen, can't you hear it? *(Sniffing)* Ahh, the smell of tear gas in the early morning hours! All this chitter chatter, chitter chatter, everybody talking, bullshit this, bullshit that—politics, Molotovs, SDS, Panthers, priests, Playboy Bunnies—all transparent, infantalized bullshit. I mean, look where everything you've tried to do has brought you? Self-serving governments still murder cute yellow people, boys still come home in boxes, black people still get lynched, women still bend over for their men and the most potent aphoristic antidote we can come up with is, "Turn on, tune in, drop out"? I mean, in all this muck, what is a truly meaningful action? Huh?

What we glimpsed that night. That. Was it merely a spectre of imbibed errant chemicals? A figment of sexual indulgence? Or was it truly a prescient experience?

MILES: Does it matter? You ran away, scared you'd be swallowed up in my maleness. You were a coward.

EIKO: I ran away because I did not have faith. *(Beat)* After I left you I wandered until the currents of tradition brought me here. The place where no one grows old and no one dies. And then, of my own volition, I stepped up onto the pedestal. Yes, I am a coward. But you don't have to be . . .

"Perfectly disappeared"? You're free to go there. *(Gives him the pill)* You have a purity, Miles. That's where courage resides. Maybe you just played at life. Maybe you lived a life of no consequence. And maybe you were just a fuck up. Until now . . .

(He stares at the pill but doesn't move to take it. EIKO suddenly puts it into her mouth. Then puts her mouth on MILES's mouth in a violent kiss. When she jerks away, it's evident she's passed the pill to MILES. MILES watches EIKO for a moment, then swallows it.)

EIKO: Until now . . .

(EIKO goes up to the obutsudan and retrieves a bundle wrapped up in a white cloth. She brings it back to MILES who opens it up. It's the aikuchi.)

EIKO: In a time of moral ambiguity, the freedom fighter addresses himself and no one else. A pure act—absolute, unequivocal, final—is the gesture of the hero.

ACT THREE

(MILES *does not respond.*)

EIKO: A pure act.

MILES: Eiko?

EIKO: I cannot go with you. But let me be with you. Do you understand?

    (*No response.*)

EIKO: Do you understand?

MILES: Yes.

EIKO: Do you promise?

    (*Long pause.*)

MILES: With this act, finally I am action.

EIKO: Yes, yes . . .

MILES: Now, I am revolution.

EIKO: Now, we are union.

    (MILES *wraps up the* aikuchi.)

EIKO: I won't go looking for you.

MILES: I won't tell you where I go.

MILES: Goodbye Mary.

EIKO: Do it . . . beautifully.

    (*He leaves.* EIKO *shuts the door and stands there in silence for a moment. Then goes to the stereo and puts on a record. "White Bird" by the band It's a Beautiful Day. Goes to the drawer and takes out the manuscript. She sits by the fire and holds it.*)

EIKO: We stand so silently. With our breaths held and minds empty, staring out over the abyss. Who will give us wings . . . By Miles Katayama . . .

    (MILES *lit with the* aikuchi.)

MILES (*musing, he's high on the hallucinogen*): Revolution. Revolution. Revolution . . . (*Thinking*) Evolution. Evolution. Evol . . . E-V-O-L. L-O-V-E . . .

EIKO: Love . . .

MILES: I am dangerous, I am dangerous, I am dangerous . . .

    (MILES *blacks out.* EIKO *tears off the page and throws it into the fire.*)

EIKO (*begins reciting*): D-lysergic acid diethylamide,—carbon 20, hydrogen 25, nitrogen 3, oxygen. Molecular weight 323.43.

Administered, oral. Threshold dose—10 to 50 micrograms. But the average "hit" sold on the street is typically around 250 micrograms . . .

(EIKO *tears off another, then more, gathering momentum and fury as she continues to recite the chemical properties of LSD. More news of Vietnam and campus strife. "White Bird" swells. Black out.)*

ACT FOUR

The following day. The room is in shadows. AUNTIE GLADYS *and* EIKO *sit across from each other. Both dressed in black. Awkward silence.* EIKO *fidgets.* AUNTIE GLADYS *is composed.* EIKO'S *moving box has been taken out and sits next to the sofa.*

EIKO: He said he was coming right here?

AUNTIE GLADYS: We took two cars so he didn't have to drive me back. He was following me.
 (Noticing EIKO.*)*

AUNTIE GLADYS: It's amazing.

EIKO: What?

AUNTIE GLADYS: Even in funeral black you look good.

EIKO: He called from your place and said you were coming so I put this on . . .

AUNTIE GLADYS *(marveling)*: How do you do it?
 (Beat.)

EIKO: So she died peacefully?

AUNTIE GLADYS: Yes. Quite beautiful actually. That's the way I want to go. Do you have any more of those chocolates I brought over?

EIKO *(realizing she hasn't offered anything)*: Oh, I'm sorry, would you like some tea or coffee or something?
 *(*EIKO *puts a pot of water on the stove.)*

AUNTIE GLADYS: I asked for chocolates. Remember the cheap ones I brought over?

EIKO: Oh.
 (She looks in a drawer and returns with a box of chocolates.)

AUNTIE GLADYS: What are these?

EIKO: Conrad Schmitz. Truffles.

AUNTIE GLADYS: What happened to the nougats I brought?

EIKO: Try one.

AUNTIE GLADYS: You threw them out didn't you?

EIKO: Try one.

> (EIKO *holds them out. Beat.* AUNTIE GLADYS *cautiously takes a truffle. Stares at it skeptically.*)

EIKO: Come on, come on.

> (AUNTIE GLADYS *takes a nibble.*)

EIKO: Over the lips and through the gums—

AUNTIE GLADYS: Oh, shut up.

> (EIKO *smirks.* AUNTIE GLADYS *chews.*)

EIKO: You like?

AUNTIE GLADYS: They're all right.

EIKO: You like?

AUNTIE GLADYS: Not bad.

EIKO: Well, then . . .

> (*She starts to take the box away when* AUNTIE GLADYS *stops her.*)

AUNTIE GLADYS: Why don't you just leave them for now.

EIKO: But I thought you didn't—

AUNTIE GLADYS: Leave them.

EIKO: But you said—

AUNTIE GLADYS: Please, leave them.

EIKO (*watches her for a beat*): Okay . . .

> (EIKO *sets them down and sits back down opposite her.* AUNTIE GLADYS *takes a truffle and pops it whole into her mouth. She slowly chews it, savoring its flavor.*)

AUNTIE GLADYS: Ahhh . . .

> (AUNTIE GLADYS *seems revived now.*)

AUNTIE GLADYS: I had to come over here. Funny, huh? Auntie Vicky's just passed away and I say to Raymond, "Quick, we must go over and tell Eiko." He says why not just phone her and I say, "No, no, we got to go over there, to the house, I need to tell her in person." So here I am and I'm not sure why I'm here . . .

> (RAYMOND *has just entered and heard the last part.*)

RAYMOND: Sorry, I'm late getting here. I had an errand to run before I came home. (*Kisses* AUNTIE GLADYS) I'm sure Eiko appreciates your thoughtfulness.

EIKO: Yes, I do appreciate you coming over and telling me in person.

ACT FOUR

AUNTIE GLADYS: It's so odd how things happen. One life leaves just as another arrives. Maybe that's why I'm here. To let you know in person that the one who's going to die, has. So the one who's supposed to arrive, can.

RAYMOND: Auntie?

AUNTIE GLADYS: What am I going to do now? What am I going to do? Maybe Auntie Vicky was the lucky one. She gets to leave first. Not be left alone. I've been taking care of her for the last twenty years, I don't know what else to do? Who am I going to care for?

EIKO: She liked the truffles.

RAYMOND: Oh. Would you like us to order you some?

AUNTIE GLADYS: They're very expensive, aren't they?

RAYMOND: It's okay, Auntie. After all, you're all I have left.

AUNTIE GLADYS: And you two are all I have left. Maybe there's something I can help you with. You're going to be needing an extra hand and that's right up my alley.

EIKO: They're from Chicago. The truffles. A small boutique shop. We have them sent over from there.

RAYMOND: Why don't you stay here for a while, you don't have to go right back. The doctor's over there and he said it would take a while for the ambulance to arrive. Seeing as it really isn't an emergency . . .

AUNTIE GLADYS: Auntie Vicky was really worried about *Hop Sing*. She was. Wrote a letter to the TV station and everything. Now that Eiko was with you, Auntie Vicky felt it her duty to understand her people better. That's why we had to watch *Bonanza*. Where did *Hop Sing* sleep? In the kitchen? They never say. In the bunkhouse with the other cowpokes? Vicky didn't think they'd want him in there with them. "Poor Hop Sing," she'd say.
   (Beat.)

AUNTIE GLADYS: It's so odd, like she was just sleeping, you know. Like she was going to wake up any moment, just like always. But when I walked over and touched her . . .

   (AUNTIE GLADYS acts it out, her hand extending. She holds it for a beat as both EIKO and RAYMOND watch her. Then she pulls it back and becomes herself again.)

AUNTIE GLADYS: When someone close leaves us, it's comforting to know that another will soon arrive.

EIKO: Would you please stop talking so cryptically, it's making me sick.

RAYMOND: Eiko, please.

(Awkward pause. EIKO *goes to the window and looks out.)*

AUNTIE GLADYS: Well, I better be going. I really should be there when they take Vicky away.

RAYMOND: You sure you don't want to stay a bit?

AUNTIE GLADYS *(shakes her head)*: They're both gone now—first your father, and now Vicky. *(Beat)* Why did I have to come here?

(She turns to leave.)

EIKO *(not looking from the window)*: Goodbye Auntie Gladys.

*(*AUNTIE GLADYS *stops and turns around to look at* EIKO. RAYMOND, *too, is surprised by* EIKO *calling her by "Auntie."* EIKO *turns to look at them both.)*

AUNTIE GLADYS: I wondered why . . .

*(*AUNTIE GLADYS *walks over to* EIKO, *stopping in front of her. She looks at* EIKO *for a moment, then slowly reaches out and touches her naked arm and holds it there as if feeling something. Then she withdraws her hand, turns, and leaves. She's her old self again. She grabs the box of truffles as she exits.)*

AUNTIE GLADYS *(calling loudly as she exits)*: You two have things to talk about. And Raymond? Maybe Eiko has something to tell you. *(Stops at the door)* I said to Auntie Vicky, "Who cares?" Hop Sing has a good thing and he knows it. This was the god-damn Ponderosa for criminy sakes!

*(*RAYMOND *sees* AUNTIE GLADYS *out.* EIKO *is feeling her arm where she was touched.* RAYMOND *returns.)*

RAYMOND: That was nice of you to call her *Auntie* Gladys. I'm still really worried, though.

EIKO: She'll be fine. She's as strong as a horse.

RAYMOND: No, I mean, about Miles.

EIKO: Do you have any news?

RAYMOND: I stopped over at his place on the way here, I wanted to tell him we had the manuscript.

ACT FOUR

EIKO: Did you see him?

RAYMOND: No, he wasn't there, but as I was leaving I ran into Rachel. She said Miles stopped by here last night.

EIKO: Yes, after you left.

RAYMOND: She said Miles told her he'd destroyed the manuscript.

EIKO: Yes.

RAYMOND: My god, he must be truly losing it. So you didn't tell him you had it?

EIKO: In the state he was in? I didn't think it was the prudent thing to do. Did you tell Rachel we had it?

RAYMOND: No.

(Awkward silence. They look at each other.)

RAYMOND: I was a bit confused because of what Rachel said Miles told her about the manuscript. I know they were here and I assumed you were present when he said what he said, I didn't understand what was going on. But. Maybe you should have told Miles. You know, when he came over?

(EIKO *remains silent.*)

RAYMOND: Well, I better take it over to him now. In his state he might do anything. Where is it? Eiko?

EIKO: I don't have it.

RAYMOND: You don't have it?

EIKO: No.

RAYMOND: Well, where is it then?

EIKO: I burned it.

RAYMOND: What?

EIKO: I burned the manuscript. Last night.

RAYMOND: Miles's paper? What—you burned it? Why would you burn it?

EIKO: I wish I had a Conrad Schmitz truffle.

RAYMOND: Are you insane? You burned his manuscript? It wasn't yours to do that to. It's Miles's. My god, this could get us in a lot of trouble Eiko. That was the only copy, you know. That was it. The whole paper, gone, you destroyed a major work. What in the world possessed you to do—

EIKO: I did it for you.

(Pause.)

RAYMOND: What?

EIKO: For you. That's why I destroyed his manuscript.

RAYMOND: What are you talking about?

EIKO: You said you envied his work. Envied him.

RAYMOND: Yes, but . . .

EIKO: This way you don't have to worry about him. His competition. You, my husband, are alone at the top of the heap.

RAYMOND: For me? You did that for me? But what if someone finds out?

EIKO: Who's going to find out? No one knows you found it, right?

RAYMOND: No.

EIKO: I didn't tell anyone. So . . .

(RAYMOND *is speechless.*)

EIKO: So you publish your new book. It comes out. It gets the full attention it deserves. Not more, not less, but exactly what it should rightfully get. Let it stand or fall on its own merits. But let's not have these other people's works floating about to detract from its deserved consideration.

RAYMOND: Eiko? You did that for me? But. I don't know what to say.

(EIKO *stares at him for a beat. She slaps him hard across the face.* RAYMOND *pulls back, stunned, almost cowering.*)

EIKO: Say, "Thank you!" Thank you my wife for having the balls to do something that will actually help me in my career, my life! But. Do tell me. You weren't thinking just a little along the same lines, I mean, why did you bring the manuscript back home in the first place? And why didn't you tell Rachel what really happened to Miles' manuscript when you just saw her? Huh?

(RAYMOND *is silent.*)

EIKO: But these are things you needn't worry your pretty head about because I've taken care of them for you. For you! For you!!!

(RAYMOND *doesn't know what to say.* EIKO *goes over to the stereo and puts on the Kinks, "You Really Got Me." Loud.*)

EIKO (*talking over the music*): And you know what else I've done for you? Know what else? Check out my profile. Notice anything? You crawl all over me every night, poking me, biting me, sticking me—didn't you feel anything different? My waist getting wider? My ass a bit larger? My nipples a little harder? Doesn't it seem to be all swelling up like a spoiled cabbage?

RAYMOND: You don't mean? You mean, you're pregnant? You are?

EIKO: I'm fat! I'm fat!

RAYMOND: Oh, Eiko, this is wonderful, this is truly a miracle!

(Music blaring.)

EIKO: It's killing me! It's killing me!

RAYMOND: Having a baby is wonderful, it's not going to kill you!

(A winded RACHEL *bursts in.)*

RACHEL: I had to come over.

*(*RAYMOND *turns off the stereo.)*

RAYMOND: Rachel?

RACHEL: I was over at the faculty housing and I overheard some-one say Miles was in the hospital. That he had some kind of accident.

RAYMOND: What happened? Is it serious?

RACHEL: I don't know. That's why I came over here to see if you knew anything.

EIKO: No, we've heard nothing.

RACHEL: I have this bad feeling, this very bad feeling. I heard what happened last night at the Fillmore and how he got arrested. He went to see that woman. Have you seen him? Did he stop by again?

EIKO: No.

RAYMOND: The last we've heard of him was when he stopped by and talked to both of you.

*(*NAKADA *bangs on the back window, then hurries around and enters from the back. He is dressed in a dark suit, carrying his briefcase.)*

DR. NAKADA: Well, everyone's here. Oh, I'm sorry about your aunt, Raymond.

RAYMOND: That's okay, thank you.

RACHEL: Do you know something about Miles?

DR. NAKADA: Oh, so you've heard?

RACHEL: Just that he had an accident and he's in the hospital.

DR. NAKADA: Nothing else?

RAYMOND: No.

DR. NAKADA: He is in the hospital. It's very serious. *(Beat)* He may not recover.

RACHEL *(overwhelmed)*: Oh Miles, I knew it, I knew it . . .

> (RAYMOND *helps her to the couch.* EIKO *removes the pendant from around her neck and lays it on the* obutsudan. NAKADA *notices.)*

EIKO: What kind of accident?

DR. NAKADA: He was stabbed.

RAYMOND: Oh, my god. How did that happen?

DR. NAKADA: He got into a fight it seems.

RACHEL: Oh Miles, I knew he was going to get himself into trouble. I knew it . . .

DR. NAKADA *(to* EIKO*)*: Do you know anything about this?

EIKO: Why would I?

DR. NAKADA: I thought you might.

EIKO: I can't say it's unexpected.

DR. NAKADA: And what do you mean by that?

EIKO: Perhaps he has fooled all of us. Fooled you, Nakada. An *accident*? Perhaps Miles found his manhood and committed a willful, intentioned act. And as such, it was anything but an accident.

> (RAYMOND *goes to get* RACHEL *some water.)*

RAYMOND *(noticing)*: Your hot water, Eiko.

> (EIKO *goes over and shuts it off.* NAKADA *has been watching her.)*

RACHEL: Maybe I should go over there.

DR. NAKADA: I don't think it's wise, right now.

RAYMOND: Just rest here for a bit. He's at the hospital, I'm sure they're doing everything they can. We can phone over later and check.

RACHEL: What about his manuscript? Did he really destroy it?

DR. NAKADA: It wasn't found with him, as far as I know. Do you folks know anything about it?

RAYMOND: Why, no.

DR. NAKADA: It's a shame, from what he read to us, it was quite original.

> (RAYMOND *looks at* EIKO.*)*

RACHEL: I can't believe there's nothing of the work we did together. Nothing.

ACT FOUR

RAYMOND: You said something about having some notes, right?

RACHEL: Yes, in my knapsack.

RAYMOND: Well, let's look at them. It's a long shot but maybe there's a way we can reconstruct some of the more important ideas.

EIKO: Raymond?

RAYMOND: I mean, we were trapped for a whole two-and-a-half hours while he read chapter headings and then did extemporaneous synopses of their contents.

EIKO: You said you didn't remember how long?

RAYMOND: And this one, like his book, it isn't an academic work, footnoted all over the place. It's more a visionary stream of consciousness . . .

RACHEL: Do you think it's actually possible to recreate the work?

RAYMOND: Of course not in its entirety, but maybe we can put together enough to publish some smaller papers on selective topics. Let's see the notes you have . . .

(NAKADA *goes to* EIKO, *who stands off to the side.*)

DR. NAKADA: I was fooled, huh?

EIKO: Tell me how it happened. I want to know every last detail.

DR. NAKADA: You are more dangerous than I thought.

EIKO: A kind of purity to leave on one's own terms, don't you think?

DR. NAKADA: He turned up at another students' rally over at Berkeley. They let him speak because of who he was but he was incoherent—babbling on and on about how one day it's going to be hip to be Asian in America—white kids in suburbs eating raw fish, black inner-city kids idolizing Japanese ballplayers. The students laughed him off the stage. Then later he turned up at the house where that band was staying. It's a known drug hangout. Seems he was still looking for whatever he thought they stole from his knapsack. He went straight to the singer's bedroom. This time she was sober and wasn't about to put up with his antics. And given his state of mind. Seems there was a struggle—

EIKO: And she stabbed him?

DR. NAKADA: More or less.

EIKO: What do you mean?

DR. NAKADA: It was in the groin. Or more specifically, she cut off his penis.

(*Silence.* EIKO *is stunned, physically revolted.*)

DR. NAKADA: I believe you're right. It couldn't have been an accident. Her aim was far too good. It's like a very bad joke and I didn't want to mention it in front of Rachel. He lost too much blood. He died on the way to the hospital.

EIKO (*recovering. To herself*): A worm is a worm is a worm . . .

(NAKADA *goes to the* obutsudan *and picks up the pendant. He finds a pill inside.*)

RAYMOND (*excitedly*): Hey, I think we'll be able to put together the first chapter!

RACHEL: Yes, I know we can do it!

(EIKO *has moved up to the kitchen to make her tea.* NAKADA *joins her with his briefcase.*)

DR. NAKADA (*holding out the pill*): There'll be an autopsy. Test his blood. And if they find any controlled substances, given the nature of his death, I'm sure they'll want to know from whom he got it. These *Marys* as they were fondly called by their *maker*.

EIKO: Really?

(EIKO *pushes by him and crosses down to get the tea she'd put away earlier.* DR. NAKADA *takes something wrapped in a cloth out of his briefcase and follows* EIKO *downstage. He pulls out the* aikuchi *from the bloodied white cloth and shows it to* EIKO.)

DR. NAKADA: As I mentioned, I have friends down at the department. (*Beat*) I asked them if given all these circumstances, could criminal charges be brought? They said without question. We're looking at an indictment, a very public trial and more than likely the humiliation of prison.

(*Silence.*)

EIKO (*notices the weather outside*): Such a beautiful day for a funeral. I was a very little girl when my mother died. Everything was white.

DR. NAKADA: It's the color of death in Japan.

EIKO: Only it's not really a color, is it? All I have left of her is that knife.

ACT FOUR

(EIKO *reaches for the* aikuchi *and* NAKADA *pulls it away.*)

EIKO: I feel you do know things about me now.

DR. NAKADA: I believe I might.

EIKO: I think I know what you're asking of me, Professor Nakada.

DR. NAKADA: Yes?

EIKO: Yes.

DR. NAKADA: We're the last of our breed. You and me. Bats. It's a whole new world now. At least for the younger ones. Not us, though. We've made our choices. And we have to live with them.

(*Silence.* EIKO *holds out her hand.* NAKADA *is hesitant.*)

DR. NAKADA: The back door, the front door, are always open. We have an understanding?

EIKO: We have an understanding.

(NAKADA *drops the pill into her hand.* EIKO *keeps it extended, wanting the* aikuchi *also.* NAKADA *cautiously places the knife-sword into her hand, holding his hand over hers.*)

DR. NAKADA: A gentleman's agreement, then.

EIKO: Yes, a *gentleman's* agreement. (*He releases the sword*) At last, I'm on equal terms.

(EIKO *moves to the shrine and places the* aikuchi *there in a reverent manner.*)

RAYMOND: Eiko, I think we might be able to do this. Well, not reconstruct the whole thing, but Rachel's notes are quite extensive and very detailed.

RACHEL: Oh, no, I wouldn't know what to do with them without Raymond.

RAYMOND: This is a very important work, a major opus and we must do everything we can to salvage it.

(EIKO *moving to them.*)

RAYMOND (*to* RACHEL): What does that line mean, the "thought unknown"?

RACHEL: A vision he had with that woman—we'll have to go back and see if we can cross-reference it, find out its meaning that way . . .

EIKO: Is there anything I can help you with?

RAYMOND: What? Oh, no, there's nothing you can do. Besides,

you must rest, remember? Why don't you go keep Dr. Nakada company.

(*They return to their work.* NAKADA *smiles at her.*)

NAKADA: How about some music? Something to soothe the nerves.

(EIKO *thinks for a beat, then moves to the stereo. She puts a record on and steps off to the side looking out the downstage window. It's Jimi Hendrix's "Purple Haze"—extremely loud.*)

RAYMOND: What the—Eiko! Eiko!

(RAYMOND *runs over and turns the music off.*)

EIKO: Yes?

RAYMOND: You can't play the music so loud when we're trying to work.

EIKO: Yes, dear.

RAYMOND: You were heating up water weren't you—Make us some tea.

EIKO: How about coffee?

RAYMOND: Tea, Eiko. (*Returning to* RACHEL) Why don't you move in to my Aunt Gladys's place, that way you'll be closer so we can continue the work.

RACHEL: Oh, yes, yes, wonderful—Auntie Gladys won't mind?

RAYMOND: She'd love your company. And the kids, too.

(*They resume.* EIKO *watches them for a beat. She looks around. Then announces.*)

EIKO: Attention. I'm making tea for everyone. *Mugi-cha*!

DR. NAKADA: Wonderful idea. Wonderful idea. I love *mugi-cha*.

RAYMOND: Hey, how ironic, I become the voice for Asian American students. Fanon would have a field day with this one!

DR. NAKADA: Maybe I'll be their faculty sponsor.

(*Erik Satie's "Trois Gymnopedie" comes on. Lighting shift so* EIKO *is highlighted in a pool of light.* EIKO *makes the tea. She places the Mary, the LSD pill, in the pot. Swirls it around. Pours out the tea into four cups. Then gets up and serves the tea on a tray.*)

DR. NAKADA: I'm feeling at home already.

EIKO: Tea?

DR. NAKADA (*taking a cup*): The first of many, I assume.

(EIKO *brings tea over to* RAYMOND *and* RACHEL. *They both take the tea without acknowledging her presence.*)

ACT FOUR

She returns to her original position and sits down in front of her lone remaining teacup. The following has an intentioned, deliberate quality, bordering on ritual. As she brings the teacup to her lips we sense she is coming to a decision. She stops, the cup held in mid-air. Then, slowly, she turns the cup over, pouring the tea onto the ground. She then places the teacup back on the tray, upside down. Music stops. A beat.

She gets up and moves with a quiet measured walk up to the shrine. She takes the aikuchi *in both hands and stands there for a moment with her head bowed.* EIKO *then returns and sits down on the sofa with the knife-sword in her lap. She looks around, taking in the scene.* RAYMOND *and* RACHEL, *engaged in their work. Then at* DR. NAKADA, *who appears lost in his own thoughts and unaware of* EIKO. *It could be a day like any other normal day.* EIKO *looks straight ahead for a beat. Then takes the* aikuchi *in hand.)*

EIKO *(proclaiming)*: My legs are unbound!

*(*EIKO *is about to slash her throat, then stops. Silence. All eyes turn to her.* EIKO *puts the* aikuchi *down, reaches into her moving box and pulls out a pistol. She turns and faces* NAKADA.*)*

EIKO: It's amazing what you can buy in America.

*(*EIKO *shoots* NAKADA. *She then turns and faces* RAYMOND. *She puts the gun to her neck and shoots herself.*

Slow fade to black. "Ferry Cross the Mersey" by Gerry and the Pacemakers is brought up. Underneath it we hear the news report. Something that completes the arc and posits the irony of the story's narrative, spins it off into the next step. E.g., the administration capitulates, the progressive President Sommers has quit, the conservative S. I. Hayakawa is now installed. And, that the Ethnic Studies Department has been established with divisions of Black American, Chicano, and Asian American Studies established. The war rages on, the body count rises.)

[END OF PLAY]

Ballad of Yachiyo

Ballad of Yachiyo had its commissioned world premiere at the Berkeley Repertory Theatre in 1995–96.

DIRECTOR: Sharon Ott

CAST –
Yachiyo Matsumoto: Sala Iwamatsu
Hiro Takamura: Lane Nishikawa
Okusan/Sumiko Takamura: Emily Kuroda
Papa/Hisao Matsumoto: Sab Shimono
Mama/Takayo Matsumoto: Dian Kobayashi
Osugi: Annie Yee
Willie Higa: Greg Watanabe

Set Design: Loy Arcenas
Lighting Design: Peter Maradudin
Costumes: Lydia Tanji
Music: Dan Kuramoto
Puppets: Bruce Schwartz

Characters
YACHIYO MATSUMOTO
HIRO TAKAMURA
OKUSAN/SUMIKO TAKAMURA
PAPA/HISAO MATSUMOTO
MAMA/TAKAYO MATSUMOTO
OSUGI
WILLIE HIGA

Time
1919

Place
Kauai

ACT ONE

Upstage a large screen for slides and video. We hear the haunting strains of a Japanese plantation working song with both traditional and contemporary accompaniments. Sepia-toned period photos of Kauai life dissolve into each other, giving a sense of the world—the cane field workers, a pottery, family life, etc. We end with a photo of the actual YACHIYO. *A series of shots moves in closer on the grainy, sepia-toned image of her face. It fills the screen.* YACHIYO *moves in front of the slide, her image's large face superimposed on her body. As she moves down stage, the slide dissolves to super titles.*

    YACHIYO *has just turned seventeen years old. She is simple in appearance, with an understated, subtle beauty. As she speaks,* TAKAMURA *is lit. He mimes what* YACHIYO *describes. Above, video/slides show what he is doing.*

YACHIYO: In front of him sits a mound of clay which he is squeezing into a tall cone. He pushes it down, then squeezes it into a tall cone again. This helps to even the consistency of the clay and makes it easier to work with. All during this he is pulling on the base of the wheel with his feet to keep it turning.

TAKAMURA *(calling out)*: I need more clay, prepare more clay for me!

YACHIYO: He is making *yunomi*, teacups. Takamura-san does this by working the clay back into a tall cone and by fashioning a measured portion at the top into a ball. He's done this so many times he knows just the amount to use by the feel. Then by inserting the thumb of his right hand he makes a deep pocket, drawing the clay up to make the walls of the cup with the same thumb and middle finger. It's all done in one motion. Now he starts to use some tools. First, he inserts a flat spatulate tool to make sure the *yunomi* has a clean surface on the inside.

ACT ONE

Then, he takes a *tombo*, dragonfly, because of the way it looks—

TAKAMURA *(looks up, interrupting gruffly)*: Yachiyo, *hayaku shiro*! Hurry up!

    (TAKAMURA *fades to black. Silence.*)

YACHIYO: Just before the sun breaks it gets very dark. Inky black and silent. As if all the light and sound has been sucked out of the air. The wind dies, night birds stop singing and everything seems to be suspended. Waiting. This is my favorite time of day. It's so dark that the boundary between the night and my body blurs and I begin to come undone, as if I am a child again, my mama's hands unbuttoning me, my papa putting me to sleep. And I can drift, let go, releasing out into this night my sweat, my breath, my thirst. My shame . . .

    (*The sun begins to slowly rise. Upstage in half-light we see the silhouettes of* PAPA *and* MAMA *stirring from sleep.*)

PAPA: Yachiyo? Yachiyo?

MAMA: What is it Papa?

PAPA: Yachiyo, is that you? Yachiyo?

    (*Morning light begins to break the horizon.* YACHIYO *turns away from* PAPA *and* MAMA *as they fade to black.*)

YACHIYO: It is a beautiful morning and the night was filled with many dreams. I cannot remember any of them, the dreams, and yet when I woke up, I was happy.

    (*She picks up a worn leather suitcase and moves across the stage.*)

YACHIYO: I was born on the island of Kauai. On the leeward side just beyond Camp Mana in an area called Saki-Mana. It's the dry side of the island. The soil is reddish in color and when you walk barefoot in it you leave a trail of red prints wherever you go.

    (*Glancing back at her path.*)

YACHIYO: Papa says you don't need to know where you came from. Mama says you do.

    (*Pause.*)

YACHIYO: The year is 1919. I am seventeen years old. My name is Yachiyo Matsumoto . . .

    (HIRO TAKAMURA *lit.* YACHIYO, *holding the suitcase, stands in*

Sala Iwamatus as Yachiyo and Emily Kuroda as Okusan in *Ballad
of Yachiyo*, Berkeley Repertory Theatre, 1995–96

Photo by Michal Daniel, courtesy Berkeley Repertory Theatre

front of a door held open by HIRO TAKAMURA. *He is fortyish,
dark, intense. He wears a work apron covered in clay and drinks
from a bottle of sake.)*

TAKAMURA: What do you want?

YACHIYO: Yachiyo Matsumoto? My father wrote to you. My father
was a good friend of your wife's father. She wrote back—

TAKAMURA: Ahh, you're the girl . . .

OKUSAN *(off)*: Who is it? Hiro? Is it Otosan's [father's] friend?

YACHIYO: I came by myself. My Papa could not come. He sent
this along.

(She offers a letter to TAKAMURA, *which he does not take.)*

TAKAMURA *(calling back to* OKUSAN*)*: No. He didn't come. Just
the girl.

TAKAMURA *(stepping aside so* YACHIYO *can enter)*: Come in. Yeah,
come right in. Eat our food. Here, drink my liquor.

*(Pushing the bottle in her face. She moves away. He gets right in
her face.)*

TAKAMURA: Please order me around. Tell me what to do. What
would you like me to do? Huh? Little girl has a mouth, tell me
what to do? Huh? Huh?

YACHIYO *(flustered)*: I want to thank you and your Okusan for
taking me into your—

*(*TAKAMURA *motions disgustedly with his hand for her to stop.
He stumbles away, singing drunkenly.* YACHIYO *stares after his
disappearing figure.* SUMIKO TAKAMURA, *or* OKUSAN, *appears.
She is mid-fortyish, older than her husband.)*

OKUSAN: Hiro . . .

*(*OKUSAN *notices* YACHIYO *watching the drunken* HIRO. YACHIYO
becomes aware of OKUSAN *and catches herself.* OKUSAN *takes
her suitcase.* YACHIYO *glances back one last time at* HIRO.
OKUSAN *notices, then she exits.*

WILLIE HIGA *is lit with a cane knife under his arm. This is*
YACHIYO'S *boyfriend. Okinawan. He is nineteen years old, stur-
dily built with a deep tan. He is a worker. Lighting a match.*
YACHIYO *watches as* WILLIE *begins to run the flame over the open
blisters on his hands. Speaks with a pidgin accent.)*

WILLIE: Yachiyo.

YACHIYO: Willie. What are you doing?

WILLIE *(trying to laugh, hiding the pain)*: Yamaguchi-san taught me this. See, it seals the blisters up so you can keep working out in the cane fields.

YACHIYO *(noticing his pain)*: Willie . . .

WILLIE: Hey, you sit down out there, the Portuge "luna" hit you with his "black snake" whip, make you bleed more. This way my blisters won't bleed.

> *(Beat.)*

WILLIE: I won't get blood on your dress like I did last time.

YACHIYO: You know how Mama and Papa feel if they catch us together.

WILLIE: Tonight, by the pump house.

> (WILLIE *lets the flame burn him, waiting for a response.)*

YACHIYO: I cannot. No.

> (YACHIYO *can't take it and blows out the flame.)*

WILLIE: I'll be waiting.

> (HISAO *and* TAKAYO MATSUMOTO *lit.* PAPA *sewing, watching* MAMA.)

MAMA: Ryoichiro! Mitsuru! Where're the boys? The food's gonna be ready soon.

> (YACHIYO *brings a bowl with a damp cloth over it.)*

MAMA: That the *tofu* [bean curd] from Mr. Sato?

YACHIYO: Un-huh. The boy brought it all the way out here.

MAMA *(to* PAPA*)*: Sato said he's willing to deliver. Trying to take away business from Hamada's store.

PAPA *(looks under the cloth)*: It's all lumpy.

MAMA: He was willing to give us credit, Papa.

PAPA *(tasting it, makes face)*: Lousy, *mazui* . . .

YACHIYO *(exiting)*: I'll go check the rice, it's almost done.

MAMA *(remembering)*: "Ara," did Mitsuru fill all the kerosene lamps?

YACHIYO *(exiting)*: Ryoichiro did it for him.

PAPA *(to* YACHIYO*)*: Come here Yachiyo.

> (PAPA *stops* YACHIYO *to see if the shirt he's making will fit her.)*

MAMA: Now where're the younger kids? Yohei! Itchan! Shigeno!

YACHIYO: Out back Mama, with Mitsuru and Ryoichiro.

ACT ONE

PAPA: You've grown, huh Yachiyo.

MAMA: Make the front bigger for her Papa. What are they doing out there?

YACHIYO *(embarrassed at her comment)*: They're getting honey. To trade at the Pake [Chinaman] store for crack seed. *(To PAPA)* You don't have to make the front *that* big.

MAMA: Where? Not the *kiabe* tree behind the horse stall again?

YACHIYO: They said the bees rebuilt the hive.

MAMA *(hurriedly exiting to the back)*: Last time they tried to smoke out the bees, the bees went crazy, bit up the poor horse.

> *(PAPA measures YACHIYO in silence. Slightly awkward, but they enjoy each other's company.)*

PAPA *(kidding)*: Maybe I should do this full time, huh? I'd be working then.

YACHIYO: Mama would like that.

PAPA *(shrugging)*: Not good enough. Just good enough for when you were all kids. *(Measuring)* I know you don't like what I make for you anymore. Not stylish like out of those catalogues you look at.

YACHIYO: I don't mind Papa.

PAPA: You thought anymore about what Mama talked about?

MAMA *(off)*: Put that fire out!

YACHIYO: Rice gonna burn, Papa.

> *(YACHIYO turns to leave. PAPA watches her exit as MAMA enters.)*

MAMA: Ryoichiro, Mitsuru, you hear me! Come inside. Bring the kids in too. And move the horse out of there! Shigeno, Itchan, Yohei—come around the side and wash your feet first!

> *(To PAPA.)*

MAMA: Did you ask her again? Papa?

PAPA *(going back to sewing)*: You worry too much about what people think.

MAMA: You want people to think your daughter is some farm girl from the *inaka*—no refinement, not good enough?

PAPA: That's not what I mean.

MAMA: I'm not worried about what people think of me, Papa. I just want Yachiyo to find a good husband.

PAPA: So she needs to learn Chanoyu? Go all the way over there to learn Tea to find a good husband? She helps out here with the cooking, takes care of the little ones—

MAMA: What? You want her to end up with someone like that Okinawan kid?

(Sees the kids off to the side, entering.)

MAMA: Ah, ah, ah—I said wash your feet first, they're all dirty.

(YACHIYO enters with a pot of rice. MAMA encourages PAPA to speak to her.)

PAPA: Yachiyo?

(YACHIYO doesn't respond)

MAMA: Papa's talking to you.

PAPA *(beat)*: Do you want to go stay with those people in Waimea?

YACHIYO: *Mada shiran yo*, I'm not sure . . .

MAMA: She doesn't know what's good for her. Sneaking around with that Willie Higa boy . . .

PAPA: You have to go live there. Move to Waimea. You understand? That far away you can't come home—

MAMA: You want to end up working twelve hours a day in the mills, come home to a batch of crying babies, too tired to take care of them, let alone take care of your husband's needs at night, 'cause—*(Continues.)*

PAPA *(overlapping)*: Mama . . .

MAMA *(continues)*: —that's the kind of life you're going to have if you don't listen to me and go—

PAPA: Mama! Let her speak. Yachiyo?

YACHIYO *(aside)*: If I open my mouth a thousand papio minnows will come shooting out going every which way . . . So I don't say anything.

MAMA: Stubborn girl.

YACHIYO: I'm not stubborn. It's just the things I feel I can't talk about yet, 'cause I don't know what to call them.

(YACHIYO runs off.)

MAMA: Yachiyo.

(Pause.)

PAPA: Mama?

(No response.)

PAPA: You shouldn't be so hard on her.

ACT ONE

MAMA: I know Yachiyo. She wants things.

PAPA: So she looks through the catalogues all the time. That doesn't mean she—

MAMA *(interrupts)*: Other things, Papa. Other things . . .
   (Pause.)

MAMA: I already wrote them. I wrote Old Man Takamura's daughter a letter.

PAPA: What?

MAMA: It's what's best for Yachiyo.

PAPA: Takayo!

MAMA: Besides, we can't afford to keep Yachiyo at home anymore. Not with the money we owe at Hamada's store and Yohei's medical bills—

PAPA: I can go over to the Knapper Plantation—see if they're hiring.

MAMA: They won't hire you and you know it.

PAPA: Then I'll go to the McDonald Plantation.

MAMA *(shaking her head)*: You can't quit working in the fields just because you're tired Papa—

PAPA: I didn't quit working, I passed out, Mama. I passed out.
   (Pause.)

MAMA: Yachiyo can earn her own keep and learn a new trade at the same time.

PAPA: Old-Man Takamura's daughter probably doesn't even remember me.

MAMA: You saved the old man's life—they owe you.

PAPA *(under his breath)*: I didn't save his life.

MAMA: Coming over on the boat from Japan he was sick, coughing up blood—you said so yourself.

PAPA: Yeah, but—

MAMA: Now they can pay you back. And what's so terrible about learning Chanoyu. Your sisters did. A young girl should learn those things so she can meet a suitable young man.

PAPA: That's all crap. You don't need those kinds of things here. You have too much refinement here, it makes you weak. People step all over you.
   (Pause.)

PAPA: You shouldn't have written them, Mama.

> (*Dim to darkness on* PAPA *and* MAMA. YACHIYO *appears holding flowers.*)

YACHIYO: Lately, I feel so many things inside of me. Sometimes I feel I'm going to burst. It is not a bad feeling, but it makes me confused. I'm always expecting something to happen. Something new. Something good.

> (OSUGI *appears.* OSUGI *is* YACHIYO'S *age. Japanese with Chinese stepfather. Night. Full moon. Lamp. High on bluff, overlooking the ocean. Drinking from a bottle of champagne. In the distance we hear music.* OSUGI *wears a maid's outfit. During the scene they pass a bottle of champagne back and forth, drinking freely.* OSUGI *speaks with a pidgin accent.*)

OSUGI *(looking out)*: That one's a pig! Okay, your turn—what's dat one?

YACHIYO: I can't tell, Osugi.

OSUGI: The cloud's changing, hurry up . . .

YACHIYO *(aside)*: Osugi is my best friend. She works at the McDonald house. I call her "head to mouth"—*atama kara kuchi e.* She thinks something, out it comes from her mouth. No in-between stops. I sometimes wish I could be more like her . . .

OSUGI: Hurry up!

YACHIYO: I don't know, what?

OSUGI: A horse, a horse, yeah?

YACHIYO: Oh yeah, yeah, a horse.

> (*Watching for a beat.*)

YACHIYO: And it's running, running—so fast its body is stretching out . . .

OSUGI: Getting long like an eel now.

YACHIYO: An eel, yeah. Umm, wouldn't you like some *unagi* right now. The way Tabuchi-san cooks it over the hibachi.

OSUGI: Umm, da best, with some hot rice.

> (*Noticing.*)

OSUGI: Ooh look, look, dat's Mrs. McDonald's butt.

YACHIYO: Dat big. Your boss's *oshiri*'s dat big?

OSUGI: Hey, if you never move, your butt get big, too. Just sit dere and do like this . . .

ACT ONE

(Starts to point in several directions.)

OSUGI: Osugi get dis, Osugi get dat. Get dis, get dat, all the time.

YACHIYO: You gonna get into trouble taking the champagne?

OSUGI *(shaking her head)*: Good, huh? The bubbles make your nose tickle.

YACHIYO: This some new kinda work, huh. Just drink and fool around.

OSUGI: They all drunk and dancing back there. Da other girls take care of everything. Hey, I get you a job here. Da Shimokawa girl, getting big, starting to show, they fire her as soon as they know.

YACHIYO: You know my parents have other plans for me. I dunno yet.

OSUGI: When I get da job at McDonalds? Happiest day of my life. I don't have to work in the fields no more. And at night I get to see Pantat. Dat's it. Big smile on my face. I have everything. I can die now. *(Passing the bottle to* YACHIYO*)* How 'bout you? What's your happiest day?

YACHIYO *(thinking for a beat while she sips)*: When they took the picture of me. Dressed up in the kimono Mama had Papa's sister send from Japan. Then, that day. As we walked to Miyatake's photo shop, everybody stare. *Bijin*, they whisper. "Matsumoto-san's daughter is growing up to be a beauty." And when I look at Mama and Papa? They almost busting open, they so proud.

OSUGI: Dat's it?

YACHIYO *(nodding)*: Un-huh.

OSUGI: Dat's your happiest day?

YACHIYO *(nodding)*: Un-huh.

OSUGI *(shaking her head)*: Un-uh. Dat's not your happiest day. Dat's *their* happiest day. You still waiting, Yachiyo. You still waiting.

*(*OSUGI *gets up and drags* YACHIYO *with her.)*

OSUGI: Come on, come on, I show you how the rich *haoles* dance.

YACHIYO: You should get Pantat to dance with you.

OSUGI: Come on, don't be such an ole fart.

(Music volume rises, an up-tempo song. It's a fun and lively ren-

dition. OSUGI *and* YACHIYO *start to dance.* OSUGI *has to guide*
YACHIYO, *pushing her along. Soon, however,* YACHIYO *is enjoy-ing herself.)*

OSUGI: Drink break, drink break . . .

YACHIYO: Hey, hey, we just get started, show me the slow one
now. Show me the slow one . . .

    *(*OSUGI *grabs the champagne bottle and* YACHIYO *pulls her back.*
    OSUGI *pulls* YACHIYO *close. Music changes to a slow tempo.)*

OSUGI: Like dis.

YACHIYO: Like dis?

OSUGI *(drinking from the bottle)*: Yeah. Just like dis.

YACHIYO: So close, yeah? The boy's body pushed up close like dis?

OSUGI: *Haoles* dance nasty, yeah. You can feel the boy's *chimpo*
and everything if he gets excited.

YACHIYO *(stopping)*: That's enough.

OSUGI: What? You and Willie don't do this kind of thing?

YACHIYO: I'm thirsty.

    *(*YACHIYO *takes the bottle and takes a big gulp.)*

OSUGI: Pantat and me, all the time do this kind of thing. Not
dancing, but you know.

YACHIYO: We don't do that kind of thing.

OSUGI: How come—Willie's cute, yeah?

YACHIYO: That kind of thing get you into trouble, Osugi.

OSUGI: You so old-fashioned Yachiyo. Everybody does it some.

YACHIYO: Do that kind of thing you end up bringing shame to
your family. Then you have nothing, no family, nothing. End
up like that Shimokawa girl.

    (During the following YACHIYO *moves away to a watery pool
of lights.)*

OSUGI: Shimokawa, she's a stupid girl, go too far. Go so far, cannot come back. And now, she don't even have no boyfriend to
take care of the baby. I've got Pantat. He always take care of
me. Just like Willie. He always take care you Yachiyo. Hey,
maybe we have a double wedding, yeah. You and Willie, me
and Pantat, at the Japanese Kaikan—all our families dere. And
lots and lottsa flowers—We'll have beautiful white blossoms
falling down around us, we'll drown in a sea of white flowers!

ACT ONE

(YACHIYO *moves down by the water. She kneels and looks at her reflection in the moving watery lights.* OSUGI *fades to black.)*

YACHIYO: The water, it's like a mirror.

(*Stares for a beat*)

YACHIYO: My face. It's changing. Or maybe it's just the inside of me looking out that's changing. All I know is that sometimes I find myself staring at a stranger. Who is she?

(*Reaches out and touches the water.*)

YACHIYO: She thinks things, wants to do things . . . I wonder what it's like to look at the world from the other side. Through her eyes.

(*Dim to darkness.* OKUSAN *is lit in her Japanese-style tea cere-mony room. She has a large Japanese doll in her lap. A lamp sits off to the side casting the puppet's moving shadow on the shoji screens behind her. We hear a variation on traditional Japanese instrumentation for Bunraku. This scene should feel slightly eerie, skewed.* OKUSAN *holds the doll. Touches it, runs her hands along the fabric, its face. She then lifts it up and sets it in her lap.* OKUSAN *begins to manipulate it, the attention shifting from* OKUSAN *to the doll as it comes to life. As if she were imbuing it with her spirit. It raises its hand to its face, tilts its head, wipes a tear from its face . . .*

OKUSAN *fades to black.*

YACHIYO *lit full. A sprig of pikake flowers sits next to her. She is cutting up a Montgomery Ward catalogue and pasting cutouts onto a paper.* WILLIE *enters. A tree branch extends out overhead. When* YACHIYO *sees* WILLIE *she looks around.)*

YACHIYO (*calling off*): Shigeno, keep an eye on Itchan and Yohei.

WILLIE: You want me to go?

YACHIYO (*shaking her head*): Mama's at church, Papa's sleeping.

(WILLIE *notices what she's doing.*)

WILLIE: You know that catalogue, your parents don't mind? Cutting it up like dat?

YACHIYO: We got the new one already.

WILLIE: Monkey Ward one okay to do that with I guess, the paper gives the butt a rash. But the Sears and Roebuck Catalogue. Dat one da kine. Ooh, so soft, everybody fights over dat one at my house. Can I look? I like dis hat, look good on your head, yeah. And dis winter coat Yachiyo. All da thick fur. *(Teasing)* You gonna wear that thing when the big snow come here?

YACHIYO: Maybe. Someday.

WILLIE *(picking up a cutout picture)*: Whoa, this dress . . . Yachiyo? You got something going on in dere no one can see on the outside—*iroppoi* [sexy], yeah. Look like some sexy *haole wahini* walking down the street.

YACHIYO *(grabs the picture back)*: It's just a game I play with Osugi. It doesn't mean anything. It's just something we do . . .

> *(Pause.)*

WILLIE: Hey, I'll get you that dress okay? Yachiyo? I'll buy it for you.

YACHIYO: You can't afford it.

> *(Pause.)*

YACHIYO: This kind of dress no one can afford. Maybe only the plantation boss's daughter.

> *(Pause.)*

YACHIYO: You ever seen snow?

WILLIE: What?

YACHIYO: Snow? You ever seen it?

WILLIE *(shaking his head)*: I know what it looks like. Seen pictures. You?

YACHIYO: No. Almost everywhere else in the world it snows. Japan, mainland. Even a little bit on the Big Island. But not here . . .

> *(Pause.)*

WILLIE: I gotta go. A meeting at Yamaguchi-san's house. We planning some things.

YACHIYO: Willie.

WILLIE: Yamaguchi-san says the union gotta stand up if it want to get noticed.

YACHIYO: You stand up, the boss gonna knock you down, you know that.

WILLIE: Then we stand up again.

> *(Starts to leave, hesitates.)*

ACT ONE

WILLIE: You gonna do what your parents say? Your Mama's telling everybody you're gonna be this *ibatte-iru* young woman, nose stuck up in the air. Too good for anybody around here maybe.

YACHIYO: I don't know yet.

(Pause. He turns and leaves. YACHIYO *picks up the sprig of flowers.)*

YACHIYO: Pikake. I put it by my pillow at night. It makes me feel like I can dream while I'm still awake.

(She inhales deeply, then looks at her cutout picture. A few white flower petals begin to drift down around her. HIRO TAKAMURA *lit, drunk. Holding a bottle.* YACHIYO *dims to half-light, watches him.)*

TAKAMURA *(teetering)*: I feel . . . I feel . . . nothing . . .

(Puts bottle to his lips and attempts to drink. Finds to his disappointment, it's empty.)

TAKAMURA: . . . Nothing.

(Looks at bottle. Examines it.)

TAKAMURA: What makes this?

(Taps bottle.)

TAKAMURA: Not the bottle but this . . .

(Runs his hand along the curve of the bottle's surface.)

TAKAMURA: What allows it to be is the nothingness. The space around the curve is what allows this line to be, to be defined in what? . . . In the nothingness around it. And what holds it up? Why, all the nothingness on the inside. In fact, look well. More nothingness than somethingness is what it is . . .

(Spins the bottle on the ground.)

TAKAMURA: In Hiroshima, we throw pots on the wheel going this way. But here, on the other side of the world . . .

(Spins bottle the opposite way.)

TAKAMURA: . . . here they throw pots with the wheel going the opposite way, the wrong way.

(Muttering.)

TAKAMURA: Nothingness. Too much nothingness . . .

(He gets up. Moving up stage he starts to urinate. He is in despair.)

TAKAMURA: The world is backwards here. There is no order. No order. I should have never left. *(Calling out)* Masako . . .

I should have stayed and married you, Masako! Who cares whether you're a whore! Who cares what anyone says!

(As he urinates, the stars come out. TAKAMURA *is overcome with the beauty as the whole stage is inundated in stars. He starts to laugh.)*

TAKAMURA: As I piss, in despair, this . . . You show me this. Are you trying to tell me something? *(Laughing.)*

TAKAMURA: I give up. You win! You win! . . .

(Lights suddenly bank up. OKUSAN *is standing there.* YACHIYO *fades to black.)*

OKUSAN: Hiro!

TAKAMURA *(buttoning up, embarrassed)*: I had to urinate.

OKUSAN: Off the lanai?

TAKAMURA: If I have to piss, I have to piss, okay?

(Pause. TAKAMURA *goes to get a drink.* OKUSAN *watches him.)*

OKUSAN: I'm going to have her come and stay with us. Papa's friend—his daughter?

TAKAMURA: You don't know who the hell they are. Then out of the blue you get this letter.

OKUSAN: I met him once. Otosan used to talk about him all the time. He saved Otosan's life. It might be nice to have his daughter in the house. Since Father passed away . . .

TAKAMURA: I'm having enough trouble getting set up. The clay's all wrong here, way too sandy. There are no materials for the right glazes—and I have no idea if this damn *nobori-gama* is even going to fire right. Back in Japan you have experts for this kind of thing, kiln building. Even my father would go ask Kayama-san, the kiln expert. He'll tell you how to build a kiln— the angle of the incline, the draw—and all it costs is a few rice balls. But here, I don't know . . .

OKUSAN: It could be fun. Like having a younger sister. And she can help out. You always complain about not having enough—

TAKAMURA *(interrupts)*: What, another worker like the last local I had to fire. These workers around here, all peasants—they have the aesthetic sense of cows.

ACT ONE

OKUSAN: It's so quiet around here in the evenings. You always go out and leave me alone.

TAKAMURA: That was our agreement, right? After work I can do whatever I damn well please. What? Your Old Man is not here anymore. We don't have to pretend.

(Pause. Softening.)

TAKAMURA: Look, the pottery will work. I know how to make pots. Wait till the first big firing. You've been firing all night, the kiln's finally cooled down, you begin to tear open the bricks covering the door—

OKUSAN *(interrupts)*: You said the kiln might not work.

TAKAMURA: I know, I know, I said that but—

OKUSAN: Matsumoto's daughter is coming. I have made up my mind, Hiro. She is coming to live with us.

TAKAMURA: Okay. Fine. You and your Old Man. "Do this, do that," like an *inu* [dog]. Okay, that's all right. But at night the dog is free to roam.

(TAKAMURA exits. OKUSAN fades to black. YACHIYO and PAPA are lit playing Go.)

YACHIYO: Papa? The farthest away I've been is Kekaha.

PAPA: Are you scared?

YACHIYO: No.

(Pause.)

YACHIYO: Maybe this is our last game, huh?

MAMA *(looks in)*: Yachiyo, go to bed. Shimasaki-san is coming by early to pick you up and I want you ready to go. He charges extra for that broken down buggy if you make him wait. Put away the game Papa.

(MAMA exits. PAPA starts to put the game away but YACHIYO stops him. They look at each other for a beat, then continue. Play for a while in silence.)

PAPA: Remember when I had all those silkworms. I had my family send them over from Japan. Do you remember that? I used to let you take them out and play with them? You remember?

YACHIYO: I remember Papa.

PAPA: I wouldn't let the boys touch them. I had to yell at Mitsuru all the time. They were feeding them to the birds. Just Yachiyo.

YACHIYO: You kept them in that shack next to the old bathhouse.

PAPA: You remember, huh? You were *chiichai* [tiny], what, five or six or something.

YACHIYO: I have to tell you something. You promise you won't get mad, Papa?

PAPA: What?

YACHIYO: I was feeding them to the birds, too.

(PAPA *stares for a beat. Then breaks into laughter.* YACHIYO *joins in.*)

MAMA *(off)*: Yachiyo, go to bed! Papa . . .

PAPA *(lowering his voice)*: Everyone around here was laughing at me, thought I was crazy. Thousands and thousands of those silly silkworms, crawling all over the place. I thought I was so smart, so smart. That's why we live way out here, so I can have my big silkworm ranch. Everybody was going to wear silk. Ship it to the Mainland. New York, San Francisco, Chicago—Hell, even ship it back to Japan. Mama tried to warn me. "Crazy . . ." Maybe they were right.

YACHIYO: It was a good idea, Papa. It was a good idea.

PAPA *(shrugs)*: Good idea, but . . .

(*Silence.*)

PAPA: Yachiyo? You sure you want to go?

(*No response.*)

PAPA: You don't have to go. You can stay at home, the whole family together.

YACHIYO: I'm all grown up now, Papa.

(PAPA *is silent. He moves a piece.*)

YACHIYO: Would you show me one of your poems?

(PAPA *stops. Looks up.*)

YACHIYO: Mama said you used to write poems.

PAPA *(stares)*: I don't have them anymore. I burned them all.

(*Beat.*)

PAPA: Time to go to bed.

(*Gets up, hesitant, then embraces her. Turns to leave.*)

MAMA *(lit in a pool of light)*: Listen to me. Flower Arrangement and Koto, too, if she is willing.

YACHIYO: Papa will be angry if he finds out.

ACT ONE

PAPA *(turns back to* YACHIYO*)*: You think you're all grown up.

MAMA: You tell Mrs. Takamura that Papa wants her to teach you those things.

YACHIYO: Mama . . .

PAPA: Be careful. The world might think you are.

> *(*PAPA *exits.* MAMA *and* YACHIYO *dim to darkness.* OKUSAN *lit with her doll in a tight pool of light. Music cue. As she manipulates it she begins to tell a story. Another person manipulates the other male doll. A few white petals fall from the branch during this scene.)*

OKUSAN: There once was a woman. She was young. She was beautiful. And she was in love with a man.

> *(Male doll lit. Manipulated by actress who plays* OSUGI*.)*

OKUSAN: He was of a proud, noble family. He was very handsome. And the woman loved him deeply.

> *(Pause. The female doll looks towards the male doll, who turns away.)*

OKUSAN: She was very lonely . . .

> *(*OKUSAN'S *doll slowly droops and becomes lifeless.*
>
> YACHIYO *lit by the water with* OSUGI. OSUGI *is upstage from her, listening.)*

YACHIYO: When I was younger this older boy held me under the water as a joke. He was below me and had me by my foot. I was trying to get to the surface, I needed to breathe so badly I could feel my face about to explode. I remember seeing the sunlight entering from above. It was cutting through the water like long, transparent knives. I wanted them to cut me open, peel me out of my skin so whatever was me, whatever was wanting, needing to breathe so badly could get out . . . I go into the water. I go in but I don't put my face in. It still scares me. I don't dive deep beneath the surface. Not yet. The farthest I've ever been is Kekaha, Osugi. I'm afraid.

OSUGI: Maybe you shouldn't go then.

WILLIE *(appears in a separate pool of light)*: We're thinking about going on strike. We're talking to the Filipinos, see if they join in with us.

> *(*WILLIE *turns to leave.)*

YACHIYO: Willie . . .

WILLIE *(stops)*: I thought you was gonna stay here. With me.

OSUGI: What about the double wedding? All the petals falling down around us?

(WILLIE and OSUGI withdraw.)

(As YACHIYO watches them leave, PAPA carrying a suitcase and MAMA enter. PAPA and MAMA and YACHIYO face each other in awkward silence.)

PAPA: *Ganbare yo.* Work hard.

MAMA *(pause)*: Don't bring us any shame.

(MAMA turns and leaves. PAPA hands YACHIYO the suitcase. She turns and moves across stage. PAPA fades to black.)

TAKAMURA *(lit, holding the door open)*: What do you want?

YACHIYO *(glances back at her tracks, then back to TAKAMURA)*: Matsumoto? My father wrote to you. My father was a good friend of your wife's father. She wrote back—

TAKAMURA: Ahh, you're the girl . . .

OKUSAN *(off)*: Who is it? Hiro? Is it Otosan's friend?

YACHIYO: I came by myself. My Papa could not come. He sent this along.

(She offers a letter to TAKAMURA, which he does not take.)

TAKAMURA *(calling back to OKUSAN)*: No. He didn't come. Just the girl.

(Stepping aside so YACHIYO can enter.)

TAKAMURA: Come in. Yeah, come right in. Eat our food. Here, drink my liquor.

(Pushing the bottle in her face. She moves away. He gets right in her face.)

TAKAMURA: Please order me around. Tell me what to do. What would you like me to do? Huh? Little girl has a mouth, tell me what to do? Huh? Huh?

YACHIYO: I want to thank you and your Okusan for taking me into your—

(Drunk, TAKAMURA stumbles away singing. OKUSAN appears.)

OKUSAN: Hiro . . .

(Notices YACHIYO watching HIRO leave.)

OKUSAN: Matsumoto-san's daughter? Yachiyo?

ACT ONE

YACHIYO: Yes.

OKUSAN: Let me take that.

(Takes her suitcase.)

YACHIYO: My Papa could not come. He sent this.

(Offering the letter.)

OKUSAN *(taking it)*: Please, please, come in.

(YACHIYO enters as OKUSAN stares in the direction of TAKAMURA'S exit, then back at YACHIYO. YACHIYO takes in OKUSAN'S house, impressed at the surroundings. OKUSAN leads YACHIYO to a meal already laid out. Two bowls of noodles with some condiments. It's a simple meal, but served in a very elegant manner on small standing trays. The chopsticks are set on small decorative stands. A pot of tea and two teacups. OKUSAN directs YACHIYO to seat herself in front of a tray.)

OKUSAN: Please have a seat. I was expecting you.

(YACHIYO eyes the bowls of steaming noodles, as the long trip has left her ravenous. She takes the invite to sit as an invitation to help herself. She immediately digs in and begins to slurp down the noodles in a noisy and messy fashion. OKUSAN pours the tea.)

OKUSAN: Would you like something to eat?

(YACHIYO is embarrassed and stops. She notices how mannered OKUSAN'S movements are and becomes intimidated. OKUSAN pushes the tea towards her. YACHIYO watches how OKUSAN drinks her tea and tries to imitate it.)

OKUSAN: It's nothing special. Just something I threw together in case you were hungry. *Doozo*, please help yourself.

(YACHIYO begins once again to eat in a noisy, slurpy fashion, when she notices how OKUSAN is eating. She slows down, watching OKUSAN and trying to follow her appropriately mannered way of eating noodles. YACHIYO and OKUSAN fade to black.

PAPA and MAMA lit. PAPA'S shirt is off, and MAMA is doing yaito [moxa burning] on his back.)

PAPA: Did you tell her about the poems?

(No response.)

PAPA: Mama?

MAMA: She asked about them so I told her.

PAPA: She asked about them?

MAMA: She remembers us fighting about them all the time.

PAPA: I burned them all didn't I?

MAMA: I didn't tell you to burn them Papa.

PAPA: You're always saying, "You don't need to write poems here. It's a waste of time. You just need to know how to work." And now you want her to learn those things.

MAMA: Because she's interested in those—

PAPA: She's not interested in Tea, she's just doing it because you tell her to. *Itai, itai!* [hurts] You trying to set me on fire . . .

MAMA: *Yaito* is good for the muscle. I told you not to lift the crates, you should have waited for the boys. Always trying to prove yourself. The heat will help. Right here?

(Testing the muscle.)

PAPA: Yeah—ahhh . . .

(MAMA puts another small ball of the salve on his back.)

PAPA: If I just soak in the *ofuro* [bath] for awhile, the hot water—

MAMA: Sit still Papa.

(They work a while in silence.)

PAPA: Mama?

MAMA: Hmm?

PAPA: What if she gets into trouble? Waimea is so far away.

MAMA: She's got a good head on her shoulders. You worry about her too much Papa.

PAPA: Old-Man Takamura's daughter was always peculiar. And his son-in-law, the potter. We don't know anything about him.

MAMA *(lighting a match)*: This is going to burn a little . . .

PAPA: I've heard rumors.

MAMA: He's not from around here. He's from Japan. A good family. His father is a famous artist I hear. *Erai* man.

PAPA: *Itai, itai . . .*

MAMA: Be good for Yachiyo to be around those kind of people. She can learn something. Make a better life for herself.

PAPA *(reaches back and takes her hand)*: I still keep worrying Mama.

(YACHIYO and TAKAMURA lit. Continuation of the opening scene. YACHIYO assists TAKAMURA, who mimes the actions while

the slides/video demonstrate the "actual" visuals as YACHIYO *describes them. All during this* TAKAMURA *is barking commands.* WILLIE *lit reading a letter.)*

YACHIYO: Then, he takes a *tombo*, dragonfly, because of the way it looks, to double-check the depth and width, but he hardly ever needs to make adjustments. He is very skilled, Willie.

*(*WILLIE *takes the letter and burns it with a match.)*

YACHIYO: Finally he takes a piece of string attached to a small stick for the handle. He lays the string around the base of the cup—and as it wraps around he pulls, perfectly cutting the cup from the rest of the clump of clay.

*(*WILLIE *exits.)*

YACHIYO: Takamura-san then lifts the cup off the clay, sets it aside and begins all over again. And through all of this the wheel never stops moving.

TAKAMURA *(overlapping last sentence)*: And through all of this the wheel never stops moving.

*(*TAKAMURA *stops and wipes his hands.)*

TAKAMURA: I want everything set up by the time I get here, understand. First thing, light the stove and heat the water. The floors must be swept. And I want tea ready. And the clay must be prepared and ready for me to throw. Oh, and just before I arrive—I don't want it prepared too early. I get here at seven o'clock sharp every morning. Pour some of the hot water into the slip buckets next to my wheel—I don't like to dip my hands into cold slip. It stiffens the fingers. I will mix all the clays until I feel I can trust you, but you must wedge it for me. I need six wedged portions ready by the time I get here in the morning and six more by ten o'clock. Then after our noon meal and nap, six more. As I stated before, don't prepare them too soon or they dry out. Keep them covered with a damp cloth. I suppose you don't know how to wedge clay, do you? No, I don't suppose you do. Watch.

(Demonstrates as he describes.)

TAKAMURA: You work in a circular motion like this. Almost looks like a rough seashell pattern. Then gradually work it into an elongated ball. What this does is to take out any inconsistencies in the clay's texture. It actually aligns the particles of sand in the clay. It's easier to work with. Now try it.

(YACHIYO attempts clumsily.)

TAKAMURA: No, no, not like that. Here, get out of the way. Now watch.

(He shows her again.)

TAKAMURA: Now you try it again.

(Montage sequence: TAKAMURA steps in and works the clay, then steps aside, and YACHIYO steps in wearing a work apron and begins to mime shoveling with a shovel. TAKAMURA, now wearing a hachimaki [headband], steps in and jerks the shovel from YACHIYO.

YACHIYO has stepped away and begins to take her apron off as she continues to speak what she has written in her letter to WILLIE. She moves towards OKUSAN.)

YACHIYO: I live in a room off of the work studio. They have given me a small oil heater but I hate to use it because it makes my hair and clothes stink—

TAKAMURA: No, no, this clay is mixed all wrong. Weren't you listening to me? It's way too sandy. Look at the texture. Feel it. You can't work it. It needs more of this red clay. The iron gives it a richer color in firing.

(TAKAMURA and YACHIYO speak simultaneously, their voices rising in volume as they attempt to be heard over each other.)

TAKAMURA: No! What the hell is wrong with you? I would send you back right now if my wife didn't want you here. A pot is only as good as the soul of the man who makes it. Within this domain where I make the pots it is your duty to see that the potter's soul is at peace. The *ochawan* [tea ceremony teacups] I do on the hand wheel. And the "foot" is the key. The way the base is trimmed is the signature of the artist.

YACHIYO: I get up at six o'clock every morning. We have an "ocha" break at ten o'clock. I work till lunch, that's at twelve-thirty. Eat, nap, then start work again at two-thirty and work till sun down. Eat dinner, bathe, then go to sleep

(YACHIYO moves to OKUSAN, who is in the middle of giving

ACT ONE

YACHIYO *a tea ceremony lesson.* OKUSAN *is holding an* ochawan *teacup and examining its base.)*

OKUSAN *(overlapping* TAKAMURA'S *last lines)*: The way the base is trimmed is the signature of the artist. If one is knowledgeable, one can recognize the artist merely by examining the foot of the pot. No, no, Yachiyo. Always with two hands. You are then less likely to drop the *ochawan*. You are showing respect for it.

*(*YACHIYO *seats herself and* OKUSAN *proceeds into the tea ceremony.* YACHIYO *is still visibly upset at* TAKAMURA'S *rough manner.* OKUSAN *places the cup in front of* YACHIYO, *who picks it up and copies her movements.* OKUSAN *reaches in and corrects her turning of the* ochawan.)*

OKUSAN: Do you have a lover?

(Pause.)

YACHIYO *(embarrassed)*: No.

OKUSAN: A girl as pretty as you could have one if she so desired.

(No response.)

OKUSAN: How old are you?

YACHIYO: Almost seventeen.

*(*YACHIYO *sips and makes a face.* OKUSAN *notices.)*

OKUSAN: Chanoyu tea is very special. It has a bitterness. But you will grow to appreciate that quality.

(Beat.)

OKUSAN: He is not always so ill-tempered. Takamura-san. He can be very gentle if he wants to be. Please be understanding of him. He doesn't mean to treat you so harshly. He is just . . . unhappy. He is the eldest son of a well-known pottery family in Japan. But he gambled too much. So his father disowned him. Hiro decided to try his luck here. He met my father, who was impressed with him. Father decided to set him up in business. We, of course met, and one thing led to another . . .

TAKAMURA *(enters, grabbing some things)*: I have to go out . . .

OKUSAN: Where are you going?

*(*TAKAMURA *ignores her.)*

OKUSAN *(sternly)*: Hiro.

*(*TAKAMURA *stops.)*

OKUSAN: You're not going into town, are you?

TAKAMURA: Seto's missing again. They need more men for the search party. He's probably passed out drunk somewhere, but you know his wife, she's half out of her mind with worry. He'll stagger home in a few days just like always, won't remember a thing.

(*To* YACHIYO.)

TAKAMURA: Don't forget to check the stove in the shed. And turn the pots, they have to dry evenly or they'll crack.

(*To* OKUSAN.)

TAKAMURA: Don't wait up for me.

(TAKAMURA *exits. Silence.*)

OKUSAN: I am glad you are here. Sometimes it is lonely. We have no children.

(OKUSAN *lost in thought.*)

YACHIYO (*uncomfortable*): Can we continue?

OKUSAN: Yes . . .

(YACHIYO *lifts the* ochawan *and rotates it in a circular fashion two times, then sips. She wipes the lip of the cup and lowers it. Notices* OKUSAN *staring at her.*)

YACHIYO (*embarrassed*): Okusan . . .

(OKUSAN *doesn't know what* YACHIYO *means.*)

YACHIYO: Please. It makes me uncomfortable. You looking at me.

OKUSAN: I am sorry. I was just noticing how beautiful you are. When I was your age that is all I would think about.

(*As she speaks,* OKUSAN'S *doll is lit, manipulated by a person dressed in black. The female doll mirrors the movements described by* OKUSAN. *Flower petals fall from the branch.*)

OKUSAN: Sometimes I would awaken at night, go to the mirror and stare at myself. In that world of shadows and dream, I would recreate my face. I would make my skin smooth and milky white like the inner shell of the abalone. My mouth like a freshly cut fig. And my eyes, the perfect arc of a wave just before it breaks.

(*Beat.*)

OKUSAN: But of course, when I awakened . . .

(*Puppet becomes lifeless and droops. Fade to black.*)

ACT ONE

OKUSAN: Do you think he is handsome?

(YACHIYO *doesn't understand.*)

OKUSAN: My husband. Takamura-san?

(Pause.)

YACHIYO *(nodding uncomfortably)*: Yes.

(OKUSAN *watches her.* OKUSAN *and* YACHIYO *fade to black.* TAKAMURA *lit with a kerosene lamp that he carries.* YACHIYO *lit standing in front of the pond of lights. Watery sound cue. Staring at the water. She kneels and dips her hand in it, letting it drip back into the water. We hear the sounds of water splashing. She begins to disrobe to go swimming.)*

TAKAMURA *(calling)*: Seto! Seto! Seto!

(Sound of a Buddhist funeral bell. Seto's body appears, floating.)

TAKAMURA: They found Seto. I guess he tried to go swimming and was too drunk . . .

(He sees YACHIYO'S *image.)*

TAKAMURA: Masako . . . Masako . . .

(He blows out lamp.

YACHIYO *lit wading in a shimmering bluish pool of lights. She reaches out to the edges of the shadows and touches something. A distance away in a pool of light we see a naked man floating on his back. Legs and arms extended upwards, slowly wafting in the current.* YACHIYO *pulls back in terror.)*

YACHIYO: Seto was naked. Floating there. His body is very muscular. You couldn't tell by just seeing him. He had come by Takamura's a couple of times trying to get work. Takamura-san would give him a drink then send him on his way. Seto was very forward. Once I caught him staring at me. At my breasts . . . I never touched a dead person before . . .

(She stares out at the body. Her fascination overcomes her fear. She tentatively reaches out to touch the body. Blackout.

OKUSAN *and* TAKAMURA *lit.* TAKAMURA *drinking sake, gesturing towards the* tokkuri *and* guinomi *[sake bottle and cups] on the table.)*

TAKAMURA *(sarcastically)*: This is wrong. This is all wrong. What's a good-looking piece of pottery like this *tokkuri* and *sakazuki* doing here. This is not right.

(OKUSAN brings out wooden bowl and places it on the table in front of TAKAMURA.)

TAKAMURA: There, that's better. What really should be here is this . . . A crude wooden bowl. That's what belongs on this table. It's more in keeping with the aesthetic sense of the people here in this town. They don't want fine pottery in their every-day lives. They want wooden bowls that they can knock on the floor and not break when they're screwing their wives on the kitchen table.

(Knocks wooden bowls to the floor.)

TAKAMURA: See. That's what peasants like. Not finite beauty with the inherent fragility of human nature . . .

(Drops the tokkuri from one hand, but saves it by catching it in the other below.)

TAKAMURA: . . . but crude, pedestrian substitutions. At least in Japan the people could appreciate a good pot. The Japanese people here, like your father . . .

(Downs a cup of sake.)

OKUSAN: I won't tolerate you talking about my father that way. After all he has done for you—

TAKAMURA *(interrupts)*: He was a petty merchant, who couldn't squeeze any more money out of the farmers who had wised up to him. Comes here and is lucky enough to figure out all the workers need things and starts a store—a shack, four walls and—

OKUSAN *(interrupts)*: Which he was smart enough to make money with. And which he sold so you could start this pottery.

(YACHIYO lit in half-light standing with her eyes closed. As if sleeping in bed. Tossing and turning.)

TAKAMURA: I should have never left Japan.

OKUSAN: This pottery where you said you could make great—

TAKAMURA *(overlapping)*: The pottery will work, it will work!

OKUSAN: —works of art like your father back in Japan!!

(YACHIYO awakens with a start.)

TAKAMURA: I should have stayed in Japan. I should have stayed there—married Masako. To hell with what anyone says . . .

(Exits.)

ACT ONE

OKUSAN: Where are you going? Hiro!

> *(Blackout on* OKUSAN.*)*

YACHIYO *(gets up)*: When I was a child I would hear sounds coming from my parents' room. I would wake up at night, hear them fighting. The walls were so thin, the sound would pass through them like dark, scary animals. In the blackness, I could feel their voices scurrying about my skin, and even though I would try to keep them out of me, my head buried beneath the covers, they would crawl inside my mind, these ugly, screaming animals.

> *(*PAPA *and* MAMA *lit in half-light making love. Soft moans.)*

YACHIYO: Sometimes I would hear moaning coming from their room. I used to think maybe Mama or Papa was having a bad dream and I would want to go in there. But something always stopped me. A feeling, inside.

> *(*PAPA *and* MAMA *fade to black.)*

YACHIYO: At night I still feel the dark scary animals scurrying around—

> *(*WILLIE *lit. Agitated.)*

WILLIE: The start of the strike has everyone nervous. Da Filipino union went ahead first, so we join in too. Nobody knows what the company gonna do. Yamaguchi-san says it might get violent.

YACHIYO: It's so hot and humid, everybody's irritable. Takamura-san and Okusan had a violent fight. He's in a bad mood because the pots are cracking as they dry.

WILLIE: I think you should come home. I thought it over and it is not good for you to be there. I talked to my cousin who lives there in Waimea and there is talk about the man and his wife.

> *(We hear thunder and rain.)*

YACHIYO *(listening)*: Thunder storms.

> *(Beat.)*

YACHIYO: At night I hear them yelling and screaming.

WILLIE: They've been married nine years and don't have any children. The wife's father had money but he was a drunken sot. And they say the son-in-law's no better.

> *(Crashing thunder and the violent flash of lightning.)*

YACHIYO: It scares me but it is quite beautiful. Why do they stay together?

WILLIE: No wonder—he's a *yoshi*. I can't see how any man would give up his own family name and take on his wife's and be some pussy-whipped male taking orders from her.

(Streaks of light.)

YACHIYO *(holding out her hand to the lightning)*: I sometimes wonder if it will strike me . . .

WILLIE: I think it's a mistake to stay there. You should come home.

(He fades. The sound and lightning slowly subside. Distant rumbles and occasional flashes in the horizon.

TAKAMURA lit in half-light in front of a small bisque firing kiln. Small flames are coming out of it.)

YACHIYO: After Takamura trims the pots they must be completely dried—this has been hard because of the humidity—and then they are baked in a low fire . . .

(Flames die out. Lights up full on TAKAMURA opening the kiln and taking the pots out gingerly.)

YACHIYO: Then they are ready to be glazed.

(Beat.)

YACHIYO: More and more I think that coming was a mistake. I miss Willie. I miss my family . . .

TAKAMURA *(handing pots to YACHIYO)*: Here. Be careful. We still have to glaze them.

YACHIYO *(noticing)*: The reddish color . . .

TAKAMURA: It's all the iron in the clay—Be careful! They're fired just hard enough to take the glazes but they can still break easily.

(He is sweating profusely, water dripping from his brow. He reaches for some water but it's out. He's about to say something when YACHIYO, anticipating his needs, hands him a newly filled water container. He stares at her. She's uncomfortable.)

TAKAMURA: How long have you been here?

YACHIYO: Four months.

TAKAMURA: You like working with me?

YACHIYO: Yes.

TAKAMURA: No, you don't. You hate my guts.

ACT ONE

YACHIYO (*flustered*): No, that's not true—

TAKAMURA: Lie to my wife. She's the one who needs it, not me. You do your work right and I don't give a shit what you think of me. Get the other pots ready for trimming. The ones I was throwing this morning—

YACHIYO: Why do you treat me like this? I'm trying so hard to do everything right. The way you want it. The studio has to be cleaned in just the right way. And the temperature in the studio—I open the window too much, I close the window too much, turn on the stove to make adjustments, then open the window again to compensate for the stove's heat—I'm trying, I'm trying Takamura-san, I'm trying! . . .

(*Silence.* TAKAMURA *stares at her.*)

TAKAMURA: Good. Good Yachiyo. Now try harder.

(TAKAMURA *goes back to work.* OKUSAN *enters with two dusters, rags tied to sticks. Hands one to* YACHIYO.)

YACHIYO (*trying to contain herself*): Okusan and I dust the pots off, otherwise the dirt and soot will keep the glazes from sticking to the surface of the pots. Then we can apply the glaze. He is very nervous as this will be the first firing of his smaller test kiln. There have been many problems—because the pots can't dry thoroughly they have been breaking in the low bisque firing—

(YACHIYO *drops a pot, shattering it.*)

TAKAMURA (*furious*): Yachiyo!

(*Beat, to* OKUSAN.)

TAKAMURA: Peasants and farmers, peasants and farmers . . .

(TAKAMURA *stomps off.* YACHIYO, *humiliated, goes to her room, takes out her suitcase and begins packing.*)

YACHIYO: When he's not there, when I'm alone in my room, I always answer back, right to his face, I always have the answer. But when he's there, in front of me, scolding me, I shrink up, and become tongue-tied—he knows everything, I know nothing, I'm stupid. I hate it, I hate it.

(OKUSAN *enters* YACHIYO'S *room. Sees her open suitcase.*)

OKUSAN: You can hear us fighting at night, can't you?

(YACHIYO *hesitates, then returns to packing.*)

YACHIYO: No.

OKUSAN: You hear us. These days he has no shame about show-ing the world how much contempt he has for me. In the begin-ning it was different. He liked me. He liked me very much. Then Otosan died and he started to change. He became mean, insulting. Began to go out at night.

(Pause.)

OKUSAN: Hiro has a lover. A young Filipino girl in town. She works at the Taxi-Dance place . . .

(YACHIYO stops packing. Silence.)

YACHIYO: Okusan? You asked me before if I had a . . . friend? Willie Higa. Back in Mana. He asked me to marry him.

OKUSAN: Do you love him?

YACHIYO: I don't know.

OKUSAN: He loves you?

YACHIYO: Yes.

OKUSAN: It is better to be loved.

(Beat.)

OKUSAN: This is for you. I want you to have it.

(She takes out a wrapped package and hands it to YACHIYO. OKUSAN turns and exits. YACHIYO opens the gift to find a beau-tiful tea ceremony ochawan. YACHIYO stares at it, then at her open suitcase.

PAPA'S letter to YACHIYO. YACHIYO lit in a pool of light with OKUSAN doing the tea ceremony with YACHIYO'S new ochawan. YACHIYO'S able to do the drinking portion of the ceremony smoothly, without a hitch. This goes on during PAPA'S monologue.)

PAPA: Dear Yachiyo. Things are very busy at home. They are con-sidering me for a job at the Knapper Plantation so I probably will start work soon. Mama will like that . . .

(Pause. Starts a new letter.)

Dear Yachiyo. How is the Takamura family? Old Man Takamura, the father—whew! When he drank, you didn't want to be around. See, there are three types of drunks. Some people when they drink, they get sad. That's your Papa. Others, they get happy. But Old Man Takamura, he was the third type. He got mean. It must have been hell for that daughter growing up in that house. He yelled, screamed obscenities, even beat up people. He liked my company. When he was sick on the boat coming over here I played Go with him. Read him some of my poetry. He liked my *tanka* verse. One time Takamura got real drunk. This was after we got here and he was better. We were outside a local gambling house and he was picking another one of his fights. Only this time the old man was very drunk and the other man very big. So, like a fool, I tried to stop him. Old Man Takamura got furious. And he hit me. He hit me again and again. The other people had to pull him off. He almost killed me. After that he started telling everyone that I saved his life coming over on the boat. He would say the same thing to me, then say if I ever needed a favor just to ask him. I guess after a while I started to believe it myself. I didn't save his life. He just felt guilty.

(Pause. Starts a new letter.)

PAPA: Dear Yachiyo . . .

(PAPA fades to black.

OKUSAN lit with dolls. YACHIYO looks on. Recounting a tale. This is a continuation of the story OKUSAN started earlier. Petals fall. Music cue.)

OKUSAN: There once was a woman. She was young. She was beautiful. And she was in love with a man. She was so lonely. Because though she loved him, he was not able to return the love. But she already carried his love within and could not release it. It grew inside her soul until she was filled with inconsolable grief. No one could help her, no one could save her. And in a fit of this sadness, the woman, young and beautiful, threw herself into the fire and perished, her ashes floating upward like a swarm of dark insects . . .

(Lighting change. Silence.)

OKUSAN: What did you think of the story?

YACHIYO: I don't know . . .

OKUSAN: You didn't like it?

(YACHIYO is silent.)

OKUSAN: Yachiyo?

YACHIYO: Why do you like it?

OKUSAN: It's a very famous story. Based on a true incident. It's very beautiful. You don't think so?

YACHIYO: Yes, but . . .

OKUSAN: Yachiyo?

YACHIYO: Why did she have to kill herself?

OKUSAN: In order to preserve her family's honor. To save face for herself and her parents. Because there was nothing else for her to do. A beautiful death. You wouldn't?

YACHIYO: No. She should have figured something out. Gone on living.

(OKUSAN stares at her. Then begins to laugh.)

OKUSAN: What did I do?

(Pause. OKUSAN becomes quiet.)

OKUSAN: Sometimes. When I'm alone, I visit my dolls. Play with them. Make them move. An arm this way. A head tilted this way. And after a while, the doll becomes me. It's my arm, it's my head. And I make up stories. About her. About me . . . *(Embarrassed.)*

OKUSAN: I like you Yachiyo. I can talk to you. You can be my friend. My only friend, okay? Okay Yachiyo?

YACHIYO: Okay . . .

(OKUSAN exits. YACHIYO pauses for a moment, staring at the dolls. She picks them up and begins to manipulate them. While speaking the following lines, the dolls come alive.)

YACHIYO: There once was a woman. She was young. She was beautiful. And she was in love with a man.

(The male doll, now lit, and the female doll begin to embrace. This is too much for YACHIYO, and she turns away, moving to the pool of water, lit by the water. She's having her period and takes out a blood-soaked cloth from between her legs. She puts it into the river and begins to clean it. We see the growing red color as it spreads. As she does this, OSUGI is lit and speaks.)

OSUGI *(working)*: They finally let the Shimokawa girl go. She was pretty big. I was walking her home when these workers from the plantation called her a prostitute and asked her to go in the bushes with them. Everybody talking, whispering behind her back—she won't go out of the house anymore. And the mother is so ashamed she won't go out either, so the little sisters have to do the shopping and everything. I don't let Pantat touch me that way no more. Not till we get married. That kind of shame . . .

(OSUGI fades to black. Seto's naked body brought up in half-light, floating. YACHIYO stares at the body. TAKAMURA staggers along drunk. Big moon in the night sky. YACHIYO hides and watches him. TAKAMURA stands at the water's edge and talks to the night.)

TAKAMURA: My soul . . . My soul, an empty bladder, shriveled up with no song. No song. It used to be such a glorious roar. Explosive and deliciously indiscriminate. At times it would scare me. It needed so much, it wanted all the time. Days and nights on end in abandoned revelry—in drunken stupor, my cock in my hand waving it at any woman who would pay attention. But always it was about the pursuit of that mysterious thing. Yes, "thing," because I can't even name it, yet I can always sense its presence. When I'm lost in drink, drenched in the scent of sexual union, it's there. Just beyond my grasp, just beyond the pale. Masako knew, Masako could understand . . .

(Holding up his hands.)

TAKAMURA: . . . these imperfect human hands . . .

(Looking at the bottle's curve.)

TAKAMURA: . . . The curve, the curve, how it hangs in space . . . How perfect.

(Looking at his hands.)

TAKAMURA: You give me the mind to imagine it, see it. And yet I cannot create it. Imperfect, perfect. My father's blood pushing through me, feeding me with his seed. And still . . . Nothing, nothing, NOTHINGNESS!!

YACHIYO *(looks at Seto's floating body)*: I never touched a dead person before. I think you have to live life now. Because tomorrow you might be dead.

(YACHIYO turns to TAKAMURA and slowly reaches out to touch him. Dim to darkness.)

[END OF ACT ONE]

ACT TWO

YACHIYO *(lit, sitting on her bed)*: Okusan thinks of me as her friend. She confided in me about her husband. I, too, confided in her about Willie. How can she stay married to Takamura-san. He is such a rude and awful—

WILLIE *(lit)*: Yamaguchi was beat up. All da workers' families getting kicked out of the camps. Some of the older workers think maybe we should give in. Not Yamaguchi-san. "Pau hana, no go work, we on strike."

(Starts to leave, then stops.)

WILLIE: Maybe it's better that you stay there.

(WILLIE, looks around furtively, then hurries away.

YACHIYO seats herself on her bed. The ochawan *sits next to her on her stand.* TAKAMURA *arrives, weary, after a night on the town. Bottle in hand. Sees something in her room, enters.)*

YACHIYO *(scared)*: Takamura.

TAKAMURA *(picking up the ochawan)*: Where'd you get this?

YACHIYO *(grabbing it back)*: Okusan gave it to me.

TAKAMURA: You don't know what you're holding, do you? Do you?

YACHIYO: It's an *ochawan*. For tea ceremony.

TAKAMURA: No, no, it's much, much more Yachiyo. It's my blood. It's what gets me up each morning, lets me live. It's what makes me die each night after a long day of failure, knowing I will never be good enough to be his son. I gave it to her. It's my wedding gift to Sumiko. My father made it.

(Laughs and sits down next to her. Drinks from his bottle.)

TAKAMURA: You remind me of someone. But then they all do now.

YACHIYO: How can you treat Okusan like this? Seeing that girl at the Taxi-Dance hall. Shame on you!

TAKAMURA *(stares at her, surprised at her fervor. He likes it)*: Here. Why don't you drink with me. Come on, drink—

(TAKAMURA puts his arm around YACHIYO and tries to make

ACT TWO

her drink from the bottle. YACHIYO *pushes the bottle away and slaps him.)*

YACHIYO *(shaking)*: GET OUT!

(Silence. TAKAMURA *stares at* YACHIYO. *Then, slowly, he rises and goes to the door. Stops.)*

TAKAMURA: What did she tell you? That she was the poor misunderstood wife? That I was cheating on her behind her back? I never lied to her. Right from the beginning she knew what I was. She knew exactly what she was getting.

(Pause.)

TAKAMURA: She liked me. Why I shall never know. She became infatuated with me. Had to have me. Begged, cajoled her father until—ahh, the father. He was a shrewd, shrewd bastard. He cared little about anything but what he could buy and sell for a profit. And he could do that better than any man I've ever met. Have you down on your knees begging him to stick his hands into your pockets. And he could smell a man's weak spot a mile away. Profit, that's all he cared about. That is, except his daughter. His only child. That was his weak spot. And since his daughter wanted me, he made sure she got me. The old man offered me a proposition. I get a second chance to be the artist, to redeem myself in my family's eyes. In exchange, I marry his daughter and—ahh, here's the catch—I give up my name.

(Pause.)

TAKAMURA: I don't know if I really cared one way or the other at the time. So you see, her father bought me for her. Like a pet dog. And she knew what I was. What she was getting.

(Pause. Unsure whether to reveal more.)

TAKAMURA: We had an agreement. This one was between Sumiko and me. Her father didn't know. I told her I didn't love her. And that she must allow me my freedom. That I would be discreet and never bring her shame. This was my side of the bargain. She agreed. Maybe I am getting a bit careless of late—ever since the old bastard died. I guess you could say I've been celebrating. He'd like me drinking, though. That's the one thing we had in common.

(Silence. He drinks from his bottle.)

TAKAMURA: You have a lover, don't you.

YACHIYO *(hesitant)*: No.

TAKAMURA: You don't have to lie to me.

YACHIYO: I'm not lying to you.

TAKAMURA: A man like me can just smell it. We have a nose for it. You aren't so easy because your heart is preoccupied. Ahh, but if it should be distracted . . . Why don't you marry him? Raise a litter of babies.

> *(No response.)*

TAKAMURA: Can't make up your mind, huh? Think maybe something better is out there.

YACHIYO: No.

TAKAMURA: Not necessarily a lover, but just something, something . . .

> *(Pause.)*

TAKAMURA: I couldn't make up my mind once. She married someone else. I began to drink too much, gamble too much. Finally my father kicked me out. I should have killed myself. I think my father would have preferred that. Instead, I left for Beikoku, America. I wanted to forget, start all over. I couldn't even do that right. I gambled my money away on the boat coming over and got stuck here. But then a man without his real name doesn't exist anymore. Not really. I guess, in a sense my father got his wish, huh.

> *(TAKAMURA staggers out of her room.)*

YACHIYO *(watching him leave)*: Hiro . . .

> *(YACHIYO notices he's left behind his hachimaki. She picks it up, touches it. Places it next to her pillow along with the pikake and lays down staring at it. Lights fade to black.)*
>
> *(Lights up. It's OKUSAN calling to waken YACHIYO.)*

OKUSAN: Yachiyo? Yachiyo? Yachiyo, wake up . . .

YACHIYO: What is it?

OKUSAN *(getting YACHIYO up and dressed)*: We have to go get Hiro. He didn't come back tonight. I'm afraid all those pots he threw will be too hard in the morning to trim . . . We have to make him come back tonight. He has to come back tonight or everything will be ruined.

ACT TWO

YACHIYO: Why don't we just put wet towels on them—

OKUSAN: They're some of his best work yet. We have to save them, we must save them for him . . . I already harnessed the horse to the carriage.

(As OKUSAN *ushers* YACHIYO *out she notices* TAKAMURA'S hachimaki *next to her pillow. She follows* YACHIYO *and they seat themselves side by side in her horse-drawn carriage. Night. The moon. We hear night sounds. Ominous feel.)*

OKUSAN: I saw a *hachimaki* on your pillow. It looked like Takamura-san's.

YACHIYO *(uncomfortable)*: I found it. I was going to return it to him.

(As they ride in silence, the world around them begins to transform. It grows dark, skewed—as if we could see the growing turmoil inside OKUSAN'S *mind reflected in the exterior world.* OKUSAN *abruptly continues her puppet story.)*

OKUSAN: She was so lonely. And though she loved him, he was not able to return the love. But she already carried his love within and could not release it. It grew inside her soul until she was filled with inconsolable grief. No one could help her. No one could save her . . .

(Long silence. YACHIYO *wonders what's wrong.)*

YACHIYO: Okusan?

OKUSAN: Until one day a young girl arrived. She befriended the woman. The pain inside subsided. The young girl made her feel happy again . . .

*(*OKUSAN *notices where they are and pulls the reins to stop the carriage. The world returns to normal. We hear the muffled sounds of music and laughter. They both stare at the Taxi-Dance hall.)*

OKUSAN: He's in there. With his girlfriend. Some farm girl from Manila they painted up to look like a woman. And he pays five cents a dance to be with her. Five cents a dance.

*(*YACHIYO *notices that* OKUSAN *doesn't move.)*

YACHIYO: I can go in. Okusan? I can go in and get him.

*(*OKUSAN *doesn't respond.* YACHIYO *gets out of the carriage and goes into the Taxi-Dance hall. Loud music is blaring out and the room is bathed in a garish red hue. A couple whirls by dancing.*

YACHIYO *stands there for a moment disoriented. She is both fright-*
ened of and drawn to the atmosphere of this world. TAKAMURA
is dancing with the young girl [played by OSUGI*].* YACHIYO
approaches him.)

YACHIYO: Takamura-san? Takamura-san?

DANCE HALL GIRL: *Lumayas ka*! He's all paid up!

(TAKAMURA *notices it's* YACHIYO. *Lets go of the other young*
woman.)

YACHIYO *(talking over the music)*: Takamura-san, Okusan is waiting outside.

TAKAMURA: Dance with me.

DANCE HALL GIRL: *Puta*!

YACHIYO: Okusan's outside.

(TAKAMURA *grabs* YACHIYO, *pulling her to him. They begin to*
dance. YACHIYO *is trying to politely get away but he holds her*
tightly. She finally relents and stumbles along with him. OKUSAN,
wondering what has happened to TAKAMURA *and* YACHIYO,
enters. She sees them dancing, together.)

(*Lighting change.* TAKAMURA *and* YACHIYO *isolated in a pool*
of light. Sound dips.)

OKUSAN: But maybe the young girl was only pretending. Maybe
she was deceitful and full of lies.

(YACHIYO *and* TAKAMURA *now dance smoothly.* YACHIYO *is*
uncomfortable but enjoying it. OKUSAN *watches. Dim to darkness.)*

YACHIYO *(lit)*: It is now five months that I've been at the pottery. Takamura was pleased with the test tiles. I have—

(TAKAMURA, *lit, opening the small test kiln. He pulls out the test*
tiles and eagerly looks at them.)

YACHIYO: —noticed a change in Takamura-san. In how he treats
me. He no longer is so mean to me. Okusan, however, seems
distant. During tea ceremony she has become very strict with
me. When I want to talk with her she says—

OKUSAN *(appears doing the tea ceremony. Her lines overlap* YACHIYO'S*)*:
It is not correct form to make small talk about our personal
lives . . .

YACHIYO: —"It is not correct form to make small talk about our
personal lives," that it somehow "breaks—

ACT TWO

OKUSAN *(overlapping)*: . . . breaks the correct mood for the appreciation of the tea . . .

YACHIYO: —the correct mood for the appreciation of the tea." I miss talking to Okusan. Her behavior towards me is confusing. I noticed something. The tea. It no longer tastes quite so bitter.

> *(OKUSAN turns to watch YACHIYO. Fades to black.*
> *TAKAMURA and YACHIYO face off. They're both hot and thirsty. They've been building the kiln.)*

TAKAMURA: The point of the *nobori-gama*, the climbing kiln, is that it reuses the heat over and over. The heat used to raise the temperature in one chamber travels up to the next chamber and heats it up. And on and on. Instead of having seven separate kiln firings you have one extended firing, saving time, money and fuel. We have to check the angle of the kiln again.

YACHIYO: Didn't we just check it?

TAKAMURA: I'm not sure, I want to look at it again.

> *(YACHIYO dips her cup into the water bucket and drinks greedily, water spilling over the front of her clothes. TAKAMURA laughs.)*

YACHIYO *(gasping for air)*: What?

TAKAMURA: It's dripping all over your clothes.

YACHIYO: I'm thirsty.

TAKAMURA: You drink like a dying horse.

> *(YACHIYO stops drinking.)*

TAKAMURA: Drink, drink some more. I enjoy watching you.

YACHIYO: I'm crude, I know. Okusan keeps telling me that in Tea. I'm trying as hard as I can.

TAKAMURA: I like it. It reminds me of when I was young. When it's hot, you sweat. When you're thirsty, you drink. There's no need to over think things, that muddies everything up. Too much thinking, too much logic makes the simplest things seem impossible. How far apart are we? Two feet? Half of two feet is what? One foot. Half of one foot is what? Half a foot.

> *(Moving his hand closer to YACHIYO'S face.)*

TAKAMURA: Half of one-half is one-quarter. Then one-eighth. Then one-sixteenth, and on and on and we'd never touch. We'd

always be a fraction of a distance away from each other, or so
the scientist would like us to believe . . . but for the artist of
course . . .

(He reaches out and touches her cheek.)

TAKAMURA: The life of an artist. You live a life of immeasurable
suffering. But there are some rewards—you get to experience
poverty and public ridicule, too. Here, let me show you something in the *nobori-gama*. I noticed it while we were working.
See, a bird is building her nest in the first chamber.

YACHIYO *(moving)*: I'll clean it out—

TAKAMURA: No, no, let it build. It'll be long gone before we have
to fire. Besides, I love the sound of baby birds chirping. Like
little children singing to us. It'll make our work easier when
we're loading all the pots into the chambers. Keep track of the
nest for us. If need be we can always move it.

YACHIYO *(going back to work)*: Hiro?

TAKAMURA: Yes?

*(She takes out a worn sheet of paper from her pocket and hands
it to TAKAMURA. It's the composite picture of YACHIYO'S Montgomery Ward ensemble.)*

TAKAMURA: What is this?

YACHIYO: It's what I'm going to look like someday. When I grow
up.

TAKAMURA: What did you do, cut this out?

YACHIYO: Un-huh. Out of the Montgomery Ward catalogue. I
make them up. I cut out different pieces of clothing and then
paste them together. It's a game I play with myself and sometimes with my friend Osugi. What we'd like to look like one
day.

(Beat.)

YACHIYO: Only for me it's not a game.

*(Pause. TAKAMURA doesn't know what to say. YACHIYO takes it
from his hands and folds it up.)*

YACHIYO: I thought you might like to see it. That's all. I just
wanted to show you.

*(YACHIYO goes back to working. TAKAMURA watches her.
TAKAMURA dims to darkness.)*

ACT TWO

YACHIYO: I feel a little guilty. I did not think about—

(OKUSAN *lit.* YACHIYO *dims to darkness. During* OKUSAN's *following monologue,* TAKAMURA *is lit holding a dress.*)

OKUSAN: Dear Mr. William Higa. This is a rather embarrassing situation, but I feel I must write to you. Your fiancée, Yachiyo Matsumoto—who as you know works with my husband and myself—has . . . How do I say this—she has developed a romantic interest in my husband. He, of course, is embarrassed by the whole situation.

(OKUSAN *freezes.* TAKAMURA *fades to black.*)

(WILLIE *lit, very agitated, bleeding. We hear the plantation siren and the commotion of men being beaten.*)

WILLIE: Dear Yachiyo. The company's goons attack us with horses and guns—we had only sticks to fight back with. The head of the Filipino Federation now siding with the company bosses— he sold his union out. I have to hide out for a while.

(*Pause.*)

WILLIE: How come you don't write?

(WILLIE *dims.* OKUSAN *unfreezes.*)

OKUSAN: . . . before she does something to embarrass all of us.

(MAMA *lit in a pool of light next to* OKUSAN.)

OKUSAN: As I do not have your address, Mr. Higa, I am sending this care of Yachiyo's mother and father. I am sure we can trust them not to take advantage of the situation and that this unfortunate circumstance will remain a secret just between the two of us.

(YACHIYO *lit, holding a dress. Continuation of* YACHIYO's *prior scene.*)

YACHIYO: I feel a little guilty. I did not think about Willie all day.

OKUSAN: Signed, very sincerely yours, Mrs. Hiro Takamura.

(OKUSAN *hands the letter to* MAMA. OKUSAN *exits.* MAMA *stares at the letter. Looks up towards* YACHIYO, *who is holding the dress.* WILLIE *appears, and* MAMA *hands him the letter. As* WILLIE *takes the letter he looks from* MAMA *to* YACHIYO, *then exits.* YACHIYO, *with her mother's eyes on her, withdraws, still clutching the dress.* MAMA *is silent for a moment. Then fade to black. As* MAMA *dims to darkness,* YACHIYO, TAKAMURA *and* OKUSAN *are lit. They are doing the tea ceremony. It is* YACHIYO'S *regular lesson; however,* OKUSAN *has insisted that* TAKAMURA *participate.* OKUSAN *whips the tea up and offers a cup to* TAKAMURA, *who drinks following all the correct movements. He is obviously trained in this.)*

OKUSAN: Yachiyo? Why don't you try on your new dress?

*(*YACHIYO *is silent.)*

OKUSAN: Hiro says the color becomes you.

YACHIYO *(embarrassed)*: I cannot accept it. I told Takamura-san.

OKUSAN: But why not?

TAKAMURA *(to* OKUSAN*)*: It's just a dress. I saw it in the store and I thought she might like it.

OKUSAN: I think it is wonderful that you think of Yachiyo.

YACHIYO: I asked Takamura-san to take it back.

OKUSAN: No, no, that is unthinkable. You must wear it for me. Please?

(Pause.)

OKUSAN: After all. It's the one you wanted, isn't it, Yachiyo?

*(*YACHIYO *is silent.* OKUSAN *takes out* YACHIYO'S *ochawan.)*

OKUSAN: Let's use this one. The one I gave you.

(She glances at TAKAMURA, *then begins to prepare* YACHIYO'S *tea, whipping it to a froth.)*

OKUSAN: I was talking to Mrs. Lee next door and she said a girl from your camp was found unconscious. She had taken ant poison. Her parents found her just in time. A Shimokawa girl. Do you know her? Maybe we should get you a hat. To go with your dress. What do you think Hiro?

(Back to YACHIYO.*)*

OKUSAN: Would you like that?

*(*YACHIYO *turns the cup three times and drinks. Wipes the lip and sets the cup down.)*

OKUSAN: How do you find the flavor now, Yachiyo. Still too bitter?

(Pause.)

YACHIYO: I'm starting to like the taste.

OKUSAN: I was once told Chanoyu tea could never be appreciated by someone of a pure nature. The flavor, the bitterness would overwhelm the innocence, the purity of the person's palate. Only when one has walked through the, how do I say this politely, the human excrement of life, is one capable of understanding, appreciating, finding pleasure in the complexity of its *ningen no aji*, its human flavor.

(*Beat.*)

OKUSAN: I'm glad you're beginning to *like* the taste.

(*As* OKUSAN *continues with the tea ceremony,* TAKAMURA *and* YACHIYO *glance at each other. Dim to darkness.*)

(MAMA *lit in a pool of light.* WILLIE *appears holding the now opened letter. His arm is bandaged.*)

WILLIE: Matsumoto-san?

MAMA: I read it. I'm sorry.

(*Pause.*)

MAMA: Do you think it's true? What Mrs. Takamura said?

WILLIE: I'm going there. To Waimea. To see Yachiyo.

(WILLIE *exits.*)

MAMA (*calling after*): I don't believe it! Mrs. Takamura lied! . . .
(*Dim to darkness.*

YACHIYO *lit in a pool of light in the upstage area. She is putting on the dress* TAKAMURA *bought for her. Her curiosity piqued, in the privacy of her room she has finally decided to actually try it on. Further downstage,* TAKAMURA-SAN *appears in the shadows silently watching* YACHIYO *dress.* YACHIYO *senses something and turns, covering herself.* TAKAMURA-SAN *ducks back into the shadows, still watching.*

YACHIYO *goes back to putting the dress on. We almost get the sense that* YACHIYO *knows who is watching and that she enjoys the sensation.*

As YACHIYO *starts to adjust the dress and comb her hair,* TAKAMURA *hears something and turns to leave.* OKUSAN *appears and they exchange looks as he exits.* OKUSAN *sees* YACHIYO *in the pool of light adjusting the dress.* YACHIYO *glances back, still assuming it's* TAKAMURA. *However, unbeknownst to* YACHIYO, *it is* OKUSAN *in the shadows watching her.* OKUSAN *glances back towards the exiting* TAKAMURA. *Fade to black.*

YACHIYO *lit.* OKUSAN *enters.* YACHIYO *is embarrassed at being caught wearing the dress.*)

OKUSAN: I think the hat would go well with your new dress. Don't you think so?

(YACHIYO *is silent.* OKUSAN *approaches her. Admires the dress, touching it.*)

OKUSAN: Do you enjoy sleeping with my husband?

YACHIYO: What?

OKUSAN: Or, maybe a shawl. Would you prefer a shawl? Hiro gave you this dress. Then I shall give—*(Continues.)*

YACHIYO *(overlapping)*: Okusan, what are you saying?

OKUSAN *(continued)*: —you a shawl.
    (Pause.)

OKUSAN: I said, "Do you enjoy sleeping with Takamura-san?"

YACHIYO: Please, Okusan, I am not sleeping—I'm not doing anything with Takamura-san. He just gave me this dress, that's all.

OKUSAN: I could tell your parents. You know that of course. Such an ungrateful . . . I trusted you. No one knows the things that I have told you. No one.

YACHIYO: Okusan . . .

OKUSAN: No. A hat. Yes. I think a hat would be better.

(OKUSAN *exits, leaving* YACHIYO *in her room.* WILLIE *approaches* OKUSAN *as she leaves.*)

WILLIE: Mrs. Takamura?

(*Pause.* OKUSAN *is not sure who he is. Then realizing.*)

OKUSAN: Willie Higa?

WILLIE: Where's Yachiyo?

(OKUSAN *gestures towards* YACHIYO'S *room, where she remains lit in half-light.* WILLIE *starts to turn, then stops. Pulls out the letter.*)

OKUSAN: From Yachiyo's parents? From you?

WILLIE (WILLIE *hands the letter to* OKUSAN): It's the letter you sent.

(WILLIE *turns and approaches* YACHIYO. OKUSAN *watches for a beat, then exits.*)

WILLIE: Yachiyo.

YACHIYO *(surprised)*: Willie . . .

(YACHIYO *stares for a beat.*)

YACHIYO: What are you doing here?

WILLIE: I came into Waimea with—*(Continues.)*

ACT TWO

YACHIYO *(overlapping)*: It's good to see you.

WILLIE *(continued)*: —my brother.

　　(Pause.)

WILLIE: I rode with him in his wagon. We rode all night.

YACHIYO *(noticing)*: What happened?

WILLIE: Just a scratch. During the fighting.

　　(Beat.)

YACHIYO: Did your brother have business here? Is that why he came to Waimea?

WILLIE: No.

　　(Awkward pause.)

WILLIE: I'm supposed to be at work. Drank a whole bottle of *shoyu*, the soy sauce made my blood pressure shoot up through the roof, my whole body, like it was crawling with ants. Fool da plantation doctor good.

　　*(*WILLIE *moves forward and they awkwardly embrace. Remembers some Okinawan food that he's brought and gives it to her.)*

WILLIE: From my mother, some *andagi*, the one you like—she made it for you special.

　　*(*WILLIE *glances around the room.)*

WILLIE: This where you live?

YACHIYO: Un-huh.

WILLIE: You look kinda skinny. Bag of bones, yeah. They feeding you good?

YACHIYO: I get plenty to eat. They treat me very well.

WILLIE: Good, good, 'cause your Mama and Papa are worried. You look good, though. I like the dress. Did you buy it here?

YACHIYO *(ignoring his question)*: It seems funny to see you standing there. In this place.

WILLIE: What do you mean?

YACHIYO: When I see you, it's like I'm trying to remember me . . .

WILLIE: A lot of things have happened at the plantation. I haven't heard from you so I don't know if you got—*(Continues.)*

YACHIYO *(overlapping)*: I've been very busy . . .

WILLIE *(continued)*: —my letters or not.

　　(Pause. During WILLIE'S *monologue* YACHIYO *moves away and watches* TAKAMURA, *who is gradually brought up in light.*

TAKAMURA *waking up. Next to him is sleeping the young woman from the dance hall.)*

WILLIE: They got rid of Fagundez. Guess who the new foreman is? Yamaguchi. Finally, a Nihonjin luna—the first Japanese foreman. They give us everything we asked for after we give in. I'm kind of important now, a big shot. Not really a big shot, like a luna or anything. But since I know Yamaguchi-san, the older men, they treat me differently now.

(As TAKAMURA *gets up, the young woman from the dance hall tries to get him to stay in bed.)*

DANCE HALL GIRL: Hiro? Hiro-chan? Come back to sleep. Hiro?

*(*TAKAMURA *looks back. Turns away in disgust and stumbles towards* YACHIYO *and* WILLIE. *Lighting change.* YACHIYO, TAKAMURA *and* WILLIE *lit.)*

TAKAMURA: Who's this?

YACHIYO: This is my friend from Mana. Willie Higa.

TAKAMURA *(staring at him)*: So you're the one.

YACHIYO: This is Takamura-san.

(Silence.)

YACHIYO: Willie and his brother had some business in Waimea. He decided to come visit.

TAKAMURA: He knows who I am.

(Pause.)

TAKAMURA: Sumiko wrote you, didn't she?

(Beat.)

YACHIYO: What did she write you Willie? Willie?

WILLIE *(to* TAKAMURA*)*: She told you?

(Pause. TAKAMURA *watches him.)*

TAKAMURA: No.

(During the following TAKAMURA *gets in* WILLIE'S *face.)*

TAKAMURA: Did she write that Yachiyo is getting quite formidable in the tea ceremony? Or that, that, Yachiyo is quite accomplished at mixing clays now and prepping the studio? Did she write that I'm not paying enough attention to her or, or that I gave Yachiyo this new dress? Did she write you about that?—*(Continues.)*

YACHIYO: Takamura-san, please . . .

ACT TWO

TAKAMURA *(continued; backing* WILLIE *up)*: —What's this? A bandage for the little cane field worker trying to bring the big bosses to their knees. You can't change things, little cane field worker, didn't you know that? Someone will always be above you, bigger than you, better than you Okinawa boy, putting you in your place, telling you what to do, slapping you around, beating you with a stick—

*(*WILLIE *wields* TAKAMURA *around and slams him against the wall.)*

WILLIE: SHUT UP! SHUT UP! SHUT UP!!!

YACHIYO: Willie, let him go! Willie! . . .

(The force of the banging causes the ochawan *to fall and shatter.* WILLIE *stops.* TAKAMURA *notices the broken* ochawan. *Stares at it. Then, bends down and picks up a piece.)*

WILLIE: Who the hell do you think you are anyway? Huh? Who the hell do you think you are?

*(*TAKAMURA *stares at the shard for a beat. Then digs it into his palm. Stares at the blood.)*

TAKAMURA: I don't know. I don't know anymore . . .

*(*TAKAMURA *stumbles away.)*

MAMA *(lit, to* WILLIE*)*: Willie?

WILLIE *(to* MAMA*)*: Everything's fine Matsumoto-san. Yachiyo's all right. Nothing's going on.

(Pause.)

MAMA: Good.

(Silence. WILLIE *and* MAMA *stare at each other.* WILLIE *turns to look at* YACHIYO. *Then* WILLIE *exits.* MAMA *looks at* YACHIYO, *then dims to darkness.*

YACHIYO *bends down and begins to pick up the pieces of the broken* ochawan. TAKAMURA *lit by the water. Bluish pond lights.* TAKAMURA *at the water's edge. Stares at himself in the water.* YACHIYO *enters and approaches him cautiously. She sits down next to him. She offers him a folded cloth with the pieces of the* ochawan.*)*

YACHIYO: Maybe we can piece it together. Re-glaze it. Fire it again.

(He stares at it, then looks away. YACHIYO *places it down beside him.)*

YACHIYO: I watched you here. One time. You couldn't see me. You were drunk.

(TAKAMURA *is silent.*)

YACHIYO: The eggs are beginning to hatch. The nest in the kiln? You can hear the babies calling for their mother to feed them. You were right. It's a nice sound. It helps the work.

(*Pause.*)

YACHIYO: I sent him home. Willie.

(*Silence.*)

TAKAMURA: We'll be firing soon. We may have to move the nest.

(YACHIYO *takes a cloth and pats* TAKAMURA'S *bleeding wound. At first he pulls away but eventually relents. She has her face close to his and is watching him. She works in silence for a beat. She leans forward and kisses him. He gently pushes her away.*)

YACHIYO: I thought . . . I don't understand Takamura-san.

(*Beat.*)

YACHIYO: I know you've been watching me. At night. When I go to bed. I know it's you. It doesn't matter. Hiro? I don't mind . . .

(TAKAMURA *doesn't respond.*)

YACHIYO: I thought this is what you wanted. I should have gone back with Willie. He asked me to, you know. He begged me to go back home with him.

TAKAMURA (*quietly, barely audible*): I can't. I just can't Yachiyo.

YACHIYO: What? Takamura-san, what?

TAKAMURA: I can't do this.

YACHIYO: Hiro.

TAKAMURA: You don't want this kind of thing. You don't, Yachiyo.

YACHIYO: Why not? Okusan's accused me of sleeping with you. She did, she thinks we're lovers. Now, Willie believes it, too. Why shouldn't I, then? Huh? Why shouldn't I?

(TAKAMURA *is silent.*)

TAKAMURA: Go home. Back to Willie. Back to your old life Yachiyo.

YACHIYO: I don't want to go back. I can't go back.

(YACHIYO *takes a piece of the broken* ochawan. *She digs it into the palm of her hand. Blood appears.*)

YACHIYO: Okusan was right. About the tea. I like it now. I like it a lot.

ACT TWO

(She reaches out and places her hand on his cut hand. YACHIYO *moves forward and kisses* TAKAMURA. *He embraces her. The water gradually washes over and becomes blood red. A rippling sound score, like wind over water. Fade to half-light. As they embrace,* OKUSAN *is lit. Upstage from her two dolls are lit. They mirror the embrace and movements of* YACHIYO *and* TAKAMURA. *As* OKUSAN *watches the dolls,* YACHIYO *and* TAKAMURA *fade to black.)*

OKUSAN *(watching the dolls)*: They do not move to my wishes. I cannot make the world inside my head be the world out there. I will make it move to my wishes.

*(*OKUSAN *dims to darkness. Lights up on* YACHIYO *watching the two dolls make love.)*

YACHIYO: His skin was not smooth like Willie's. It was both coarse and smooth. His face, his hands were rough. But under his arm, the back side of his thigh, his skin was like a little boy's. I would run my fingers over those places and he would laugh because it tickled him and his joy would fill me with childish pleasure. But when I touched his stomach he would grow quiet and the laughter would become thick with musty, sweet odors. And I could feel my own breath growing heavy, the air inside me a prickly heat and I would want his sex, now hard in my hand, to carry me on its swollen current.

(Dolls fade to black.)

YACHIYO: When I look in the mirror, I cannot see myself the way I used to. Just me, my face looking back at me. My own thoughts, my own feelings. I can only see myself through his eyes now. How does he see this face? How do I look to him? Am I pretty enough? I cannot tell where my face ends and his eyes begin. *(*TAKAMURA *lit. He moves in behind her.)*

YACHIYO: And when he touches me, I want his hands to grow into my body, taking hold, sending roots deep into my flesh. Each touch a new root pushing into the deepest part of me, taking hold, so we would always be together, nothing could ever separate us.

*(*TAKAMURA *withdraws.)*

YACHIYO: I am in pain and yet it is so pleasurable. At times I cannot think, I cannot breathe. And to be apart from him for even an instant feels as if time has stopped and I am only waiting, waiting. Until he is there again and I can breathe. I wish it would stop, this feeling. I wish it would never end.

(TAKAMURA *lit at the small test kiln. Hurriedly opening it and taking out the pots. They are still hot and he tosses one after another aside, as they are not good.* YACHIYO *finds one and stares at it.* TAKAMURA *takes out a red cloth and wipes it off. Holds it up and stares at it with satisfaction.*)

TAKAMURA: Yachiyo, look!

(*As* YACHIYO *is about to move towards* TAKAMURA, OKUSAN *is lit.* TAKAMURA *sees* OKUSAN. *Wraps the pot in the red cloth and reluctantly hands it to her.* OKUSAN *stares at the pot, then at* YACHIYO *and* TAKAMURA.)

OKUSAN: I'm beginning to understand.

(TAKAMURA *and* OKUSAN *fade to black.*

YACHIYO *moves into another light. Loud, rhythmic sound. Feeling is fast paced, hurried with no sentimentality.*

MAMA *and* PAPA *lit.* WILLIE *lit playing Hana. He slaps the cards down and makes loud exclamatory sounds.* OSUGI *lit doing housework.*)

MAMA: Yachiyo?

PAPA: Yachiyo?

OSUGI: Yachiyo?

WILLIE: *Chikusho* [dammit].

MAMA: Yachiyo.

PAPA: I started writing poems again.

MAMA: We haven't heard from you.

PAPA: Mama doesn't know.

OSUGI: The Shimokawa girl.

MAMA: How are you?

PAPA: They aren't half bad.

OSUGI: She go so far.

MAMA: Papa and I were talking.

PAPA: You stay there. Study—(*Continues.*)

MAMA (*overlapping*): Maybe you should come home . . .

ACT TWO

PAPA *(continued)*: —Tea, flower arrangement . . .

OSUGI: Cannot come back.

MAMA: Yachiyo.

WILLIE: Yamaguchi . . .

PAPA: Yachiyo.

WILLIE: He's siding . . .

OSUGI: Yachiyo.

WILLIE: With the company bosses . . .

> *(Pause.)*

MAMA: Are you friendly with Mr. Takamura?

WILLIE: CHIKUSHO!!! . . .

> *(Sound punctuation. They all move hurriedly past* YACHIYO *as she attempts to talk to them. They quickly cross and exit, leaving her alone.* TAKAMURA *enters. Distracted.)*

YACHIYO: Hiro?

TAKAMURA: Not now, not now—we have work to do. Is the clay prepared? I'm going to try some new designs . . .

> *(They work in silence. Yachiyo watches* TAKAMURA. *He notices her staring.)*

TAKAMURA: Stop doing that.

YACHIYO: What?

TAKAMURA: You're looking at me. Staring at me.

YACHIYO *(aside)*: I can't help myself. I find myself watching him all the time. It's as if I have no control over myself. And the more he tells me not to look, the more I must watch him, as if my eyes had their own hunger . . .

> *(They work in silence.)*

YACHIYO: Do you think about going back to Japan?

> *(No response.)*

YACHIYO: I wouldn't mind going there.

> *(No response.)*

YACHIYO: Your pottery has become so good. Okusan said so. You could be famous. More famous than your father. Maybe he would take you back if you showed him some of your pots. You could return home. I would go back with you Hiro—

TAKAMURA: My father is dead.

YACHIYO: I don't understand. You said he was still alive—

TAKAMURA: He's dead and so am I. Now leave me alone, I need to work.

> (OKUSAN *is lit doing the tea ceremony.* YACHIYO *moves over and joins her.*)

OKUSAN: You turn it two times.

YACHIYO *(seating herself)*: What?

OKUSAN: You turn it two times, not three.

> (YACHIYO *turns it two times, then drinks in several sips of the thick, astringent tea. Then, silence.*)

OKUSAN: Takamura-san is working so hard these days.

YACHIYO: He is not nice to me.

OKUSAN: When he works, he is happy. I have you to thank for that. Don't I.

YACHIYO: What do you mean?

OKUSAN: When Takamura-san is happy, I am happy. And he is happy now.

> (*Holds pot up. Admires it.*)

OKUSAN: He made it in the smaller test kiln. It is his best piece, yet. You cannot tell, can you? It is quite beautiful.

YACHIYO: Pots. That's all he cares about. This damn pottery. Day and night, night and day.

> (*Pause.*)

YACHIYO: Why is he ignoring me now? What did I do?

> (OKUSAN *doesn't respond, continues looking at the pot.*)

YACHIYO: I'm sick of this pottery. And this damn tea ceremony, too.

> (YACHIYO *exits angrily.* OKUSAN *is alone.*)

OKUSAN: You did everything you could be expected to do. But now. Now he needs something more.

> (*Holding pot, quietly smiling to herself. Dim to darkness.* PAPA *lit.*)

PAPA: Yachiyo. Mama finally put her foot down. She made me go to Hamada's store to talk about our . . . money problem. You know how I hate that kind of thing, having to argue with people. It wasn't so bad. Hamada was actually understanding of our situation with me not working right now. When I happened to mention I was writing poetry he asked if I could write letters for him. I said, "What, Hamada-san you can write." He said, "No, for the workers. Love letters."

(MAMA *lit in pool of light working.* YACHIYO *lit.*)

YACHIYO: Mama?

(MAMA *stops and looks towards* YACHIYO. *Continuation of the earlier scene.*)

YACHIYO: Yes. I am friendly with Mr. Takamura.

PAPA: *Sensei*—that's what the workers call me. "Sensei, tell her I've got muscles as hard as stone, can work a twenty-four-hour day and that we won't have to live down below, but high on the hill in a huge house above the lunas, or even the plantation boss! Make her want me so badly, she'll swim here!" . . . I write letters for the workers who want wives back in Japan. They send pictures and exchange letters. And they pay me for my services. Not a lot, Hamada gets a percentage. But I'm working. Mama is happy. Mama?

YACHIYO: Mama?

(*Pause.*)

YACHIYO: I love him.

MAMA: Yachiyo . . .

(*Fade to black.* TAKAMURA *and* OKUSAN *lit.*)

TAKAMURA (*upset*): I don't know, I don't know— My father was right.

OKUSAN: Hiro . . .

TAKAMURA: What if the clays can't hold this type of heat, they didn't even work in the test kiln—

OKUSAN: It worked, it worked, you made your best piece—

TAKAMURA: But everything else cracked—was it the clay, the heat, the kiln, I'm not even sure what I did to make that one pot? And the *nobori-gama* is totally different. Much more complicated. What if the angle is all wrong? We've wasted all these months building a useless kiln, your father's money all used up on this—(*Continues.*)

OKUSAN (*overlapping*): Hiro! Hiro, listen to me . . .

TAKAMURA (*continued*): —goddamn kiln that won't even fire . . .

(*Pause.*)

OKUSAN: It's all right, don't worry. It will work. I know you can do it.

TAKAMURA: I keep seeing his face watching me, my father's face. I become paralyzed. I can't do it, I just can't do it . . .

(TAKAMURA *breaks down;* OKUSAN *comforts him like a small boy.*)

OKUSAN: He's not here. It's not important what he thinks. I will help you . . .

(TAKAMURA *and* OKUSAN *dim to half-light.* YACHIYO *lit.* YACHIYO *sees* OKUSAN *comforting* TAKAMURA *like a small crying child. She is confused to see* TAKAMURA *acting so uncharacteristically. And seeking comfort with* OKUSAN. YACHIYO *approaches them.*)

YACHIYO: Hiro? Hiro, what's the matter? Hiro?

OKUSAN (*waving her away*): Yachiyo . . .

YACHIYO (*persisting*): Hiro? It's me, Yachiyo. Are you all right? Hiro?

TAKAMURA (*angrily*): Get out! Get out of here!

(YACHIYO, *confused, withdraws. Dim to darkness on* OKUSAN *comforting* TAKAMURA. YACHIYO *lit by the kiln.*)

YACHIYO (*upset*): Sometimes I would awaken at night, go to the mirror and stare at myself. In that world of shadows and dream I would recreate . . .

(*Pause, thinking.*)

YACHIYO: Recreate . . .

(*The male and female dolls are lit making love.*)

YACHIYO: . . . and he loved her very deeply . . .

(YACHIYO *watches them for a moment.*)

YACHIYO: Yes. Just like that.

(MAMA *lit. Continuation of the earlier sequence.*)

MAMA: You, *what*? You "love him"?

YACHIYO: Mama . . .

(*Pause.*)

MAMA: Your Papa, his family was so against our marriage. I didn't come from a good family, wasn't trained in the arts the way young girls are supposed to be. Papa didn't care. He married me anyway. I went to live with his family. They all looked down their noses at me. Especially the sisters, oh, his two older sisters . . . Papa could tell how much I hated being treated like that. Finally, he decided—and he made up his own mind— that we would come here and start all over. He came first, then soon after called me over. Left his family, the life he knew, so I could be happy. He did that for me.

(*Beat.*)

MAMA: "You love him" . . . He's married Yachiyo. What's this man going to do for you?

(*Pause.*)

MAMA: Are you sleeping with him? Yachiyo?

YACHIYO: I want to come home. Can I come home? Mama?

(*Pause.*)

MAMA: If you want to.

(YACHIYO *dims to half-light.* PAPA *lit.*)

PAPA: Since I started doing all his business correspondence we can have anything we want at the store now. I'm practically handling all his negotiations—a whole new line of things from Japan and from San Francisco. Hamada said we can even order the Singer sewing machines . . .

(*He moves to* MAMA.)

PAPA: Did you hear what I said? Are you upset with me? We paid everything off—

MAMA: Do you still think about going back? To Japan?

PAPA: What?

MAMA: Do you regret coming here?

PAPA: I'm working again, it's more suited to what I can do. I'm good at it. And we don't have to ask my sisters for any more help.

MAMA: Hisao?

(*Pause.*)

PAPA: Yes. I do regret it.

(PAPA *and* MAMA *fade to black.*
YACHIYO *lit by the water. In half-light we see* OKUSAN *putting the dolls into the kiln's first wood-burning chamber.*)

YACHIYO: I missed my period again.

(OKUSAN *moves away.*

YACHIYO *takes the cloth from between her legs and washes it in the water. There is no blood.* YACHIYO *frantically washes the cloth in hopes that it will show a trace of blood. Sound of birds.)*

YACHIYO: I love the sound. The mother bird comes and goes bringing food to the babies. I think we will be firing the kiln soon so we will have to move the nest.

(TAKAMURA *lit, working.* YACHIYO *approaches* TAKAMURA.*)*

YACHIYO: Hiro.

TAKAMURA: Not now, Yachiyo.

YACHIYO: Hiro, I have to—

TAKAMURA: Prepare some mortar so we can seal up the doors on the upper chambers—

YACHIYO: Takamura!

(Pause.)

YACHIYO: You have to stop this. Stop ignoring me. You have to start paying attention to me. Like you used to.

TAKAMURA: I don't have time for this now, there're so many things I have to—

YACHIYO: I'm pregnant.

(Silence. TAKAMURA *goes back to work.)*

TAKAMURA: I've got work to do. I have to ready everything.

YACHIYO: What are you doing, did you hear what I said?

TAKAMURA: What do you want me to do? What? I'm married, Yachiyo.

YACHIYO: I don't care, I don't care—let's go away. Let's run away together. Osugi's parents did it. Her mother was a picture bride and didn't like her real father so she ran off with Mr. Chong, that's why she has a Pake last name and a Japanese first name—

TAKAMURA: I can't do that, I just can't do that.

YACHIYO: Why not, why can't you Hiro?

TAKAMURA: Yachiyo, look at me. Look at me. I'm not a young man.

YACHIYO: We can be happy, we'll be so happy together . . .

TAKAMURA: I ran away once before. I just can't do that anymore.

YACHIYO: We can go to the Mainland or back to Japan and you can build a pottery, start all over. We can have the baby, get married there and no one will have to know—

ACT TWO

TAKAMURA: Yachiyo! Yachiyo!

> (*Silence.*)

TAKAMURA: I'm not strong enough. I'm weak. That's always been my problem. My father knew it. He always knew it. Maybe that's why I hate him so much. This is my last chance. I need this. I need to be strong enough this time. Go back to Willie. He'll marry you.

> (*The kiln explodes with flames.*)

TAKAMURA: My god, she lit the kiln. She started the firing . . .

> (TAKAMURA *runs to the kiln where* OKUSAN *stands watching.*)

YACHIYO: The nest, the nest . . .

> (*As the kiln burns, a flaming bird soars out of it into the night air.* YACHIYO *stares in horror as the mother bird, engulfed in flames, thrashes wildly about.*)

OKUSAN: Look, look, what a glorious sight!

YACHIYO: The mother bird . . .

OKUSAN: You have to grow up now, Hiro . . .

YACHIYO: Her wings, whole body . . .

OKUSAN: . . . or you lose everything . . .

YACHIYO: . . . on fire . . .

OKUSAN: You have no time to be scared of your father.

> (*Looking at the flames.*)

OKUSAN: This is my gift to you.

> (TAKAMURA *stares at* OKUSAN *for a beat. Then runs up and pulls a plug out of a kiln portal opening and looks at the flame.*)

TAKAMURA: The wood we stocked in earlier seems to be allowing the fire to burn correctly. The pull seems a little strong up the center. We need some smaller, hotter burning wood for the edges—it'll help pull the flame to the sides. Yachiyo, more wood! Sumiko, make the mortar so we can shut the sixth and seventh chambers!

> (*As* YACHIYO *watches,* SUMIKO *turns and stares at her. For a moment* YACHIYO *returns the look. Then, she slowly moves away. The kiln flames die and the scene fades to black on* TAKAMURA *and* OKUSAN. TAKAMURA *glances back at* YACHIYO *as he dims to darkness.*)

YACHIYO: And he loved her very deeply. He loved her very deeply.

(A night sky. A moon.)

YACHIYO: I walked all night. Through the reddish soil. By early morning I had reached Mana.

WILLIE *(lit, returning from a night of drinking and gambling)*: What are you doing here?

YACHIYO: I've come back home. I missed you.

WILLIE: Things have been busy, yeah. That's why I haven't written. Some of the Japanese and Filipinos are starting a new union. Yamaguchi and I have to keep an eye on them. For the company bosses.

(Beat.)

WILLIE: I'm making good money now.

(Pause.)

YACHIYO: Willie? Let's get married.

(WILLIE doesn't respond.)

Willie? Please . . .

(Instead of responding, WILLIE moves to embrace her. He is rough, forcing himself on her. YACHIYO pushes him away.)

WILLIE: You let him, didn't you?

(Pause.)

WILLIE: All right. I'll marry you.

(YACHIYO doesn't respond.)

WILLIE: I said I'll marry you.

(Silence.)

YACHIYO *(quiety)*: No . . .

(WILLIE withdraws.)

YACHIYO: . . . to preserve her family's honor. To save face for herself and her parents. Because there was nothing else for her to do . . .

(Upstage MAMA and PAPA lit in half-light, sleeping. YACHIYO stares at bluish watery pool of lights that appears before her. The watery lights begin to move over her.)

YACHIYO: Polihale Beach. The sun is just beginning to rise. The water. It's like a mirror. I will see the world from the other side. Through her eyes. I enter the water and swim out far beyond the breaking waves. My arms ache and my legs already weary

from walking all night begin to cramp. But I continue to push
out until the shore appears a distant shadow.
  (Noticing.)
YACHIYO: The sun . . .
  (YACHIYO watches the sun breaking the horizon.)
YACHIYO: And then I dive. Deep beneath the surface.
  (Lights and sound.)
YACHIYO: My face feeling the cold lick of salt and wetness. Deeper
and deeper, straining my arms, kicking with my legs. Forcing
myself to go farther and farther down. The water is bone-
chilling, blackness everywhere, my air running out. Still I push
myself down, down—I must go so far. So far that I cannot come
back . . .
  *(Pause. Realizing she has no air left. Panicking, changing her
  mind. Overhead a light appears, representing the surface above.
  Sound cue builds through this.)*
YACHIYO: No air, no air left, I'm choking, suffocating—I have
to get back to the surface, I need to breathe, I need to breathe
so badly I can feel my face about to explode. I see the sunlight
entering from above. Cutting through the water like long transparent knives. I want them to cut me open, peel me out of my
skin so whatever is me, whatever is wanting, needing to breathe
so badly can get out . . .
  *(Struggling fiercely. Black out. Deep, echoing crash. MAMA and
  PAPA sleeping in half-light begin to stir.)*
PAPA: Yachiyo? Yachiyo?
MAMA: What is it Papa?
PAPA: Yachiyo, is that you? Yachiyo . . .
  *(YACHIYO lit. Light goes from warm to a brighter and brighter
  light.)*
YACHIYO: Lately I feel so many things. Sometimes I feel I am
going to burst. It is not a bad feeling, but it makes me con-
fused. I'm always expecting something to happen. Something
new. Something good.
  *(Light is tightly focused, a very intense white light. Very slow fade
  to black on YACHIYO. As YACHIYO fades to black, TAKAMURA*

lit at the kiln pulling the bricks out of a chamber door. In a pool of half-light, OKUSAN *is lit watching him.*
As TAKAMURA *takes out the pots, one after the other, they are all extraordinary in their complexity and humanness.)*

TAKAMURA *(staring at the pots)*: My god . . . They're beautiful . . .
*(*TAKAMURA *embraces the pot and bows his head in despair.* OKUSAN *holds up a pot and stares at it. She smiles and begins to hum a lullaby to herself.* YACHIYO, *who has dimmed to half-light, pulses for a beat to brightness, petals falling around her.*
Light quickly fades to black.)
Super titles appear:

DEDICATED TO THE MEMORY OF YACHIYO GOTANDA
1902–1919

[END OF PLAY]

Under the Rainbow, a Play of Two One Acts
Number 3 in the series "the garage band plays"

Author's thanks to Diane Takei, John Lew, Kathy Lu, Dr. Roland Minami, Prof. Neil Gotanda, Prof. Lisa Ikemoto, Prof. Karen Shimakawa, Campo Santo + Intersection, Locus Arts, Annette Koh, Julia Kim, Tim Yamamura, Danny Wolohan, and Rania Ho. Special thanks to Carl Mulert and the Joyce Ketay Agency.

Curtain Raiser
"In Praise of Yellow Women"

Under the Rainbow, a Play of Two One Acts had its world premiere at the Asian American Theater Company, San Francisco, in 2005.

DIRECTOR: Philip Kan Gotanda

NATALIE WOOD IS DEAD

CAST –
Kiyoko Dalhauser: Diane Emiko Takei
Natalie Hayashi: Pearl Wong
A Man: Danny Wolohan

WHITE MANIFESTO, or, GOT RICE?

Richard Saugus: Danny Wolohan

Woman #1 Prize Show Girl: Suzi Takeda
Woman #2 Prize Show Girl: Pearl Wong

Lighting Design: Heather Basarab
Costumes: Lucy Karanfilian
Original Music/Sound: Yvette Janine Jackson
Movement: Erika Chong Shuch
Stage Manager: Sunnia Eastwood
Assistant Director: Wesley Wu

PLAY ONE

Natalie Wood Is Dead

For Nobu McCarthy

Characters

KIYOKO DALHAUSER
NATALIE HAYASHI
A MAN

Time

June 2001

Place

Burbank

KIYOKO *helps* NATALIE *bring in her luggage.* KIYOKO *is in her mid-sixties and done-up, almost overly done-up.* NATALIE, *in her early thirties, has no makeup on and is dressed casually for traveling.*

KIYOKO: You look horrible, didn't you drink water like I told you? Lottsa and lottsa water . . .
    *(*NATALIE *goes to the couch and collapses.)*
KIYOKO: . . . and I carry a spritzer for my skin. Only problem is if you sit in the middle or next to the window, then you have to keep getting up to go to the bathroom . . .
NATALIE: I slept.
KIYOKO: You have to climb over everyone, I hate that.
NATALIE: I slept.
KIYOKO: What was the movie?
    *(*KIYOKO *notices* NATALIE'S *stare, goes to put her coat away.)*
KIYOKO *(as she walks away)*: I heard they lower the oxygen. In the plane, to make you sleepy.
NATALIE: It's the opposite of the casinos. They pump oxygen in, to wake you up. No clocks. Day is night. Night is day. People

in bed when they should be out working and out working when they should be in bed.

(NATALIE *takes off her shoes and puts her feet up.*)

NATALIE: It's great for the dancers, though. The oxygen. You never get tired. Keeps you from cramping up, too. You know, just dancing the night away . . .

(KIYOKO *brings* NATALIE *a glass of water. She stands over her and downs her own glass in one gulp.* NATALIE *watches, then puts her glass aside.*)

KIYOKO *(examining)*: Let me get a good look at you.

NATALIE: What?

KIYOKO: We're going to have to get you a facial and on some kind of skin regime.

NATALIE: I've been in a plane for the last six hours, how do you expect me to look?

KIYOKO *(touches under cheek)*: You look fat, too.

NATALIE: Mom . . .

KIYOKO: You watching your diet? And I still think your tits are too small. Even for a dancer. Though I like the nose and I'm glad you did that. Oriental noses . . . jeez, like their tits except there's only one . . .

NATALIE: Got anything to drink? *(Notices* KIYOKO'S *look)* No, like a soda or something . . .

(KIYOKO *grabs the glass of water and holds it out to her.* NATALIE *relents and takes a sip.*)

KIYOKO: Well, I'm glad you're back dear. This is where you belong, not way over there. You weren't doing topless, were you?

NATALIE: No.

KIYOKO: Good, those things catch up with you. You know who I saw while shopping? Carol Baker. I'd like to know her surgeon.

NATALIE: Why didn't you ask her?

KIYOKO: I did, she ignored me. You don't mind sleeping there, do you? This place isn't big like our old house. It's good enough, though. And what doesn't kill you can only make you stronger.

(KIYOKO *goes and retrieves a small bottle.*)

NATALIE *(repeats, overlapping)*: —Yeah, make you stronger,

yeah . . . And the good die young, Humpty Dumpty sat on a wall, bend over and see the world . . .

(KIYOKO *returns with the bottle.*)

KIYOKO: A new line. Just came out. They sent it overnight express. I asked them to. No one has it in America yet.

NATALIE: It's probably illegal . . .

KIYOKO *(ignoring)*: Always let them think you're eager and ready to do anything and you get special treatment. You'll have so much energy you'll never get depressed.

NATALIE *(sipping water)*: I don't want any.

KIYOKO: You tried some.

(*Nodding to her cup of water.*)

NATALIE: Don't do that, okay?

KIYOKO: How do you feel?

(NATALIE *puts her glass down.*)

NATALIE: You always do that.

KIYOKO: How do you feel?

NATALIE *(thinking)*: Six years old.

KIYOKO: So what are your plans?

NATALIE: Mommy? I just got here. May I have permission to go to the pee-pee room?

(NATALIE *gets up and moves towards the hall to go to the bathroom.*)

KIYOKO: I know but I figured you must have made some plans. Have you talked to anyone about getting an agent? Or maybe Harry Edelstein will take you back.

NATALIE: No. Let me at least unpack, all right?

KIYOKO: Web sites.

(NATALIE *closes the door and locks it.*)

NATALIE *(calling through the door)*: What?

KIYOKO: Everybody's got 'em. I'm building one. A kid in the building is helping me. We need to build one for you, too. You have a lot of catching up. Oh, and everything's global—global, global, global—I'm studying French. "Dis donc où est la bibliothèque?"

(KIYOKO *begins to ease towards the bathroom door.*)

KIYOKO: Harry sent me out on the audition for a spaghetti western. Only it was a detective story. A spaghetti film noir. Only it was Chinese, so it was a chow fun-film noir. The director and producers were there—there was Chinese, Italian, English, everything flying around and they just shoot it and dub it in later depending on the country—*(Continues.)*

*(*KIYOKO *now has her ear pressed against the door, listening.)*

KIYOKO *(continued)*: —they release it all over the world, east is west, west is east . . .

NATALIE *(calling from inside)*: Black is white . . .

KIYOKO: It's an amazing time . . .

NATALIE *(calling)*: Everything's mud . . .

KIYOKO: It's all converging.

NATALIE *(calling)*: Why are you studying French?

KIYOKO: You never know.

NATALIE: What?

KIYOKO: "Dis donc où est la bibliothèque?" . . .

NATALIE: What?

*(*KIYOKO *whips the door open.)*

NATALIE: Ahhh! Jesus, what the hell you doing Mom?

KIYOKO *(closing door)*: Just checking.

(Hear flushing.)

NATALIE *(emerging, pulling up her pants)*: What? You fixed the lock, didn't you? So it wouldn't lock.

KIYOKO: You're my baby, I love you, I only want the best for you.

NATALIE: Don't do that, don't do that, okay?

KIYOKO: When's the rest of your things coming?

NATALIE: Don't do that, Mom.

KIYOKO: Hmmm?

*(*NATALIE *gives up.)*

NATALIE: I said I'd tell them when I found a place.

KIYOKO: You can stay here as long as you like Natalie.

NATALIE: I'm not even sure I want to do all that stuff anymore.

(No response.)

NATALIE: Hear what I said?

KIYOKO: We'll talk about that later.

NATALIE: I'll find a place right away. I won't be in your way.

KIYOKO: Mr. Taniguchi said a two bedroom might be opening up. *(Beat)* I was glad to hear you were dancing again. I'd have come to see you if I'd known.

NATALIE: It's a long flight, I wouldn't recommend it.

(Beat.)

KIYOKO: That's why I thought when you said you were moving back . . . That's what you wanted to do again. Or maybe try acting again . . .

NATALIE: I just took the dancing gig because it paid well. *(Beat)* Trying? I wasn't trying acting. I was acting, okay? And you make it sound like I gave up, I didn't quit, I stopped, that's a big difference. Okay? Most people quit 'cause they can't get work but I was getting work, I just got tired of doing the work I was getting. Besides I'd just get fucked in the end . . .

(KIYOKO stares at NATALIE.)

KIYOKO: I don't want to get into this now. *(Beat)* And that movie was a good movie—who gives a shit what a bunch of these political assholes think? Okay, it was a so-so movie. But it was a good career move.

(Silence.)

KIYOKO: How are you going to make a living then? What you going to do?

(NATALIE sits down, exhausted.)

NATALIE: Some more dancing maybe, I don't know.

KIYOKO: At least I didn't waste money on all those lessons. You better lose some weight, though. And we have to do something about your hair. We should lighten it up. Go blonde, maybe . . . It limits what you go out for, but at your age maybe it's better to make one strong statement so if there is someone out there who wants that particular look, you'll stick out like a sore thumb.

(Beat.)

KIYOKO: I want to show you something.

(KIYOKO pulls up her blouse.)

KIYOKO: See.

NATALIE: Oh, Mom . . .

KIYOKO: They don't droop anymore.

NATALIE: Fine, fine, put them away.

KIYOKO: Same doctor did Racquel Welch's tits.

NATALIE: Oh, jeez . . .

KIYOKO: That's what you have to do. Let's see yours.

NATALIE: No, no, mine are fine.

KIYOKO: They're like mosquito bites.

NATALIE: My breasts are fine.

KIYOKO: How you going to compete with all these young girls, you're not an ingénue anymore. Look, I did a movie last year, it's coming out this month. Know why I got it?
    (Shows her breasts again.)

NATALIE: Oh god, you didn't . . .

KIYOKO: No, no, of course not—they wanted an older woman, but see, they don't really want an older woman. They want an older woman with breasts up high, firm ass, slender thighs, dark hair, smooth skin—and I, your mother, me, got the role.

NATALIE: I'm happy for you . . .

KIYOKO: Stand up, let's see your ass. You're a dancer so it's got a longer shelf life . . .
    *(*NATALIE *hides her head in the cushions. We hear a muffled scream.)*

KIYOKO: You all right?

NATALIE: I just need some food in my stomach.

KIYOKO: You sure you should be eating?

NATALIE: I want to eat!

KIYOKO: We can go down the street and eat some Chinese.

NATALIE: Can't we have a home-cooked meal? Like everyone else, Jesus Christ . . .

KIYOKO: I work all day, then I have to rush home to meet my daughter who I haven't seen in two years and then she says, "Can't we have a home cooked meal?"

NATALIE: All right, all right, I'm sorry. Then let's order in.

KIYOKO: You have to wash dishes. You have to *have* dishes.

NATALIE: Okay, okay—we'll go out, just let me rest for a bit.
    *(*KIYOKO *tries to look at* NATALIE'S *butt.)*

NATALIE: It's not sagging and it's not too big.
    *(*NATALIE *settles back on the couch and covers her eyes with her arm.)*

NATALIE WOOD IS DEAD

KIYOKO: So how was Atlantic City?

    (No response.)

KIYOKO: Was it fun?

NATALIE: Disneyland for grown-ups. No one grows old and no one dies. And if you can afford the e-ticket, you can have anything you want.

KIYOKO: I wouldn't know. I've never been. No one's ever invited me.

NATALIE: You're either winning or losing. No gray areas. There's something perversely comforting about knowing your place on the food chain. Cute little minnow swimming along, chomp, eaten by a perch, chomp, eaten by a bass, chomp, eaten by a— *(Continues.)*

KIYOKO *(overlapping)*: That's cause you've accepted losing and you're a winner.

NATALIE *(continued)*: —tuna, chomp, eaten by a shark, chomp, chomp, chomp . . .

KIYOKO: You're a winner, come on, come on say it—"I am a winner. Natalie Hayashi is a winner." Come on, come on baby. "Natalie Hayashi is a winner. Her mother's a winner and she's a winner. Natalie Hayashi is a winner." Please? Natalie?

NATALIE: Why?

KIYOKO: Please, please . . .

    (Pause.)

NATALIE *(quietly)*: Natalie Hayashi . . .

KIYOKO *(coaxing)*: . . . is a winner.

NATALIE: . . . is dead. I'm going back to my real name. I'm not using Natalie Hayashi anymore.

KIYOKO: Natalie Hayashi is not dead, she just forgot how to believe in herself. And how to do the things she needs to do to allow herself to believe in herself. It's something that you have to keep working on yesterday, today and tomorrow, 'cause others are, who aren't as lazy, who are younger—

NATALIE: With perkier tits and tighter asses—

KIYOKO: Yes and hungrier and who are getting ahead of you even as we speak. It's not funny, it's the way things are in this town . . .

NATALIE: There's nothing wrong with growing old, you know.

KIYOKO: Yes there is.

NATALIE: See, that's what's so goddamn fucked up about this place. Can't I be happy growing old? My butt sagging, my tits drooping, it's what happens.

KIYOKO: Not if you got a good surgeon . . .

NATALIE: We all die in the end.

KIYOKO: Yes, but do you have to grow old?

NATALIE: Maybe getting old and dying *is* living. It's a process. A state of becoming.

KIYOKO: What, a prune?

NATALIE: It's just this young girl thing that's got us all cutting up our bodies, sucking fat out and god knows what else, pumping synthetic fluids into our breasts, injecting poison into our foreheads—has anyone thought that to truly live life is to feel that very process we're trying to run away from. Know it, intimately, without disturbing its natural course from beginning to the bitter, bitter end.

KIYOKO: So when you get there, what? You got there first, you win? I want to live life as long as I can and look good as long as I'm living. You didn't die of polio, did you? Know why?

NATALIE: 'Cause I had my nose done?

KIYOKO: Advances in science, that's why you're alive. What, turn your back on them? Better living through cosmetic surgery. *(Opens a small bottle and downs it.)*

KIYOKO: And herbal chemistry. Placenta of birthing Kobe cows . . .

NATALIE: Yuck . . . That's not an herb.

KIYOKO: They eat grass.

(KIYOKO *flicks off lights. Blackness.)*

KIYOKO: See that?

NATALIE: See what?

(Lights come up.)

KIYOKO: That's my point. Eternal night. And that's where you want to be? It's coming, believe me it's coming and you or I can't stop it. But while the sun is out, enjoy it as long as you humanly and surgically can—run around Natalie, take off your clothes, show off your tits, flash those beautiful legs, get laid. 'Cause it's going to be pitch black sooner than you know it.

NATALIE WOOD IS DEAD

(Turns the dial and slowly takes it to darkness. Flicks it back on.)

KIYOKO: That was for dramatic effect. *(Noticing the lighting, playing with it)* We can do play readings here . . .

NATALIE: Maybe I'll bleach my skin, you know they do it in Korea. To make themselves lighter.

KIYOKO: I never heard of them doing that . . .

NATALIE: It must be a universal thing—Blacks have high yellow, Latinos, coffee con leche—

KIYOKO: And the *grays* have Michael Jackson. What, just because I used some visual aids, now you're being sarcastic . . .

NATALIE: Oh am I? They're getting into the DNA now. Genomics? Proteomics? Why bother later when you can start sooner? Let's bypass Kiyoko Dalhauser, that's an old, imperfect model. And while we're at it, that Natalie Hayashi blueprint doesn't work either, needs a higher nose, double eyelids, longer legs—

KIYOKO: Your legs are fine—

NATALIE: Bigger bust, blonder hair, lighter skin, skinnier frame, and oh, the mother, the way her brain works, let's go into there and do some genetic tinkering so it's more linear and less exponentially expansive . . .

KIYOKO: Now you're going too far, messing with my brain, it's fine just the way it is. 'Course if you can actually rejuvenate the brain cells . . .

NATALIE: I'm not being sarcastic, I'm not. But where does it stop, huh? Where?

KIYOKO: You're talking about the extreme. You're taking what is good now and extending it so far down the road that anything is bad by then. It's like giving rats doses a million times more than what humans would take and saying, "Look, the rat died"—of course it did, it drowned.

NATALIE: What are you talking about?

KIYOKO: That was a bad one, let me try again—okay, what about using cars—use them and one day, what happens? Our legs will shrivel up and we won't be able to walk. Or, or, medicines—we'll conquer all disease so when aliens with runny noses land, we won't have any defenses and all die.

NATALIE: That's *War of the Worlds'* plot, but mixed up . . .

KIYOKO: It was late, I was falling asleep. Okay, okay, I got it. How about this? If we keep messing around with all this scientific stuff, one day everyone will be beautiful, happy, smart, rich and have nice-looking feet. Now. What the hell's wrong with that? Huh? What the hell's wrong with that? You ever look at people when you walk down the street? You ever look at the people on Jerry Springer? What's wrong with making people beautiful, happy, smart, rich and with nice feet? I'll take it. I'll take half of that, just beautiful with nice feet. Where do I go to be destroyed by being too perfect? Bring it on, bring on the science.

(KIYOKO's cell phone vibrates. Looks at it. Moves away.)

KIYOKO: I have to take this call . . .

(KIYOKO takes the call.)

NATALIE: I was talking to this guy. He asked me—

(MAN appears.)

MAN: What would you do if I gave you a million dollars?

(NATALIE stares at him. MAN withdraws.)

NATALIE: I told him I'd buy a plane that ran on moonlight, wind. That was soundless as night and never had to land. I'd bathe in the rain clouds, dry myself on the morning sun. And I'd only wear white.

KIYOKO *(on cell phone, calling to* NATALIE*)*: What would you live on? And whatever it is, not too much.

NATALIE: Melted snow water from Tibetan mountains. Mangoes from the island of Kauai. And when I was done with them I'd throw the seeds overboard in my wake and not even think about it. And when I died and the plane touched down, you would know where I'd been by following the trail of sprouting mango trees. From there, all the way to here . . .

(KIYOKO returns. Stares at NATALIE.)

KIYOKO: You on something?

NATALIE: It's just how I'm feeling. I want a soft landing.

KIYOKO: Natalie?

NATALIE: I'm not on anything.

KIYOKO: 'Cause if you are I want you to tell me right now and we can deal with it.

NATALIE: No. I'm not. I'm just tired, I haven't slept too well . . .

NATALIE WOOD IS DEAD

KIYOKO: You slept on the plane.

NATALIE: I take it back, you don't sleep on planes, you lie in a state of suspended agitation. I was cranky when I got here, now I've reached "pissed off."

KIYOKO: You're not pissed off, you're just dehydrated.

NATALIE: I'm pissed off!

(KIYOKO *picks up the glass of unfinished water.*)

KIYOKO: Drink, drink.

(KIYOKO *holding cup out. Long pause.* NATALIE *takes it, drinks some and hands it back.* KIYOKO *downs the rest. Pulls out driving gloves.*)

KIYOKO *(slipping them on)*: Work calls.

NATALIE: I thought you quit when you started the vitamin line?

KIYOKO: I never "quit" anything. *Stopped?*

(NATALIE *stares.*)

NATALIE: Okay. I thought you *stopped.*

KIYOKO: Not yet—it's easy work and the hours flexible in case I have an audition. And the old farts all remember me from my heyday as a Tokyo teen model and get a kick out of being driven around by Kiyoko Uesugi. They even ask for my autograph. Cool, huh.

NATALIE: Yeah, cool . . .

(KIYOKO *stops at the door.*)

KIYOKO: A pizza. Order a pizza. You can eat out of the box with your hands.

(*Blackout.*

Night. NATALIE *watching a video of* Geisha Boy, *half-eaten pizza sits in an opened box. A bottle of Skyy vodka and a glass sit next to her.* NATALIE *hears the door and puts the bottle and glass under the table.* NATALIE *has had a few drinks but is not drunk.* KIYOKO *enters and sits down next to her. She's wearing a chauffeur's cap.*)

KIYOKO: I'm surprised you're still up. What time is it, you're three hours ahead, right?

NATALIE: What's in that stuff you gave me?

KIYOKO: Good stuff, huh.

(KIYOKO *takes out a bottle of pills.*)

NATALIE: Well, it's about six in the morning my time and I feel like running a marathon. I've been trying to get myself to come down.

KIYOKO: Here . . .

NATALIE: What is it?

(Offering her some pills. Downs some herself.)

KIYOKO: Kava-kava.

NATALIE: Oh, I like kava-kava . . .

*(*KIYOKO *downs a few. They look at the video playing.)*

KIYOKO: I haven't seen this one in a while. Where'd you find it?

NATALIE: In one of the boxes.

KIYOKO: Oh yeah, I picked up a bunch of my films on video.

NATALIE: God, when did you make this, you've got a great figure.

KIYOKO: I still do.

NATALIE: Jerry Lewis's hair never changes, how does he do that?

KIYOKO: It never moves either.

(Both watching and enjoying.)

KIYOKO: My English is pretty bad. Can you understand me?

NATALIE: Not a word.

KIYOKO: But I look great.

NATALIE: I'm surprised they don't show this more often. It's funny.

KIYOKO: Oh, somebody sent me something . . .

(Grabs a book.)

KIYOKO: Hey, let me read you something. Written for an Asian American journal, published out of some college back East. Let's see . . . *(Reads)* "Geisha Boy . . . I know many people consider this a silly vehicle for Jerry Lewis. But when I saw this film, I saw myself in the small boy. And most surprising is, who does Jerry Lewis choose? He doesn't choose Marie McDonald. He chooses Kiyoko Dalhauser"—me. "The corollary to Sam Fuller's also conversely placed *Crimson Kimono*— Victoria Shaw choosing James Shigeta over Glenn Corbett. In *Geisha Boy*, Jerry Lewis chooses Dalhauser's character, Michiko Okada, over Marie McDonald. A triumphant moment of the reversal of the *Madame Butterfly* syndrome."

NATALIE: You go girl . . . Hey, I thought you said this Asian American stuff is a crock.

NATALIE WOOD IS DEAD

(KIYOKO *looks around for a tape.*)

KIYOKO *(innocently)*: I did?

NATALIE: You're awful.

KIYOKO *(finding one)*: Here, put this in—

(*5* Gates to Hell. *Machine-gun sounds and bombs going off.*)

KIYOKO: Oh, I love this one . . .

NATALIE *(moaning)*: Oh, no . . .

KIYOKO *(reads)*: . . . "And then there's *5* Gates to Hell. Kiyoko Dalhauser, half naked, machine guns in both hands, barrels blazing away against enemy soldiers. No squeamish, cowering female waiting for some man to rescue her. Sigourney Weaver in *Alien*? Hello? Kiyoko Dalhauser's Chioko was shooting aliens decades before." *(Continues.)*

(NATALIE *takes over reading while* KIYOKO *stands next to the screen basking in the compliments. She directs attention to the screen like a professional prize shower.*)

NATALIE *(continued)*: "They may appear on the surface as trivial moments in cinematic history that deserve to be discarded and lost in the dust bin of 'B' movies. But they have insinuated themselves into filmic lore and affected the course of women in cinema and in particular Asian women and perceptions of victimization and empowerment. Kiyoko Dalhauser is a hero. A cultural icon. I've seen every film and TV episode she's ever done and I'm a better human being because of it."

KIYOKO *(snatching book away)*: The rest of the article is not as interesting.

NATALIE: Not about you, huh. *(Noticing the movie)* You're pretty good.

KIYOKO: You used to hate it, machine gun mama, both barrels blazing.

NATALIE: It grows on you.

KIYOKO: Did you look at any of your tapes, they're in there, too.

NATALIE: Oh-oh, here's where you die. Ahhh . . .

(*We hear gun shots and an explosion.*)

NATALIE: Wow, was that a stunt double?

KIYOKO: Hell, no. Look how they made me die with my legs spread like that, so when they cut to Ken Scott's POV, you could see up my dress. The producer wanted that. Nowadays, I'd have to do it with no underwear. I wonder if I'd do it?

NATALIE: You'd do it.

KIYOKO: Yeah, probably.

(KIYOKO gets up and goes to the tape box and rummages through it.)

NATALIE: What wouldn't you do?

KIYOKO: When your father left us, you were about what—three, four years old. Do you remember much about that time?

NATALIE: Just a little.

KIYOKO: Do you ever remember being hungry? Or cold? Or without a place to sleep?

NATALIE: No.

KIYOKO: Know why?

NATALIE: Do I want to know?

(Returning with a tape.)

KIYOKO: See, you joke about it. But what you're really saying is that your mother would do anything, things socially unacceptable in proper company. Things beneath anything you'd ever consider. I did what I could. I did it every day, morning to night. And it was nothing to be ashamed of. It just wasn't pretty. And sometimes I was hungry. And sometimes I was cold. But you never were, were you?

NATALIE: Mom? You were a serial wife. You had three husbands— they had jobs, they had homes, they made money to buy us clothes and food.

KIYOKO: Actually it was two husbands, not counting your father—I didn't marry Warner. Yeah, you didn't know that. Sorry. I liked Warner.

(KIYOKO puts in a new video and turns it on.)

NATALIE: Yeah, he was nice.

KIYOKO: He was, wasn't he?

NATALIE: His hairpiece, though—What is this?

KIYOKO: I made a reel for you. When I heard you were coming back. He wouldn't take it off at night, until the lights were off. I'd already have my clothes off, standing there stark naked.

Warner'd be very shy, "Turn off the lights please, I have to take my hair off."

(KIYOKO *notices* NATALIE *staring at the video.*)

KIYOKO: Surprised? Pretty good, huh. The best of Natalie Hayashi. Notice the red super titles, that was my idea. Oh, your recurring part on *General Hospital* . . .

NATALIE *(watching)*: What'd you do, cut them all altogether?

KIYOKO: Un-huh. Here comes Nurse Kim . . . Here comes Nurse Kim . . . Oh-oh, here comes Nurse Kim again—oh a variation . . .

NATALIE: I thought carrying the files in front made me look more efficient . . .

KIYOKO: Oh hey, here she comes with *x-rays* now, expanding on your character, huh?

NATALIE: I had to fight for those x-rays . . .

KIYOKO: Here she comes again . . . And here you go, this is it, this is it, get ready . . . "Dr. Kennedy? Your wife had an accident. She's in a coma" . . .

NATALIE *(overlapping)*: . . . She's in a coma! . . . Yeah, yeah . . .

(They high five. NATALIE *stops and stares.)*

NATALIE: Oh, wow, oh wow . . .

KIYOKO: A special surprise . . .

NATALIE: I've never seen this . . .

KIYOKO: The pilot you did in the early nineties, *Nuns on the Run*.

NATALIE: But it was never aired. Where'd you get this?

KIYOKO: I have the only known or unknown copy in existence.

NATALIE: The network disposed of all their old tapes.

KIYOKO: A bootleg. Edelstein had a friend in the archival department at CBS and he made it just before they dumped all the backlog of unwanted tapes.

NATALIE: Oh, god, look at my hair, that's beyond big hair . . .

KIYOKO: That's an oak tree.

NATALIE: That's Rupaul's wig on steroids . . .

KIYOKO: And your bust, look, look . . .

NATALIE: They padded my bra—oh, what happened?

(The tape has skipped ahead, garbled sound.)

KIYOKO: The tape wasn't in good shape . . .

(Playing again. We hear early-nineties action TV music.)

NATALIE: See, the premise is that we're all former nuns from all over the world who've decided to give up our cloistered lives in order to fight crime. We traded in our nun's habits for mini-skirts and high heels.

KIYOKO: A white girl, a black girl, you . . .

NATALIE: That was the idea, a United Nations of nuns serving god by day, fighting crime by night.

KIYOKO: They seem to have you girls doing a lot of kicks . . .

NATALIE: The execs all thought this was going to be the hottest new thing—nuns, mini-skirts, very high kicks . . .

(Watching.)

KIYOKO: See, you're not that bad . . .

NATALIE *(nodding)*: I'm not, huh . . .

(The excerpt changes. NATALIE'S *mood suddenly turns.)*

NATALIE: Oh, no . . . turn it off.

KIYOKO: Watch, watch . . .

NATALIE: Why do you do this?

KIYOKO: Jeez, this scene is hotter than I remember it—

NATALIE: Turn it off!

*(*KIYOKO *switches it off.)*

NATALIE: You always do that.

KIYOKO: What?

NATALIE: You know I don't want to look at that.

KIYOKO: Why not?

NATALIE: Why not? You know why not.

KIYOKO: It was years ago and it's time for you to move on—

NATALIE: See, see, don't do that.

KIYOKO: What am I doing?

NATALIE: You're taking over and not letting me feel what I feel—

KIYOKO: How am I doing that for god's sake—

NATALIE: About things, things that happen to me, like that, I know what I feel, not you, let me feel what I feel about them, don't take that away from me by telling me, "It's time to move on, forget about it, it's nothing"—it's what I feel. I'll decide when it's time to move on.

NATALIE WOOD IS DEAD

(Long silence.)

KIYOKO: Okay. Well. Don't you think it is time to move on?

(NATALIE doesn't respond.)

KIYOKO: Can't you give me some credit for knowing a few things about life, just maybe, you don't know? Not that you won't know these things when you're my age, but by the sheer virtue of me living a teeny bit longer? Just a teeny bit longer, mind you.

NATALIE: Yeah, like what? What do you know?

(KIYOKO thinking.)

KIYOKO: Well . . . When you were four years old you got chicken pox and you had a bad habit of scratching them and I was worried you'd get scars so I stayed up with you for three days and nights. To make sure you didn't pick at them on your face so you'd be pretty when you grew up. Did you know that?

(Silence.)

KIYOKO: And. Let's see . . . That a week before I had you, your father left me. I lied when I said he was around. And I was so miserable and quite frankly not too good in the head that I considered killing myself and probably would have except I didn't have anything to do it with. But when you were born and they placed you on me and I looked at your tiny face, I thought, "No, this baby is special," and that from that moment on, my life could only be good.

(NATALIE reaches down and pulls out the bottle and glass and pours herself a drink.)

KIYOKO: What are you doing?

NATALIE: Trying to find an answer.

KIYOKO: Well, you won't find it in that.

NATALIE: How do you know? I mean, really, how do you know?

KIYOKO: Ahh, jeez, we're back to "what do you know that I don't know"?

(KIYOKO reaches over and drinks the glass of vodka.)

KIYOKO: There. I saved your life. That's what I know that you don't know.

NATALIE: You're happy now, aren't you?

KIYOKO: What?

NATALIE: You think you did something good for me.

KIYOKO: No, in your eyes I can never do anything good for you. Now I do good things for you for me. Totally selfish. Nothing to do with you. I saved your life and yes, I'm happy now.
(NATALIE *pours herself a drink.*)

NATALIE: Actually, I hate to burst your bubble of smugness, but I already had a drink. Several, as a matter of fact. Don't worry. I drink because I want to. Not because I have to.

KIYOKO: That's not the feeling I got before you left. Drinking, along with all that other stuff you were doing . . .

NATALIE: You know that movie.

KIYOKO: "That movie"?

NATALIE: You know that movie, *that* movie?

KIYOKO: Oh wow, it's now like *Macbeth*? *That* movie. Oh, you mean the East-Germanish one?

NATALIE: *Iron Curtain.*

KIYOKO *(looking around)*: I'm waiting for the sky to fall.

NATALIE: *Iron Curtain*, the one I did because you wanted me to.

KIYOKO: So you did a nude scene with a white guy, what's the big deal? What's the big deal? It's normal now. Asian woman with a white guy, that's what people want and if enough people do it, say it, live it, film it, it's normal. And who's to say two people, any two people can't love each other on screen, huh?

NATALIE: I agree. I never had a problem with that.

KIYOKO: Look, look at *Miss Saigon*. All those Asian hookers on stage sucking white guys' cocks and who's in the audience cheering? Orientals, Asians. Yeah, they love coming to see that shit. "It's our people!" They come in by the busloads. What's the big deal? If they want to see it, why shouldn't someone do it. And why shouldn't that someone be you. Huh. Why do you care what those political nitwits think? They obviously don't even know what their own people want. Face it, you quit. You let them get to you and you walked away.

NATALIE: That's not why I stopped. Because of that. I didn't quit 'cause I was getting so much flak from everybody for doing that scene.

KIYOKO: Then why? Why?
(*Silence.*)

NATALIE WOOD IS DEAD

KIYOKO: You should go to sleep.

NATALIE: I can't. Remember the drink?

KIYOKO *(moving to get it)*: Here's more kava-kava, and valerian if you need something stronger. It'll help you sleep.

NATALIE: Actually, I'm on casino hours, too. Day is night, night is day.

KIYOKO: I thought you came back to start over.

> *(*KIYOKO *goes into her room.* NATALIE *stands there for a beat. Picks up the remote and turns on the video of her film. She sits down and stares at it. Looks at her drink. Then back to video.* KIYOKO *emerges carrying a small battery pack with a wire that extends up to a pad that's pasted on her cheek. It makes her face twitch.)*

KIYOKO: I need a drink of water.

> *(*NATALIE *ignores her.* KIYOKO *gets the water.)*

KIYOKO *(noticing the film)*: See, you're pretty good.

> *(*KIYOKO *walks over, picks up* NATALIE'S *drink, downs it and places it back.)*

KIYOKO: Saved your life.

> *(*NATALIE *notices* KIYOKO'S *face twitching.)*

KIYOKO *(explaining the device)*: Sends electrical impulses to the skin to stimulate the epidermal tissues. Makes me twitch, though. Hey, look, I'm winking at you . . .

> *(*KIYOKO *goes into her room.* NATALIE *stares at the empty glass. Then grabs the bottle and takes a big swig.*
>
> *She watches the screen. Gets up and walks around the place, glancing into boxes. Happens to notice a video underneath some pictures. Picks it up and places it into the video player.*
>
> *Lights dim and* NATALIE'S *face is lit by the screen. She leans forward to watch.*
>
> KIYOKO *pokes her head out when she hears the voices. She comes over and sits down next to* NATALIE *and watches with her. Silence.)*

NATALIE: That him?

KIYOKO: Un-huh.

NATALIE: What'd you do, have it transferred to video?

KIYOKO: A few years back.

NATALIE: That's what he looked like?

KIYOKO: Un-huh.

NATALIE: That me in your stomach?

KIYOKO: Un-huh, about eight months along. This was taken a few weeks before he left.

NATALIE: So the pictures you showed me before weren't him?

KIYOKO: No.

NATALIE: Who were they then?

KIYOKO: I don't know. I found them at a photo-mat. Someone had thrown them away. I thought he had a kind face.

NATALIE: Why?

KIYOKO: They were thrown away, nobody cared.

NATALIE: No, why didn't you show me my real father's picture. Why all this . . . deceit, or, whatever.

KIYOKO: I wasn't hiding it from you. I just didn't want to think about him. You were a baby, you didn't care.

NATALIE: Why'd you keep this?

KIYOKO: I never looked at it. Just kept it.

NATALIE: All these years?

KIYOKO: Just a small piece of him tucked away. Just in case.

NATALIE: In case of what?

KIYOKO: I dunno.

NATALIE: Why'd he leave?

KIYOKO: 'Cause that's what he did. Some men are like that. You have his eyes.

NATALIE: Have you ever heard from him? Like did he want to know about me?

KIYOKO: No.
        (Pause.)

NATALIE: Know where he is?

KIYOKO: No. I don't even know if the name he gave was his real name.

NATALIE: What did he do?

KIYOKO: He left. That's all I remember him doing now. I have a feeling he might be dead by now.
        (Silence.)

KIYOKO: Can I have a drink?

(NATALIE gets out the bottle and pours her a drink. KIYOKO gulps it down.)

KIYOKO: Saved your life. Mind if I save your life again?

(NATALIE pours her another shot.)

NATALIE: You think he's dead?

(No response.)

NATALIE: What was he, a drug dealer or something?

(No response.)

NATALIE: Was he a pimp?

(KIYOKO looks at NATALIE.)

KIYOKO: Why would you say something like that? Huh? Why?

NATALIE: I don't know. What was he then?

KIYOKO: He was your father and he was my husband. Then he left 'cause that's what he did. That's all. That was enough.

NATALIE: Am I like him at all?

KIYOKO: Why you asking all these questions now? You never asked about your father before.

NATALIE: Well, it was hard keeping track of who my father was. They kept changing all the time, remember?

KIYOKO: Yes. You are like him.

NATALIE: How?

KIYOKO: He was weak. He could never commit to anything. Stick with it. Anything got too hard, he just moved on.

NATALIE: That's a terrible thing to say to me. Why do you say things like that?

KIYOKO: 'Cause you wanted the truth, right? That's why you're asking all these questions, aren't you? To know the truth, so I'm telling you.

NATALIE: Maybe you drove him away.

KIYOKO: You don't know anything.

(Pause.)

NATALIE: Know why I left? Why I "quit"?

(KIYOKO doesn't respond.)

NATALIE: It's not 'cause I'm like my father.

KIYOKO: Then why, huh?

(Pause.)

NATALIE: The scene in *Iron Curtain*? The scene in bed? I didn't want to do it nude. It was in the contract. A body double or I get to wear a body stocking. The director said it would show and everyone was so nice. "What about the integrity of the scene?" A body double wouldn't work. They had shot some stuff but they needed some shots that showed us both or it would look fake. I said no, but they kept on me, made me feel like I was letting everyone down, making the film less than what it could be *artistically*. They like to use that one—it questions your integrity as a serious artist.

KIYOKO: You go on and on about this . . .

NATALIE: So I finally said okay, but that I wanted to wear one of those panty guards. And he had to wear one, too. The director takes me aside and says it'll look unrealistic, he needs me to not have one. He'll have Jason wear one as we can't show penises anyway without getting an X-rating. I don't want to but he says it's important and that there's nothing to worry about and nothing will show in the final cut and it allows for more realism and the scene is about how explosive their sexuality is. I say it isn't a rape scene, is it? And he says no and yes.

KIYOKO: You couldn't see anything.

NATALIE: So we get into bed and Jason doesn't have a cover on his penis. What am I supposed to do, everyone's on the set, we're all in bed and what am I supposed to do? "Stop, tell Jason to put his penis guard on."

KIYOKO: Well, if it bothered you so much . . .

NATALIE: Mama, you were standing there watching. You were standing next to the director, remember? You seemed to be having a good time. You said, "Go ahead baby, it's all right."

So we're into it and Jason whispers, "Don't worry, relax," he'll be careful . . . He stuck it in me, Mama, while everyone was watching. He forced his cock into me. I was shocked but he kept forcing it into me and what was I supposed to do with everyone watching, they all thought I was acting and I was but I wasn't too.

KIYOKO: Well, you seemed happy. Everyone was happy. We even went out for a drink, you guys were holding hands.

NATALIE: We weren't holding hands.

NATALIE WOOD IS DEAD

KIYOKO: He had his arm around you. I even have pictures of that.

NATALIE: So what? So fucking what? He still stuck his penis in me and I didn't want him to and he wasn't supposed to. He raped me. In front of everyone. And you applauded. Everyone applauded.

KIYOKO: That wasn't rape.

NATALIE: It was too.

KIYOKO: No, it wasn't. And you were smiling.

NATALIE: I wasn't smiling.

KIYOKO: You were smiling and happy at the bar.

NATALIE: I mean I was but I wasn't really. Not afterwards. Afterwards when I went home.

KIYOKO: Why are you telling me this now? To make me feel bad. To make me feel ashamed for having made you do the movie?

NATALIE: No, I just want you to know what really happened. The truth?

KIYOKO: And you're blaming me for it, right? You're telling me this so I can feel sorry for you, poor, poor Natalie, that's why she quit and it's all her mother's fault. So what you say happened, so what? So fucking what? Grow up. Most of us have to screw some old geezer just to get to go to the right parties and all you had to do is get in bed naked with the lead, who's quite good-looking I might add. Someone I would have gladly fucked in my day. Grow up. This is the real world. People are dying of starvation in the Sudanese desert, small microbes eat up the insides of homosexual men, young girls throw newborn babies in dumpsters then go to the prom, daughters are used like whores by soldiers in Kosovo, then shot and dumped in holes their mothers had to dig. You weren't killed, you aren't dying, you aren't dead. Wake up. People get fucked all the time. You just got to make sure you're getting fucked for the right reasons. Who's the fucker, who's the fuckee. That makes all the difference in the world.

NATALIE: So you're telling me it's okay?—

KIYOKO: No, no—

NATALIE: —It's all right to be raped?

KIYOKO: —No, no, of course not!

NATALIE: Have you taken money? For sex?

KIYOKO: What?

NATALIE: Have you?

KIYOKO: All I was saying was people are always using other people. Screwing? As in a metaphor?

NATALIE: Who do you rent this place from?

KIYOKO: Mr. Taniguchi.

NATALIE: He's one of your bosses, isn't he?

KIYOKO: What are you saying?

NATALIE: Well, you said everybody does it. So I guess you must mean everybody, including you. You did say you'd do anything.

KIYOKO: Oh, grow up, will you.

NATALIE: At the age of thirty-three, I finally know who my father is, I'm grown-up now. So do you get favors for sex? Like in this apartment you live in.

KIYOKO: I'm an actress. Maybe you aren't, but I still am. Okay, maybe I don't get as much work as I used to, so I do part-time work with Mr. Taniguchi's company. I drive visitors around, they get a kick out of having me do it for them. A former famous model. A novelty.

NATALIE: That's all?

KIYOKO: Oh, and I sell Japanese health products.

NATALIE: That's all?

KIYOKO: Some of us don't have the luxury of worrying whether our feelings get bruised a little.

NATALIE: Bruised?

KIYOKO: No one forced you to do anything. No one forced you to take off your clothes and get into bed with Jason Dayne. And no one forced you to open up your legs and let him get inside of you. You weren't some naive fifteen year old—you were, what? Twenty-seven,-eight? You act like you suddenly woke up and found him sticking it in you—"How'd I get here, what time is it?" "My god, is that a penis?" You put yourself there. You. Take some responsibility for what you do and what you let be done to you. It's your body, not mine, not the director's, yours. He didn't force himself on you and you didn't get raped. You let him. And you let him because being good in the scene, looking good for the camera, selling yourself to the public, yes "selling yourself," was more important than the inconvenience of having Jason's wayward cock momentarily misplaced in your vagina. Not 'cause everyone was watching, not 'cause I had somehow conspired over the years of your upbringing to make you some kind of deer in the headlights, an unwilling victim, victimized by her overbearing mother and her need to please her . . .

(Realizing.)

KIYOKO: You know what it is? You know what it is? You're an actress darling. You keep saying, "I don't know if I want to do it anymore"—Oh, I don't think so. I think you do. Hell, you want it more than me. Face it. You're an actress, you're an actress, too . . .

(Silence.)

NATALIE: I saw it. The movie? The one you said you made, that's coming out soon? I already saw it.

(Pause.)

KIYOKO: My movie?

NATALIE: Yes.

KIYOKO: Where?

(Pause.)

NATALIE: On the plane coming over. In between the pretzels and the meatless lasagna. They didn't release it Mama. This fancy movie you keep talking about you were in. They didn't sell it to cable, they didn't even send it to video. They gave it to United for their flights. Not even international, domestic.

(Silence.)

KIYOKO: How was I?

NATALIE: It was hard to tell. The Japanese neighbor was on for a very, very brief moment.

KIYOKO: So were you sleeping or awake, huh? Make up your mind. Here, this'll wake you up.

(Grabs the journal.)

KIYOKO *(reading)*: . . . "Her daughter on the other hand seems to make choices that confound even the most hardened critic of political correctness, having chosen to appear in the wretched, Asian male-hating classic *Iron Curtain*, wherein she ignores every Asian male, handsome or otherwise, only to immediately fall for the first white male who happens along, who's just come from killing her brother, looks like Charlie Manson, and has at that moment, no evident socially redeeming qualities other than his whiteness. What does she do? She immediately jumps into the sack with him. This hateful, big budget action movie sets the cause of Asian American males, and Asian American portrayals in general, back fifty years" . . . Shall I continue?

NATALIE: No.

KIYOKO: Did that hurt? 'Cause that's what I didn't read to you when I could have.

NATALIE: Yes, it hurt Mama. You hurt me.

KIYOKO: I could've read it before but I didn't, okay? I wanted to protect you from that.

(*Long pause.*)

NATALIE: Aren't you tired, Mama? Just a little? 'Cause I am. And all the Japanese herbs and vitamins aren't going to change it. I'm not like you. I won't do just anything. Not 'cause I'm better than you or looking down at you. I'm just too goddamn, fucking tired. And I guess there's a point where it is okay to say, I quit. And it's okay to say I'm not an actress. It's okay to grow old, it's okay to gain weight, it's okay to have a drooping ass and even small breasts.

KIYOKO: You hate me, don't you?

NATALIE: I don't hate you . . .

KIYOKO: You have that luxury, because on the day you were born I said you were special. And because I said from that day on life was going to be good. And it was. For you. And do you know why? 'Cause I made it good. I did. Not life, not the world, not your father or fathers, not your *Asian American* community friends who turned on you, I might add. No, me. Me. I did. And do you know how I was able to do it?

NATALIE: By doing anything?

KIYOKO: By having something worth doing anything for. A beautiful baby girl.

NATALIE WOOD IS DEAD

(Silence. The morning sun is coming up.)

NATALIE: Maybe I should get one.

KIYOKO: Maybe you should, you'd learn a lot more about yourself.

NATALIE: Then again, maybe I shouldn't. Maybe I don't want something that'll make me do anything for it.

KIYOKO: Then you'll never succeed, 'cause that's what it takes. In this business. And in life.

NATALIE: You're a winner. Kiyoko Dalhauser is a winner.

KIYOKO: Yes, I am. And Natalie Hayashi? What is she?

(Pause.

The MAN *appears upstage in a pool of light.)*

NATALIE: I was telling this man why my name was Hayashi. It means forest or woods in Japanese. Natalie Wood? Get it? Natalie Hayashi, Natalie Wood? My mother gave it to me. He looked at me kinda funny—

MAN: Natalie Wood is dead, isn't she?

NATALIE: And so she is, Mama.

(Pause.)

NATALIE: I didn't ask for a million. I just said a couple hundred would get me home.

(She looks at the MAN *and he flashes a wad of bills, then withdraws.)*

NATALIE: You don't have to do just anything anymore. You can do just what you want to do and not do what you don't want to do. I'm leaving. I guess you're right. I am my father's daughter.

*(*NATALIE *grabs her stuff and leaves.* KIYOKO *stands there for a moment. Notices the sun coming up. Then goes to the video player and changes tapes. Sits down on the chair. She pours herself a drink. Flicks on the video and watches 5* Gates of Hell. *Sips. We hear gunfire and bombs going off.)*

KIYOKO *(repeating to herself)*: Dis donc où est la bibliothèque, dis donc où est la bibliothèque, dis donc où est la bibliothèque . . .

(She turns up the volume. Fade to black.)

[END OF PLAY]

PLAY TWO

White Manifesto and Other Perfumed Tales of Self-Entitlement, or, Got Rice?

Characters
RICHARD SAUGUS
WOMAN #1 PRIZE SHOW GIRL
WOMAN #2 PRIZE SHOW GIRL

Time
2000

Place
Palo Alto

Prelude
*An average-looking guy in his late twenties. On each side of him stands
a woman. Pretty, they look and act like professional prize showers from
a game show. Each holds several large flash cards.*

    *On the small table next to the guy are set a tie and coat along with
a bottle of opened wine, a wine glass. He is in his socks, and his shoes
are on the ground next to his feet.*

    WOMAN #1 *holds up a large card with an Asian male face, geeky—
black-frame glasses, spikey greased-up hair, stupid grin.* WOMAN #2
poses beside her, showing WOMAN #1 *displaying the flash card. The
two women takes turns displaying and showing while the guy narrates.*

WHITE MANIFESTO, OR, GOT RICE?

GUY: Japanese foreign exchange student.

 (WOMAN #1 *starts to lower the card, then stops.*)

GUY: Wrong.

 (WOMAN #1 *holds it up again.*)

GUY: Been here five generations, forefathers fought in World War II, Korea, Vietnam. I.e., a bona fide red, white and blue American through and through, spilled blood, rooted for Joe DiMaggio, paid taxes, the whole nine yards.

 (GUY *shakes his head disgustedly, muttering.*)

GUY: Japanese foreign student, you should be ashamed . . . Walking down the street at night. It's dark and no one's around. See a person coming towards you . . .

 (WOMAN #2 *holds up card—good-looking white male in a suit and tie. Holds it for a beat. Takes it down.*)

GUY: It's dark and no one's around. See this person coming towards you . . .

 (WOMAN #1 *holds up a menacing black male face, like the* Green Mile *guy. Holds it for a long beat. Takes it down.*)

GUY: You're horny, you just want to fuck your brains out . . .

 (WOMAN #2 *holds up an exotic-looking Asian woman. Takes it down. Then, holds up a black man, Ken Norton from mandingo-type, takes it down. Then holds up same geeky-looking Asian guy, takes it down.*)

GUY: Your plane is taking off after a long weather delay. It's stormy and the flight promises to be turbulent, maybe even dangerous. This is your pilot . . .

 (WOMAN #1 *holds up cards. First, a sexy, model-esque white woman, anorexic Kate Moss type. Then the black male face. Then the white male in the suit.*)

GUY: You're forced to cut back on your work force, to keep up

your profit margin—Silicon Valley, has to do with wireless tele-
com. Who do you keep as your lead programmer—
(WOMAN #2 holds up the white male suit.)
GUY: Or . . .
(WOMAN #1 holds up geeky Asian guy.)
GUY: Hmmm . . . not quite so easy, huh. It's the Superbowl, three
secs remaining on the clock, you're on the five-yard line, it's fourth
down, you're trailing by four, field goal won't work and your quar-
terback has the wing of a chicken. You got to take it in . . .
(WOMAN #1 holds up the geeky Asian guy. He starts busting up.)
GUY: That's funny. Okay, okay, let's try another one—sings and
moves like a sultry cat . . .
(WOMAN #2 holds up a black woman.)
GUY: That was easy. Or . . .
(WOMAN #1 holds up Barry Manilow.)
GUY: Just funning you. Uncool?
(WOMAN #1 holds up the Asian guy. He nods sadly.)
GUY: 'Fraid so. Likes watermelon?
(WOMAN #2 holds up the white male.)
GUY: Having fun with you again. *(Mexican accent)* Likes big
families . . .
*(WOMAN #1 holds up a large Mexican family, all wearing
sombreros.)*
GUY: Hey, ask Reggie White, the football player. He said it man.
(WOMAN #2 holds up picture of GUY.)
GUY: W.M.W.A. Wm-wa [pronounced wimm-waaah]. White
male with attitude.
(Dim to darkness. End of prelude.
*In half light, the two women begin to dress the guy. One helps
him with his coat while the other kneels below him and puts his
shoes on. Sexual overtones.*
*Done, they move upstage to two chairs on opposite sides of the
guy. They should sit, facing upstage, in a relaxed manner, chang-
ing poses occasionally but not distracting.*
*Lights up. Same normal, average-looking young male in his late
twenties. Pours a glass of wine.)*
GUY: *(recites)*: Perfect wave. Imperfect me. I sip my Opus One.

WHITE MANIFESTO, OR, GOT RICE?

(Sips.)

GUY: Still a little tight. Let it unwind a bit.

(Checks himself out in the mirror. Begins putting tie on.)

GUY: Hello. You don't know me but I know you. But before I get into talking to you about you, let me do what I love best—me talking about me. Wasn't that refreshing to hear? Everybody wants to talk about themselves, only they lack the confidence and sense of self-belief to let themselves go there. Not me. Why? That's sort of what I'm going to talk about.

My name is Richard Saugus. Nice to meet you. Don't ask me where that family name came from. Just about everywhere on the European continent, I think. I grew up in a small city outside Seattle: Lynnwood. This is pre–Bill Gates. The eighties and early nineties. No Microsoft, no Paul Allen–Frank Gehry rock and roll futuristic turd, Jimi's long dead, grunge is the musical arc of my years there, Kurt and Courtney are about to meet, mate and follow through with their ordained destinies—who could have thunk, huh, Courtney? Shame for thinking she was just a slut. She's a talented slut. And coffee was just coffee but has just split from Peet's and is about to become the evil empire, on and on.

Nice childhood. Happy, clean, soccer, Boy Scouts, no sicknesses or health problems. Wait, take that back, cold sores. Used to get them all the time. School years, most everybody was white. No incest, abuse, alcoholism or perversion that I can remember. Family wasn't overly religious but we were raised Methodist and attended church regularly. Father's a banker, and, get this, growing up he talked to me. Communicated. Most of my friends' fathers did. Mother was a grammar school teacher—she's retired now, does volunteer work reading for the blind and has become a tennis nut. Still has a nice figure for a fifty-six-year-old woman. She'd like me saying that. I have a younger sister whom I alternately loved and hated growing up. I'm sure she felt the same. We're at the loving-each-other stage and I expect it'll stay that way from here on out. Lisa's in residency in upstate New York—Stonybrook. Radiologist. She's engaged to a Jewish fellow, oncologist. I can't quite figure out that combination. Radiologist-oncologist, but I'm not privy to the romantic workings of my sister and nor do I want to be.

Hmm, I went to Stanford as an undergrad and got my MBA at Wharton. Had considered going for an additional law degree but once I'd graduated with my MBA I said, "Fuck it." I did, I really said it out loud. "Fuck it!" I figure I could go just as far and get there sooner with my MBA. We shall see but so far so good.

Oh, and I had a dog growing up. An Irish setter, Wiggy. And he was and he was. I loved that dog. Too bad about the accident.

(Shrugs innocently, like, "oh, well.")

GUY: A funny pickup line—

(WOMEN #1 and #2 stand, turn, and strike poses as if at a bar— drinks in hand, primping.)

GUY: —you walk up to a bunch of girls and say, "Excuse me, have you seen keys to a Ferrari?"

(They pretend to be laughing, abruptly stop, become expressionless, turn and sit.)

MAN: Okay. Let's discuss terminology first. When I say Asian, for our conversation's sake, I mean Asian American, or AA for short, except when I say Asian and mean just that, non-American-born Asians, though living in the U.S. *One point fivers* are kids who were born abroad but came here quite young. And yes, these terms are constantly changing, can be regional and also dependent on the user who may put her own English on it, so if they're not what you think is current or correct . . .

(Shrugs innocently, like, "oh, well.")

WOMEN #1 and #2: A disclaimer . . .

GUY: Yes, of course, I'm speaking in generalizations here, and of course, I'm not talking about everybody. I'm talking about a certain sector of the populace of Asian girls and a certain sector of the populace of white guys. This isn't about true, one-of-a-kind love, leading to vows of monogamy and eternal bliss and whose parties just happen to be an Asian female and a white male. No, no, that's love. No more, no less, just love. So *happas* and *quappas* and mixed race couples, please don't get your asses in a rash, this isn't about you. That is, unless it is about you.

WHITE MANIFESTO, OR, GOT RICE?

I'm talking about what I know. What I do. What *I've* done. I'm talking about white guys into Asian girls. Yes, we can say it out loud. It's not some ugly myth, a conspiracy theory made up by young disenfranchised Asian males. No, we're talking yellow fever. Kimono-my-house-and-I'll-show-you-my-koto guys. And to a lesser extent the Asian girls who like them. And to even a lesser degree, the Asian guys and white girls who orbit in and about this white and yellow, male-female dynamic.

This is about guys going to college, or guys out there doing the club scene or guys working their asses off at start-ups waiting to cash in on their stock options. All study and no play, all work and no fun—and all this makes Mr. Heterosexual white guy very frustrated and in need of a big release.

Asian girls are easier. Yes, you heard me right. For an average white guy like me, Asian girls are easier. It's true, ask any dude who's into them.

Hey, I'm being honest here, okay. I'm not talking educated, liberal, politically correct Caucasian Man hobnobbing in the middle of culturally and ethnically diverse cocktail party who would never think to say something like that. No, I'm talking white guy shop-talk, in-house versus out-house, what white guys into rice all know and may never say out loud or even acknowledge they know or even sometimes know they know 'cause it's so crass and uncool and unliberal. But who we kidding here. We know. And we know.

I'm talking about the sweet, perfumed smell of young skin and the brush of just-washed hair falling around you like those mythical pink blossoms—whose world it evokes really no longer exists, but allow a white guy to indulge a little in a white guy's fantasy here—falling around you like pink blossoms—I love that imagery—as you settle in for the sweet, perfumed ride, your loins wrapping around this gorgeous, exquisite Oriental—I know that's not PC, but we're post-PC now—exquisite oriental snow princess who looks up at you like you were the most noble being on the face of the earth and wants you to fuck her silly.

It's a jungle out there in the singles' world. Dating, hooking up with the right girl? You kidding? The competition is fierce, the demands on your time and emotional space enormous, believe me I've been out there and I know what is and what ain't. And what is, is so fine and that fineness can be yours, Mr. W.M.W.A. And what ain't, is your hand in your pocket going 'round feeling cocky all day.

(Sips.)

GUY: Gotta breathe a bit more . . .

(WOMEN #1 and #2 stand and strike another pose.)

GUY: Here's another one, demands more balls, though—you walk up to a girl and look at the tag on the back of her shirt. She says something like—

WOMAN #1: Hey, what you doing?

GUY: You say, "Exactly what I thought—made in heaven."

(They titter, abruptly stop, sit.)

GUY: Look, I can get an A Asian girl whereas I could only get a C or B-plus white girl. On an average. I hit on an A white girl I may or may not get a look—let's say one out of four times. But an A Asian girl, three out of four times. Now, you can't just walk up and say, me white man, you Asian chick, no, of course not. In fact, usually, there's hesitation, especially if they haven't tried Caucasian male before so you got to get over, be sensitive to the situation, open your eyes, open their eyes, do your homework.

For example, don't even think of bringing up the Asian thing. No, no, no. That's what they're expecting and unless they're Caucasian junkies, they'll be turned off. Instead be smart. Be cool. Be honest. Just be the you they want you to be.

Treat her like you don't notice she's Asian. Yes. You don't notice that she's got different skin, different hair, different psychology, a totally different history of being in a historically anti-Asian racialized America—spanning first, second, third, fourth, fifth generations of assimilation, specific modes of communication—indirect, direct, unspoken, repressed—and that even though they're so many generations removed, that they still carry the seeds though they themselves may not even know it—let alone cultural issues or seemingly non-cultural issues of gender: role playing, identification with, what constitutes beauty, masculinity, courtship, sex—you-don't-look-like-my-father and that's a turn off or turn on or . . . well, you get the picture.

Suffice it to say, you just don't notice it. The Asian thing. You're blind to it . . .

(Pause, thinking, looks at his ass in the mirror.)

WOMEN #1 and #2 *(leaning forward)*: Oooohhh . . .

GUY: No, I take that back. This is tricky as I'm still working on this but why not discourse and muse openly here, maybe come up with some new theories.

What I've sussed out is that if you *really* want to score points, it's this—they want you to not see it but still see it. Got that? What I mean is they want you to think you're staring at the mythical generic all-American girl but who's still Asian.

And so it begs the question, can that beast even exist, that is the mythical all-American girl who's still Asian because—let me get this straight—wouldn't that be a blonde, raven-haired, blue-eyed, brown-eyed, light-skinned, dark-complexioned girl who massages your feet and kicks your ass at the same time?

It's like a koan—you have to make this leap into an irrational area of non-logic where dwells the soul of internalized racism— yes I used the "R" word—and with that, an acute self-awareness of this internalization and subsequent resentment of it, and, the helpless embracing of it and consequent issues of self-hate— thus the push and pull of a mind at war with itself. And as she's a smart, ambitious woman, the indignant awareness of the club exclusion that the stigma of yellowness carries and yet at the same time wanting to participate with full membership in this exclusive club which, of course, really can never allow her full membership because it wouldn't be the same exclusive club that she (with her issues of self-hate) wanted to be in in the first place and you know that old joke, yada, yada, yada . . .

(Shrugs.)

GUY: I didn't say this was a perfect science . . .

(Recites.)

GUY:

Perfect cloud

    Imperfect mind

    My Armani suit

    (Tastes wine again.)

GUY: Hmm, almost but not quite there . . .

    (He abruptly stops. Becomes quiet. Lighting shift.)

WOMAN #1: His eyes are open.

WOMAN #2: He must be awake.

WOMAN #1: Is he awake?

GUY: Am I awake?

WOMAN #2: He is awake.

WOMAN #1: He is awake.

WOMAN #2: He feels something creeping about the edges . . .

WOMAN #1: His mind races, what is it?—

WOMAN #2: An intruder going to steal his *munakata* woodblock print—

WOMAN #1: Rape and defile his virgin-like wife—

WOMAN #2: Kidnap his almost immaculate children—

WOMAN #1: Or the fourteen-year-old hooker who keeps calling his pager has sneaked into his bed and—

WOMAN #2: Or, or—

WOMAN #1: Or, or—

WOMAN #2: Maybe I'm imagining this whole thing . . .

WOMAN #1: And yet—

WOMAN #2: And yet—

WOMAN #1: Maybe I'm imagining this whole thing—

    (Light shift. GUY *suddenly upbeat again. Checking his watch.)*

GUY: I better hurry up here.

    Okay, the approach. Check out how they look. No, not like, "Is she a dawg or not." No, we're way beyond that, to have to even consider that would be a *bummer*—isn't Sixties jargon cool, *bummer*—it's understood, of course, she's a *twentieth-century fox*, ooh, so retro—or you wouldn't be staring into her—never say *almond-shaped* eyes, in the first place. But we're getting ahead of ourselves.

    How she looks. What she looks like. What she is. Now, nowhere will anyone admit to being able to tell the difference, unless you're William Randolph Hearst and it's World War II, but sometimes and most often, you can. Chinese, Japanese, Korean, Filipino,—etcetera, etcetera. Yes, I, white guy me, usually can. And quite frankly, most informed folks, can. They just never say it 'cause it's uncool and oh so un-liberal.

A caveat, my accuracy rate drops radically with southeast Asians—I always blow it 'cause I'm not totally up on Thai, Cambodian, Vietnamese, the various Laotian tribes, let alone Hmong and let's not even go to central Asians—Uzbekistan, Kazakhstan . . . You know, for the sake of this discussion, let's just stick with Chinese, Japanese and Korean, 'cause it's what I have most experience in bed with anyway.

Chinese girls—I've found that just by sheer odds, she's probably that. Tend to be taller and fairer than say Filipinas, more slender and longer-legged than Japanese, a bit more severe in appearance and feel than say Koreans who are interestingly— if you know your history—closer to Japanese. I'm showing a bit of a Northern Chinese bias here with the tall slender thing, and yes, I know you can get into the whole discussion of northern versus southern, Shanghainese versus Cantonese versus Hakka versus Toisan and arguments about class, upper, lower, provinces and ethnics in other countries—look, too much, too much. Ignore it. You can get lost in that mire and from the time you make eye contact to your opening line, the window is very minuscule, so you got to focus and pick out one thing you know and stay with that. Name, type of accent or sans accent are good ones. These you'll have to read within the first few words out of her mouth, you don't have time to to go, "duh" . . .

WOMEN #1 and #2: A slight digression—

GUY: I have a Chinese friend who talks about the "dragon lady syndrome" which of course, as all good liberals and progressive AA's know, is supposed to be a stereotype. Let's just say if you ever cheat, don't leave any knives around. Oh, and here we're getting on dicey ground, but it's post-PC, Howard Stern, Jerry Springer live—I'm talking white guy truth—there's the money thing. Chinese are the Jews of the East, they know how to handle your money and how to not let you handle their money. Jews and Chinese have diasporic mercantile traditions. Cheap? Did I say that? Hey, O.T.R.—difference between Chinese and Japanese in business? An old Chinese guy told me. One Chinese working by himself is a dragon, one Japanese working by himself a worm. Several Chinese working together is a worm, several Japanese working together is a dragon.

(Looks at the audience, like "think about that one.")

GUY: I like Chinese girls, more adventuresome in bed than Japanese. But not Korean girls, whew, I'll get to that. Chinese girls, you tend to get the message pretty quick—*(Thumbs up, thumbs down)*—but don't leave any knives around, could be hasta la vista Long John *choda*, hola Senor Bobbitt, all over again.

WOMEN #1 and #2: but he digresses . . .

GUY: Japanese girls. If they're *shin-issei*, that is, F.O.B. girls, then don't even worry, the black ships have landed, the pearly gates are open. They like any color but yellow anyway. Ethno-centric as all get out, which means, no Koreans, Chinese, Filipinos— remember their history?—and no J.A.'s, that's as in Japanese Americans. They consider it a faux Japanese culture, in-authentic, a kind of bastard child they'd just rather forget. So white's big, black, too, among the counter-culture ones. Whoa, the counter-culture ones—must be 'cause they have to break out from such a rigid society of conformity when they do break out, they really explode . . .

(WOMEN #1 and #2 start screeching, imitating Yoko Ono's famous singing wail.)

WOMEN #1 and #2: Ahhhhhhhhhhhh . . .

GUY *(hollering over their screeching)*: Can you say, *Yoko Ono*?

(WOMEN #1 and #2 abruptly stop.)

WOMEN #1 and #2: But he digresses—

GUY: Back to what they think of J.A.'s, Koreans, Chinese, etcetera—you'll never get any Japanese to admit any of this. Inscrutable? Is the Pope Catholic, can fish swim? So that brings us back to F.O.B. F.O.B.? Not what it meant in the junky made-in-Japan Fifties, believe me. That's for the older folks. F.O.B.? Means "fuck off buddy," unless you're a white guy. That's me, here I am. And I am.

WHITE MANIFESTO, OR, GOT RICE?

Japanese names, everybody knows—hey, I heard this joke. What if the Japanese had won the war? We'd be eating California rolls, driving Toyotas, watching Beat Takeshi movies, getting our news on a Sony TV from female Japanese newscasters, making phone calls on a Nokia—that's not Japanese, that's foreign white folks trying to disguise themselves as Japanese which, if you think about it, still fits the category— and hey, let's take in the great American pastime. An interleague matchup between the Mariners and the Mets. Let's check in on the action—it's Mets' homeboy, Masato Yoshii, facing Seattle's local favorite, Ichiro! I rest my case.

WOMEN #1 and #2: But he digresses . . .

GUY: The thing about *yonsei* and *gosei* J.A.'s—surprised I know that *yonsei, gosei* stuff huh, pillow talk, amazing what you pick up from fourth and fifth generation girls—they know less about Japanese stuff than most white folks. Like somewhere along the line someone decided actively to run as far away as possible from being Japanese. Maybe it's just the number of generations removed from the old country or as some J.A. scholars think now—the camps. The camps. Not summer camp, but the internment camps, not relocation, internment camps. Scarred them, made them feel ashamed and fearful about who they were and made them not want to be who they were and to run as far away as possible to being American, that is, Caucasian American.

Ever see a white guy dance? Music please . . .

(WOMEN #1 and #2 join him. GUY starts dancing. He's bad, spastic, has no rhythm. "Play That Funky Music" by Wild Cherry.)

GUY: Who says we can't dance? Hey, wanna see my jump shot . . .

(Attempts to jump but barely leaves the ground.
Turns and smiles slyly at the audience.)

GUY: Just kidding . . .

Korean girls—tend to be first and second generation simply because of the later immigration patterns, so look for traces of the old country there. And a certain directness in their approach and at times an emotional volatility, which I'll address shortly. Classic look is the moon face and that—and this is what I love and makes them so, so unique and what might be related to the emotional volatility thing—that inherent, soulful, internalized yet physically manifested tormented quality, that comes of a people having been historically subjugated over and over. Like the Irish, you know, so it permeates all aspects of life with a melancholy feel and look. That trait, in Korean called *hahn*.

(Imitates a look.)

GUY: Pillow talk. They can have the short, squat legs—there is corollary in J.A. vernacular, *daikon ashi*—which I'm not too fond of in either J.A. or Koreans. Korean girls, I like the delicate, willowy ones, soft round moon face, high cheekbones are an added bonus. There is an interesting phenomenon I notice about Koreans and cosmetic surgery. They seem to wholeheartedly embrace it—eyes, nose, even a bleaching of the skin to lighten complexion.

Also, in bed, remember that soulfulness I was talking about, *hahn*? Whoa, in bed, it's a killer. If you hit what I call the "K.G.G.", "Korean girl g-spot," be prepared for a howl that is like nothin' you ever heard before. A kind of a deep-seated wail of Korean national pain and pleasure, makes you want to get on your knees and bow. Except make sure she hasn't been eating Korean food before you take her back to your place. How do you know? Can you say the words, kim chee and raw garlic?

(Shrugs again.)

GUY: So let's say, you've culled together as much info as you can, made your decisions about what you can say, not say, should do or not do, and if anything, you now feel more confident because me, W.M.W.A., has given you, soon-to-be W.M.W.A., the secret knowledge to get to the head of the class.

You're out on the town. And hopefully you have a decent ride, more than decent threads, and a hot set of CDs. You park, you walk, you enter the den of hope and desire where frequent the women of whom we speak. All right. We've talked the talk, now walk the walk. Go ahead, go ahead . . . "play that funky music white boy" . . .

WHITE MANIFESTO, OR, GOT RICE?

Opening lines? You've heard a couple already—oh, this is a funny one. You walk up to a girl and say—

(WOMEN #1 *and* #2 *strike a pose.*)

GUY: —"Hey, I have a magic watch, it can tell what you're wearing." They usually go—

WOMAN #1: "Yeah, sure."

GUY: "It says you're not wearing panties."

WOMAN #1: "Sorry, I am."

GUY: "Damn, it's running fast."

But see, the great thing is, you don't need a line. Remember the word, entitlement? All you do is walk up and say, "Hi, my name is Richard Saugus. What's yours?" She tells you. You say, "How do you do" whatever her name is, shake hands so you touch skin, important, get her used to W.M.W.A. meat in a non-threatening way. And then just smile. And let your whiteness do the rest. Remember you're a charter club member, step off into space and hey, be effortlessly supported by the kamikazes of white world fandango.

Wait—

WOMEN #1 and #2: He must digress—

GUY: There are exceptions to this—immigrant girls or 1 point fivers, harder. Especially if they're in a group of girls. And especially if there are any 1 point fiver guys, then forget it, better to leave well enough alone. You get—as they say in the islands—the stink eye. You can get punched, too.

WOMEN #1 and #2: He digresses from his digression—

GUY: Asian guys aren't wimps. Again, it's simply part of the big lie created by dominant culture—namely white guys, but don't blame me, this is really old dead white guys, you know, forefather-type white guys—made to perpetuate certain convenient and self-serving falsehoods—dependent on the winds of political and economic need—about yellow men for white male advantage. Take for example the small dick myth—

WOMEN #1 and #2: Eeek!

(*Looks at the two women.*)

GUY: The Asian male dick thing—

WOMEN #1 and #2 *(slightly irritated)*: Eeek!

GUY: I'd like to clear the air on this small dick thing—*(Continues.)*

WOMEN #1 and #2 *(overlapping, now intrigued)*: Oooh . . .

GUY *(continued; hurriedly plowing through)*: —of which a great deal of eunich representation has been pawned off as truth and which, I'm a victim just like the next brown, yellow, red, black guy or mixed-race combination thereof, cause if one man's dick—

WOMEN #1 and #2 *(overlapping; too much)*: Stop . . .

GUY: —is demeaned, so is mine. *(Beat)* In-house white male shop talk? Asian male dicks?

WOMEN #1 and #2: *(not sure but they like it)*: Yeow . . .

GUY: Not small. Big as mine. Fact, lot of them got really big ones. *(Defensively)* At the gym, okay—hey, I gotta shower after my workout, don't I? And I hear. I *hear*, okay. From my sources that—pillow talk okay—they know what to do with it, you know. How to make the fat lady sing. Not this boom-boom fortissimo one-note jock stuff. No.

> *(WOMEN #1 and #2 respond with appropriate repeated "yes's" and "no's" accompanying the guy's descriptions.)*

GUY: Entry—hard but sensual, dominating but sensitive. Stroke— *sotto voce*, building, crescendo, going for the gusto, then backing off. Yes, can you imagine a male doing that, backing off? *Pianissimo*, just strings, then, slowly taking it up, okay, bring in the woodwinds, you begin to feel the power—cymbals, now the tympanis, you hear the crashing of waves, fuck *sotto voce*, the sky is cracking open, lightning the size of elephant tusks rips through the blackness!! . . .

> *(They all climax. He composes himself.)*

GUY: *Her* words, not mine. Big ones. Know how to use 'em— think cello, think Yo-Yo Ma, fat lady. Her words.

> *(Sips wine.)*

GUY: Hmm, it's really opened up now. This isn't bad. Go good with a very rare steak.

WOMEN: But he digresses . . .

GUY: Ahh, yes, another phenomenon—sort of a corollary to what I've been talking about. And if you haven't been offended yet, this should put you over the top. *(Beat)* Homely white girls

and good-looking Asian guys. You know what I'm talking
about—

WOMEN #1 and #2: That *is* offensive.

GUY: You don't like to hear this, I don't like talking about it—

WOMEN #1 and #2: And not always true.

GUY: It's embarrassing. It's sad. It's pathetic. I feel for the guys—
hey, what's going on here? And you never see an ugly Asian
girl with a handsome white guy, do you? Do you?

Shall I tell you what's going on? Good-looking, successful
Asian American guy, totally hoodwinked into thinking he got
to have a white girl or he ain't in the game. I think there's a
black and Latino corollary here but let's not go there.

WOMEN #1 and #2: But he digresses . . .

GUY: But I digress, back to the poor Asian guy with the ugly white
girl. He doesn't realize it, but he got the self-esteem of a shriveled up peanut. That is, with white girls. And he don't want
an Asian girl—you know the joke I was talking about earlier
about not wanting to be a member of a club that would have
you as a member? Back to the white girl hang-up—doesn't
think he can really go up to some white girl. Even though this
Asian guy's tall, handsome, got his J.D., M.D., Ph.D., Porsche
Boxter, six-figure salary, can cook Northern Italian, a wonderful
conversationalist, speaks five languages fluently—all Romance,
none Asian—knows martial arts though never cops to it, is a
superb tennis player and freestyle mountain climber, and he's
got a huge ham bone—this sorryass nincompoop still believes
he can't get over with this A white girl.

Which ain't true, though can be true, however, beside the
point for this discussion—so then when some B-minus or more
likely C-plus white girl comes along and says, hi, what's your
name, he's all, wiggling his tail like a puppy dog—thank you,
thank you for noticing me. Meanwhile the yellow sisters are—
at least the ones into their brothers—are puking up.

(WOMAN #2 *holds up card of Asian girl puking.*

WOMAN #1 *notices her next card. Isn't sure what to do. Tries to
get the* GUY'S *attention.*)

WOMAN #1: Pssst! Pssst!

GUY *(grabs the card)*: What?

WOMAN #1: It's blank.

> *(Stares at it, getting upset.)*

GUY: Someone fucking around with my props? *(To audience)* It always comes down to this, doesn't it?

> *(Throws it aside, pissed.*
> *Stops. Becomes quiet. Lighting shift.)*

WOMAN #2: He's having dinner at Masami's. He's there with his virgin-like wife and almost-immaculate sons. His beeper goes off. He retires to the bar to check the call and glances up at the TV—

WOMAN #1: There's a war going on somewhere. The people are dark, faces emaciated, clothes filthy, a mother holds a dead baby, the father's legs blown off. He suddenly wants a blow job. He wants the fourteen-year-old hooker to suck him off.

WOMAN #2: He takes TV remote and switches to the football game. Blinding lights flash up on the windows. From a passing vehicle? An explosion? The next thing he knows, he's seated with his virgin-like wife, almost-immaculate kids, chewing on a piece of squab. His youngest son turns to look at him—

GUY: "Are you all right, daddy?"

> *(Lighting shift.* GUY *abruptly returns to upbeat self.)*

WOMEN: But he digresses . . .

GUY: Okay, what about the Asian girl with the white dude? Okay, you want me to talk about that? Okay, okay.

WOMEN: A corollary to the original corollary—

GUY: One reason—pillow talk again—the girl, she can't stand the thought of being on a date with an Asian guy. I know it's weird but it's true. Every day of their lives their fathers and mothers—who happen to be Asian—have been pounding it into them to marry some nice Asian boy. And though they love their daddies, they couldn't date anyone who looked like him—black hair, yellow skin, glasses. In other words, uncool. And getting into bed, even with a decent-looking one, would be like screwing their brother. Yuck.

Another reason I think is more inside the heads of the girls. That is, why not be with someone who seems to move so

smoothly through the world, who doesn't have these continual hang-ups about masculinity, inferiority and whose every
action is measured up against a society that is systematically
trying to emasculate and infantalize them. Why be on the arm
of that guy and thus be included by insinuation?

Okay, she wants to be supportive of the Asian male, but when
you get right down to it, I mean, all things being equal—which
of course can't be—Why not be with the one who is the natural. Who fits in and who moves through the world as if it
were tailor-made for him. Now, isn't that a whole lot easier?
And lo and behold, on the arm of a white guy, you get to enter,
a free pass, no toll. And whatever it was about being Asian that
made the male insignificant and demonized, you find makes
the female special, exotic and sought after. Welcome to the club.
Congratulations. You're a member now.

(Lighting shift. MAN *becomes silent)*

WOMAN #2: He gets up, drinks his coffee, reads the paper—the
headlines, "This is the end of history," kisses his wife and kids
goodbye. Gets in his car—

GUY: What kind?

WOMAN #2: No, not yet—

WOMAN #1: He turns left out of his suburban driveway, his mind
clear, his eyes keen—

(Loud, crashing sound. The lights on the GUY *go dark.)*

WOMEN #1: He blacks out. He wakes up.

(Harsh lights up on the GUY.*)*

WOMAN #2: Chaos, smoke, fire, people running every which
way—

WOMAN #1: A collision? A bomb? A plane crash? He smells burning flesh.

WOMAN #2: He kicks something—my god, it's a human hand, a
wedding ring still on the finger—

WOMAN #1: A small boy, his face on fire, writhes on the ground.
The man gags—"Did I cause this?"

WOMAN #2: "Who's responsible?" someone shouts—

WOMAN #1: "Who did this?" another yells—

WOMAN #2 *(quietly)*: "Not me," the Guy says. "It's not my fault . . ."

WOMAN #1: "It's not my fault!"—

WOMEN #1 and 2: "It's not my fault!!"

GUY (*trying to convince himself, others*): It's not my fault—
    (*Lights change. Abrupt mood change.*)

GUY: Now you ask me, how come I can say this? How dare he? And why should we take his word for it anyway? Because I'm a white guy. And hey, aren't you happy that I'm not complaining for a change, griping about how I've been disenfranchised, I'm the minority, reverse racism, what about my rights—and finally, I'm so pissed off I'm moving to Idaho next to Mark Furman, we're starting our own country. I mean, that is sooo "last millennium."

Look it, there's a long and accepted tradition of white males speaking on behalf of Asians, for Asians, through Asians, and more recently Asian Americans. As an example—I can write a book that's full of Asian characters—about how they feel, love, believe, hate, I can write about them. There's no problem, is there? Of course not, it's okay. I can even write as a female Asian. I know it seems like a stretch, but I'm telling you, I can and it's okay. Author Edward Said cites as an early example, in his seminal book, *Orientalism*, Flaubert's courtesan, Kuchuk Hanem, she never spoke for herself. Flaubert spoke for her, through her, represented her.

"They cannot represent themselves; they must be represented." Karl Marx. Hey, gotta do your homework.

WOMEN #1 and #2: Caveat.

GUY: Do not do it for African Americans, write a story, presume to talk for them, through them—oh no, never get away with it. Be skinned alive. And black women? White, heterosexual man speaking on behalf of and through black women? Hello, hello! Bell hooks et al., "have you hanging by your shrunken, honky cojones!"

But hey, *Snow Falling on Cedars*—I loved that book.

And *Geisha*? Can you believe that book? Now that mother fucker white male can write. Okay, I think he's a Jew, but it's still in that grand tradition.

Remember Flaubert, remember Karl Marx . . .

WHITE MANIFESTO, OR, GOT RICE?

So you see, me talking on behalf of, through, for Asian Americans, is because I'm supposed to. Because it's expected. Because I'm damn good at it, had years, no, centuries of experience. And because I say it the way it's *supposed* to be said. In a language that everyone knows. With words and symbology that represent the highest level of shared intellectual and *institutionalized* learning. White guy language. W.G.L. *(Like Elvis)* Thank you very much.

(A sudden loud boom.)

WOMAN #1: He wakes up—

WOMAN #2: He wakes up—

WOMAN #1: He walks out into the living room—

GUY: The TV is on—

WOMAN #2: A family having dinner—

WOMAN #1: A man, a wife, his kids—

(A loud crash, glass breaking, gunfire, screams.)

WOMAN #2: A car crash, a bomb, exploding land mine—

(The gunfire continues, more screams.)

WOMAN #1: His wife is being dragged out the door by nameless dark soldiers—

WOMAN #2: His kids are screaming for help as they are bayoneted, held up like wriggling lollipops—

GUY: He sits, glued to the vision on the screen—the beautiful man, his wife, his kids—

WOMAN #1: This is the end of history—

GUY: I am asleep—

WOMAN #2: This is the end of history—

GUY: I am asleep!

(Beat.)

WOMAN #2: He is asleep—

WOMAN #1: He stares at the TV screen . . .

(Lighting shift. Abrupt mood shift. GUY stands there for a moment, primping in front of the mirror.
Silence.

WOMEN #1 and #2 come down next to him. They stand on either side of him.)

GUY: That's it, you ask? Isn't there more? Where's the who, what and why of him? Doesn't he want more from a relationship? Maybe. Maybe not. And maybe this has nothing to do with relationships but more about what really makes the whole thing rev up and kick ass. Power.—

(WOMEN #1 and #2 kneel in front of him and begin to remove his shoes, then his socks.)

GUY: —Everything in the end comes down to power and its relationship to it. Everything. You, me, my words, actions, nonactions, and yes, even the act of making love. Who's on top and who's on the bottom. Who has to go down and who gets to stand up. Who gets to come while the other has to go. In other words, who's the fucker and who's the fuckee. N'est-ce pas?

The act itself? To quote a great man, "Love between unequals is always *perverse.*"

(Shoots an approving nasty look. The women, still on their knees, turn to the audience.)

WOMEN #1 and #2 *(silently mouthing, overlapping)*: James Baldwin . . .

GUY: James Baldwin . . .

(One last look at himself. WOMEN #1 and #2 have removed his shoes and socks and set them neatly aside.

He grabs his car keys.

Stops. Becomes quiet.

WOMEN #1 and #2 slowly stand and pull back.)

WOMAN #1: He knows a lot.

GUY: If you're a smart white guy, you pick it up, you have to. It's just like what being black, brown or yellow used to be. Growing up, you had to know what the man was thinking, 'cause that's the world you had to live in when you left the house. So you lived in both worlds. Your own and theirs. The center and the margins. This day and age, for a white guy to have game, it's the same thing.

WOMAN #2: Sometimes he gets sad, though.

GUY: I do. I get very sad. And I think, maybe it's better not to know so much. Isn't that what everybody expects. How can he ever know what it's like to be one of us? It's in his genes, a back-ass Professor Shockley thing, the inverted bell curve, he'll always

be a dumb white guy. Much like Asians always being foreign-
ers. Black conservatives never really being black. No matter if
the white guy's dressed in a suit or not—when it comes to matters of race, he might as well have a straw hat on, overalls and
a corncob pipe sticking out of his mouth.

*(WOMEN #1 and #2 begin to provide accompaniment, like back-
up singers, humming an underscoring.)*

GUY: I know what I am. I know what people think of me. You
think it's fun walking down the street knowing people are looking at you? Knowing that they always think you're forever igno-
rant. That somehow your whiteness means you can never ever
be right again. That anything you say in defense of yourself
or even offered as constructive criticism will be taken the
wrong way?

WOMEN #1 and #2 *(singing in harmony)*: Don't white folks have a
right to an opinion?

*(WOMEN #1 and #2 continue singing this phrase through this. The
guy talks over this like an evangelist on fire.)*

GUY: "Excuse me, but regarding war-time monetary redress for
JA's, isn't that setting a dangerous precedent?" "Maybe Wen
Ho Lee isn't just a naive, absent-minded scientist and aren't
these yellow students just a little too smart for their own good—
fuck, forget trying to get into Med School." "Really, don't we
have to do something about illegal aliens, downtown LA—it's
a goddamn third-world country and if we continue to let them
speak Spanish in school, hello, Los Angeles, the new capital
of Nuevo America." "Excuse me, but don't you think Al
Sharpton is a bit greasy, Louis Farrakhan is anti-Semitic and
just maybe Mumia Abu-Jamal really killed the cop?"

*(Silence. Then the GUY begins to scream, on the verge of being
out of control.)*

GUY: "Racist! Racist! Mother fucker cracker ass white male
racist!"

*(Beat. WOMEN #1 and #2 are unsure what to make of this. The
GUY calms down.*

*(Back-up singers begin again, cautiously. Builds into a more rhyth-
mic, contemporary beat.)*

GUY: And to know that from now until the end of time, whatever contributions, sacrifices, goodness your people have done
or will ever do for this country, will be tainted by that label of
racist, oppressor, stupid white guy and thus relegated to the
margins of history? See, I know. I do understand. Or, he can't
possibly know. Remember, stupid white guy can't jump? He
can't dance?

As I walk down the street, pieces are being cut out of me for
no other reason than this face. This face, look at it. I'm not
becoming part of the new world, I'm being excluded, becoming extinct. That's not me whining, that's me willing myself
to be brave and look, and to really see. I'm going the way of
the dinosaur, yes, and one has to ask, really ask, if that's what's
best for this country?

(Back-up singers continue.)

GUY: But until that time comes. Until I'm really disappeared and
that resilient, ever-coursing, ever-adapting, ever-pumping,
deep river of entitlement has gone with it, I am here. I am alive.
And yes, I am white.

WOMAN #1: Final white guy haiku, opus #3.

WOMAN #2: The rubber band theory of the universe—

GUY:

Power.

Snaps back always

Ping!!

How do I look? Fine? Hey, I got a date. Who with?
Remember what the white guy said, "They're easier."

(Sips wine.)

GUY: Hmm, it's really opened up.

*(Starts to leave, then stops and performs a tricky dance move—
elegant and deft. Shoots the audience one last knowing look.
Exits, barefoot, shaking his car keys, singing. Like the song,* Volare,
with the two women doing back-up.)

GUY: *Fer-ra-ri, oh-oh-oh-oh . . .*

(Dim to darkness.)

[END OF PLAY]